THE SIEGE

Also by Clara Claiborne Park:

You Are Not Alone: Understanding and Dealing with Mental Illness (with Leon N. Shapiro, M.D.)

Clara Claiborne Park
THE SIEGE

The First Eight Years
of an Autistic Child
With an Epilogue, Fifteen Years Later

An Atlantic Monthly Press Book
Little, Brown and Company · Boston Toronto

LIBRARY OF CONGRESS CATALOG CARD NO. 82–80654

ATLANTIC–LITTLE, BROWN BOOKS
ARE PUBLISHED BY
LITTLE, BROWN AND COMPANY
IN ASSOCIATION WITH
THE ATLANTIC MONTHLY PRESS

BP
*Published simultaneously in Canada
by Little, Brown & Company (Canada) Limited*

PRINTED IN THE UNITED STATES OF AMERICA

To those behind walls,

and to all their besiegers

Contents

THE SIEGE

1 · The Changeling

WE START with an image—a tiny, golden child on hands and knees, circling round and round a spot on the floor in mysterious, self-absorbed delight. She does not look up, though she is smiling and laughing; she does not call our attention to the mysterious object of her pleasure. She does not see us at all. She and the spot are all there is, and though she is eighteen months old, an age for touching, tasting, pointing, pushing, exploring, she is doing none of these. She does not walk, or crawl up stairs, or pull herself to her feet to reach for objects. She doesn't *want* any objects. Instead, she circles her spot. Or she sits, a long chain in her hand, snaking it up and down, up and down, watching it coil and uncoil, for twenty minutes, half an hour—until someone comes, moves her or feeds her or gives her another toy, or perhaps a book.

We are a bookish family. She too likes books. Rapidly, expertly, decisively, she flips the pages, one by one by one. Bright pictures or text are the same to her; one could not say she doesn't see them, or that she does. Rapidly, with uninterrupted rhythm, the pages turn.

One speaks to her, loudly or softly. There is no response. She is deaf, perhaps. That would explain a lot of things—her total inattention to simple commands and requests, which we thought

3

stubbornness; the fact that as month follows month she speaks no more than one word or two, and these only once or twice in a week; even, perhaps, her self-absorption. But we do not really think she is deaf. She turns, when you least expect it, at a sudden noise. The soft whirr as the water enters the washing machine makes her wheel round. And there are the words. If she were deaf there would be no words. But out of nowhere they appear. And into nowhere they disappear; each new word displaces its predecessor. At any given time she has a word, not a vocabulary.

Twenty-two months. Still not walking, talking, or responding to speech. The doctor is worried, and she is observed for three days in the hospital. There they find no evidence of phenyl-ketonuria, or of any other physical deficiencies. (From babyhood she had been unusually healthy; her temperature had never even risen high enough to tempt me to take it.) The doctors watched her, remote and withdrawn in her hospital crib. She would not let the nurses feed her. They smiled at her; she looked through them. The doctors spoke; she heard nothing. They whistled; she turned round. Her movements were quick, decisive; her expression, alert. They told us she was still within the curve of normal development, although at the very bottom; we should wait six months and then begin to worry. "She seems like a child who has been raised very much alone."

Alone? In a house with three older brothers and sisters, neighbors' children constantly in and out? She was alone, but she created her aloneness, sought it, guarded it. When we put her on the floor to watch the children play, she grizzled and fretted. Crawling in the garden, alone in her crib, she was happy. I would put her in for a nap after lunch. At five she would still be content there—sleeping, bouncing, laughing, rocking, back and forth, back and forth. I began to realize that I could put her there with a supply of food and drink and she would *never* be ready to come out. She sought enclosed spaces; every time she saw a playpen, she tried to get in. If there was no physical fence between her

4

and the world, she erected one. She looked through human beings as if they were glass. She created solitude in the midst of company, silence in the midst of chatter.

Another image; she is at the beach, two years old now, walking easily (when she was ready, she simply began; there was no physical difficulty, there never had been any). A bronzed, gold baby of unusual beauty, she walks along the sand. Many people are looking at her because she is so pretty, but she is looking at no one. On she walks, into family groups, by picnic baskets, sand castles, and buckets. She grazes human beings by a quarter of an inch. You would think she did not see them. But she does see them, because no matter how close she comes, her eyes fixed, it seems, on some point beyond them or to one side, she never touches them. On she goes. The beach is lonelier down this way. The blank sand stretches into the distance. Her silhouette, small to start with, grows smaller and smaller. When I can hardly see her, I begin to run. She might have walked straight ahead, delicately swerving to avoid an occasional collision, without a backward look, forever, so little did she need of human contact.

Once a friend, seeing for the first time her pale skin and straight yellow hair, her clear blue eyes and the dancing grace of her body, called her a fairy child. And there was a fairy lightness in her movements, a fairy purity in her detached gaze. As time passed and she grew taller, leaner, older, her face seemed not to record time's passage. She carried none of the stigmata of the defective; nothing distinguished her from other children except that in some undefinable way she looked younger. The Irish name for fairyland is the Land of Youth. There live the Good People, who bear the human shape without the burden of the human heart. There is no malice in the Good People; they do not will the pain they cause to others. If they seem cruel, it is not real cruelty—only a certain remoteness, an inability to comprehend our desires, our needs, and our warmth. It is because the fairies have no hearts that they do not grow old. Elly's eerie imperviousness, her serene self-sufficiency, belonged to those who, like the fairies, can live somehow untouched by the human experience.

Young children are a complex of needs and desires. They find themselves fed, clothed, kept clean, but that is only the barest beginning of what they want. They want sister's cookie, they want the toy that's out of reach, they want a ride in the wagon. "Mommy—I need—I want—Give me—" things, attention, love. It is hard to remember the first stirrings of doubt about a baby, but I remember a day when I took Elly to the supermarket. She was nineteen months old. She sat in the shopping cart, alert and intent, her eyes taking in the objects on the shelves as she rolled along. We passed a friend with her little girl, just Elly's age. I looked at the child carefully. My friend had had a difficult delivery. Transfusions had been necessary, the baby had lacked oxygen. There had been some anxiety that the brain had been affected. The little girl looked fine, however; sitting up in her cart, she had Elly's alertness but not her gravity. She turned, she looked up at her mother. As I watched, I saw her point to a box of candy.

I thought then that I had never seen Elly point.

To point is so simple, so spontaneous, so primary an action that it seems ridiculous to analyze it. All babies point, do they not? To stretch out the arm and the finger is, symbolically and literally, to stretch out the self into the world—in order to remark on an object, to call it to another's attention, perhaps to want it for oneself. From pointing comes the question "What's that?" that unlocks the varied world. To point, to reach, to stretch, to grab, is to make a relation between oneself and the outside. To need is to relate.

My neighbor's little boy is almost three and very slow to talk—they are worried about him. He wanders over to me, looks up at my face, points to the swing. The noise he makes is totally unintelligible, but I understand it: "I want." I put him in the swing. Not to worry; *he'll* come out of it. Elly is eight years old now. I have still never seen her point. She has a vocabulary of hundreds of words. But although it includes "rectangle," "square," and "hexagon," it does not include "What's that?"

Children vary in the intensity of their desires, and the aggressiveness with which they express them. Some babies are reasonably self-sufficient from birth—"good" babies, active and contented in their playpens, cheerful among their toys. Others are demanding and dependent. These we try to reassure, to lead gently toward self-sufficiency. We think of self-sufficiency as a virtue, even among babies—as a forerunner of independence, of inner resource.

It is some time before it occurs to a busy mother, with three other children, that a baby can be too self-sufficient.

Elly did not point. Nor did she try to get objects that were not within her reach; she seemed unconscious they were there. Content in crib or pen, when removed from them she crawled freely from room to room. But it was motion, not exploration. She did not push or poke, open drawers, pull at lamps or tables. At twelve months, when she began to crawl, I got ready the gates that we had used to keep the other three children from falling downstairs. I never used them. Elly did not try to go down, and there was never a question of her falling. Unconscious of so much, she was conscious of the location of every edge or limit; she could be left safely on any bed. She accepted limits, with an acceptance so natural it seems clear that it was a welcome. She made no move to climb the stairs, but one day, in play, her sister taught her to crawl up. She learned easily enough, and I thought the new skill would mean the usual extension of a baby's possibilities. She learned on a Friday. We went away that weekend to a stairless household, and when we came back the Sunday it did not occur to us to review her new skill. It was six months before she crawled upstairs again.

She had eaten at the table with us ever since she was old enough to sit upright. We put food on her plate, as for any baby; she picked it up in her fingers and ate it, or allowed me to feed it to her, or refused it; she did not see or ask for anything anyone else was eating. She asked for nothing, reached for nothing. She was content. Not impassive—she smiled, even laughed—but content.

Only now and then something went wrong, something trivial in everything but its effect on Elly. Her milk was served in a glass, perhaps, instead of her silver cup, or it was offered her after the meal instead of before. It was difficult to guess what was wrong, since she gave us no clue, but it was important to find out, for she would cry violently until we managed to get things right again, crying that seemed all the more remarkable in contrast with her usual serenity.

We had not thought of retardation, but after the hospital examination we thought of it constantly as we waited for the six months to pass. If a two-year-old is late walking, does not talk or understand, plays repetitively or not at all, what should she be but retarded? We thought and the doctors thought we saw alertness, but a child's look of intelligence is an intangible, a construct of the imagination. What is tangible, what is operational, is what a child does, and from one day's end to another, this child did almost nothing. Why should her look of self-absorption be interpreted as focused or intent simply because it seemed so to us? Was not the simple truth that what we were seeing, in our inexperience, was the misted stare of the retardate, that her withdrawal was in fact the natural motion of the defective faced with a world he is powerless to comprehend? In an adolescent— even an older child—we are sickeningly familiar with the discrepancies between what a person *can* do and what he does in fact. But in a baby? Elly had been something over a year old when her progress had begun to slow. Nothing had happened to her—no illness, no absence, no change in the environment. At that age, surely, the organism should be spontaneous. What it can, it does. If Elly did not do things, the presumption must surely be that she could not.

Yet however we schooled ourselves to accept this hypothesis, we could not make it fit. I did not know much about the retarded, but I imagined they would try to do things, and fail. Elly didn't try, but the few things she had learned to do she had done neatly and successfully the first time she got around to it. She was never sloppy, never hesitant. I pictured the movements of the retarded as fuzzy, clumsy, and uncertain. Elly's touch was firm, her motions deliberate, eerily controlled. She did not stumble, did not fall, did not spill or drop things. How beautifully her chain moved up and down! Yet how reluctant she was to use her small, efficient fingers! As time went on, though she still needed little in comparison to an ordinary child, she began to acknowledge some rudimentary desires. She wanted something after all—a piece of cake, perhaps, as we sat at table. She did not ask for it verbally, of course, or by any sound, whether grunt or cry. But neither did she reach for it herself. Instead, she firmly picked up the human arm that happened to be nearest her and threw it toward the object desired. She used that other arm and hand as her tool—as if the human being it belonged to did not exist.

It was not possible to give her a meaningful intelligence test. She would have looked through any tester to the wall behind him. Every test assumes communication; without it, there would be no way of making her comprehend what she was expected to do—indeed the very idea that one human being could have expectations of another was foreign to her. We could not test her—but I could watch her. A friend, a trained psychologist, mentioned that a two-year-old should be able to build a four-block tower. Elly had blocks. Occasionally she used one to tap, repetitively, on the pages of a book as she flipped them past. That was all.

One day, sitting on the floor beside her, I built a four-block

9

tower. Neatly, block by block, she dismantled it—no free-sweeping destructiveness for her. I picked up her hand, used it as *my* tool to build the next tower. Then easily, neatly, she built the third. It was the same with pegs in holes, rings on a stick. Always the passivity, the apparent incapacity—yet when the initiative came from outside, she could grasp both principle and technique at once.

In those years, only once or twice did I ever know Elly to imitate as other children do—spontaneously repeating a word or an action after someone else. Elly did so little that anyone else did. And such words as she had, such actions as she performed, originated not in a social context, but seemingly out of nowhere. In search of contact, I did what she would not; if she would not or could not do what I did, I would do what she did. So with paper and pencil I lay low beside her—she crayoning on her paper with random scribbles, I doing the same. For a normal adult, scribbling soon palls; after a while I made circles, as well as a face or two and a couple of fish. Elly paid no attention and went on scribbling.

The next day, however, she did not scribble. She made her first closed figures. Three days after I had made a cross, she made one. Surely it took more intelligence to copy a figure from memory at a remove of three days than to imitate it immediately afterward as a normal child would do? What credit would she get on an intelligence test for this?

But these were lights that flickered and went out. Like Elly's words, they did not build into usable skills. Elly made block towers for a few months. More surprisingly, she spontaneously evolved her own block play, arranging eighty or one hundred blocks in perfect parallel rows. She did this over and over again, as she had played with her chain. Again and again we saw it happen; the new accomplishment, instead of leading to more complex activity, became as sterile and repetitive as the old and was finally abandoned. After three weeks, she drew no more circles. After six months, she made no more block towers. So complete was her abandonment that I could hardly believe I had ever seen her do these things. Two years later, when for a year she had not touched crayon to paper, I looked at her sheafs of circles with helpless wonder.

And there were the things she did not repeat, but did once and once only. The day she came home from the hospital she saw a pair of scissors lying on the playroom floor, and suddenly, spontaneously, pronounced that difficult word with exemplary clarity. She repeated it, less clearly. She never said it again. One day she took the dustpan and brush and brushed the floor, just like any little girl who wants to be like her mother. One day she fed some cereal to a doll—once, and once only. Actions are past in a moment and time runs over them. One distrusts the senses, one distrusts memory. Had I seen these things? Had she done them at all?

How much did she take in of the world around her? Almost nothing, it appeared. Yet one day, several months before her third birthday, as we lay and scribbled, a pencil point broke. Elly got up in a businesslike manner, put the pencil into my hand, and propelled me toward the door. I hung back; I could not believe she knew where she was going. I wanted to test her. She pushed me through two rooms and into a third, straight to the pencil sharpener. I had not known she knew there *was* a pencil sharpener, let alone its location and its purpose. If she knew this, how much else did she know?

The doctor saw her again—the same intelligent GP who had delivered her, who had spotted her abnormality, who had supervised her first tests. Watching her precise and accurate line-up of the pegs in the holes of one of his office toys he could not, he said, think she was retarded. It could—he paused. It could be something else. If it were psychological—that he knew nothing about.

And neither did I.

I knew only that my fourth child was not like the others, who needed me and loved me, as I loved them. The fairies had stolen away the human baby and left one of their own. There she moved, every day, among us but not of us, acquiescent when we approached, untouched when we retreated, serene, detached, in perfect equilibrium. Existing among us, she had her being elsewhere. As long as no demands were made upon her, she was content. If smiles and laughter mean happiness, she was happy inside the invisible walls that surrounded her. She dwelt in a solitary citadel, compelling and self-made, complete and valid. Yet we could not leave her there. We must intrude, attack, invade, not because she was unhappy inside it, for she was not, but because the equilibrium she had found, perfect as it was, denied the possibility of growth. We had not demanded; now we must. We had accepted; now we must try to change. A terrible arrogance, for what had we to offer her? Which of us could call ourselves as content as Elly was? The world we would tempt her into was the world of risk, failure, and frustration, of unfulfilled desire, of pain as well as activity and love. There in Nirvana, why should she ever come out? Yet she was ours as well as her own, and we wanted her with us. If what we had to offer was not enough, we had nothing beside it. Confronted with a tiny child's refusal of life, all existential hesitations evaporate. We had no choice. We would use every stratagem we could invent to assail her fortress, to beguile, entice, seduce her into the human condition.

2 ⟩ Ourselves

ELLY only seemed to live in isolation. In fact she lived with us. There were five other human beings in her house. We passed, we spoke, we touched, we provided. It is time to introduce ourselves, the family that should have made up Elly's world.

Elly's father is a professor. He learns, he teaches, he writes. His work is varied, demanding, and in the main satisfying. The college is small and very good. Professors there are teachers as well as scholars, and their students (note the personal pronoun) learn not merely by watching them operate at a distance but by working with them. It may be an exaggeration to say that these professors work here in this isolated valley instead of at one of the exciting intellectual factories for which their abilities qualify them, because they believe with Forster that "the personal is all that matters." Yet most of the faculty is here by choice, and the choice has involved some such factor. My husband and I have spent almost all our lives in one school or another. Deep inside us, unspoken and unanalyzed until Elly made us analyze it, is the conviction that all good learning is at last a matter of what is now called, with a show of scientific objectivity, "interpersonal relations." We believed this, but we could not have guessed how deeply we were to test our belief.

We are a very academic family. My husband is a professor's

son; my mother was sent north to college from a small, provincial Southern town long ago at a time when to educate one's girls at all was by no means the conventional thing to do. I, who tell this story, was when Elly was born a typical college-bred housewife, of the sort that forms the backbone of the League of Women Voters all over the country. I had had a fine education; I even had an M.A., picked up at the same university where my husband did his graduate work, but I had gone no further. When David completed his Ph.D. we had been four years married, and although I enjoyed academic work and did it well I had no clear goals of the sort that would have been expected of me if I had been a man. As David entered on his professional life, it seemed reasonable for me to do what almost every other woman my age was doing—to start having babies. Before Elly came I had had three. Sara was seven when I learned Elly was on the way. Rebecca was six, Matthew three. It was a rounded, well-planned family, two girls and a boy.

There are thousands of families like us in this happy land. We live in a big house in a homogeneous community where neighbors are friends, wide lawns run into each other, and children find it safe to roam—a woman's magazine daydream which happens to be true. Our town is an ideal place to rear children, if an ideal place is one which is free from insecurity and danger. Within two hundred yards of our house were fifteen or twenty children for Sara and Becky and Matt to know. A selection of these streamed steadily through our house, depositing balls, gum wrappers, and anonymous pieces of clothing; our children streamed correspondingly through the houses nearby. These children were attractive and alert, brought up with care and considerable success by mothers like me, the mothers of the forties and fifties for whom Dr. Spock had replaced the conventional wisdom. Of professional ability, most of us, we had made motherhood our profession. We read, we discussed our problems with each other. We were very knowledgeable. If I was unusual in anything, it was that I was less educated than most in the theoretical ins and outs of the infant psyche. Having studied no psychology in college, I eschewed the more recondite writings on the subject, lost patience with Gesell's heavy detail which never seemed to describe my own babies, and stuck to the common sense of Spock, freely corrected, as time went on, by my own. But I was like my friends in putting my full resources of intelligence and intuition into the task of bringing up my children. Every mother her own Piaget. I had observed, fascinated, their first approaches to language: how one small consciousness would begin with nouns, another with verbs—and speculated on what significance this might have as a key to their orientation to the world. I had watched their first slow movement from the domain of people and objects to the making of primitive abstractions. When Becky, at two, responded to her lot of low man on the neighborhood totem-pole by remarking, "Sara bang me—Johnny bang me," and then, slowly and philosophically, "*Elly*body bang me," I had sympathized, and laughed, and rejoiced at the spectacle of a mind unfolding. There had been so much to do. I had looked at books with them and later read them aloud. I had provided them with clay and batter and cleaned up the results. I had kept track of the innumerable but not interchangeable pieces of their educational toys. I had taught them letters and numbers and how to sound out words. I had seen to it that on their shelves were the children's classics that would feed the imagination as well as inform the mind. I had punished and rewarded; I had tried to make them generous and self-controlled and unsuspicious and good. I had washed and cooked and coaxed and wrangled. I had used to exhaustion the full abilities of a grown-up woman in overseeing the first years of these small humans, and I was terribly proud of what I had done. Anyone would have said—many people did say—that I had three lovely children.

If I were to describe them this would be the place to do it. Their separate characteristics, the weaknesses and strengths of each one of them, are part of Elly's story. But it is a part that must remain incomplete, even at the risk of unreality. Our children have put up with a lot of things because of Elly; they will not have to put up with reading their mother's summation of their personalities printed in a book. I set down only what is obvious, what is attested by teachers, friends, and neighbors. It is all that is necessary here. Our children were intelligent, responsive, and adaptable. They were also—quite irrelevantly—beautiful, with a pink-and-gold beauty which seemed to belong not to the real world but to the illustrations of old-fashioned storybooks. I luxuriated in their beauty; it seemed to me that I had unaccountably given birth to two princesses and a prince. As I looked at them, remembering my own bespectacled childhood, they seemed a special and continuing miracle. It is our eyes that we believe. Irrationally, it was their beauty, with which I had had nothing whatever to do, that summed up my pride in them. It shone around them, an astonishing, almost palpable fact, as if to symbolize their less superficial successes—their intelligence and their affection.

That year, the year of Elly's beginning, a friend had visited us, one with whom we had long been out of touch. A man with a gift for intimacy, he formulated a single question to bring us close together again: "Tell me," he said, "what have you done in the past five years of which you are most proud?" He, a man of considerable attainments as a scientist, was proudest of his successful psychoanalysis. I was proudest of my children. Clearly he, a married man childless by choice, was astonished and unsatisfied by my answer as I was by his. To each his own achievement, and his own pride in it. I was terribly proud to have produced three such children. But it was my thought that the job was nearly over. Like my husband's, it had been demanding, varied, and in the main satisfying. I had done it well. Now I would grope my way back toward some of the other things I knew how to do.

I had begun to discover, in the long hours of fragmented attention while I listened to small people's chatter, what I had been too dim and too timid to perceive in graduate school. I was no natural homebody. I had the stirrings of a vocation. I had done some teaching while I was at the university—pickup work, freshman composition in the years of the great postwar teacher shortage. I was sure now of what I had only suspected then—that this was what I wanted to do. I had spent seven years teaching little people, with some success. Now I wanted to teach people whose minds could in some measure answer my own. In two years all the children would be in school. My days would be my own again; I could have again the forgotten experience of being alone. I would have time to read, to bring my knowledge up to date. I could perhaps write. I could locate a school in which I could teach part time.

It was in this forward-looking state of mind that I learned that I was pregnant for the fourth time and that the job was to be done all over again.

Except for the initial depression as the gates clanged shut, the pregnancy was uneventful. The household was full and active, I had no choice but to be busy, and depression gave way to an intermittent, semi-comic rage that was much easier to handle. The only way to deal with the jokes played by feminine biology is to agree that they are funny. Nothing unusual happened until I was in my sixth month, when the children picked up measles. I had not had it. For a pregnant woman, "measles" is a frightening word, but my doctor reassured me. It was not the severe disease that was dangerous, but the milder German measles: there was nothing to indicate it would affect the unborn baby, who was in any case advanced beyond the vulnerable stage of development. Besides, I was probably mistaken; most adults had had measles; it was easy to forget these things. I was still worried enough to call a doctor in Boston, a personal friend. She concurred. Accordingly, I received gamma globulin from my own doctor, enough to modify the disease but not to prevent it. When it came, I was very sick, but only for a week, and I recovered without aftereffects.

Three months later, on July 20, 1958, on schedule and without complications, the baby exploded into life. Once again it was over, this birthing, this experience unassimilable to any other, in which brain and familiar personality are incredibly harnessed to an enormous body whose work and pain spreads from the center to take in every remotest nerve-end and at last the whole world. Doctor and nurse moving dreamlike above me, I lay in the delivery room worn out, in the state of heightened emotional perception that accompanies an experience that has involved totally everything that one is. What had I made this time? The nurse anticipated my question. "You have a lovely little boy."

But that wasn't true. I didn't have a little boy at all. She had made a mistake, a slip of the tongue perhaps, corrected inside the minute. But one is very vulnerable after prolonged pain. Until they took my little boy away I did not realize how much I had wanted him—a brother for Matt, who would now be isolated among three sisters—a boy, because one can dream bigger dreams for a boy than for a girl. But the baby was a girl, and the doctor had been right. The measles had left no trace. She was healthy and perfect.

And then there was the matter of the name. For three days Elly lived nameless, as none of my other babies had had to do. We had thought we had a name ready. She—if she was a girl—was to be Hester, a restrained New England name which my husband and I thought beautiful. But complications arose, the silly complications of a happy modern family in which everybody's ideas count. Sara hated the name Hester, she thought it was awful. It had been agreed for months that this baby, born within a month of her birthday, was to be in a special sense hers, as Matthew had been Rebecca's birthday present almost four years before. Sara's very own baby couldn't have a name she thought was awful—we all saw that. So the little bundle went unnamed as we tried to suit everybody and finally settled on a compromise that nobody liked or objected to very much. The baby would be Elinor. It was a strange, uncertain beginning. First sex unclear, then name, in which, irrationally, so much of personality seems to inhere. David Copperfield was born with a caul. A nineteenth-century novelist could have imagined no more fitting introduction for a child whom twentieth-century psychiatrists would see as suffering from a condition which Erik Erikson calls early ego failure, in which the very boundaries of the self are confused and undefined.

But nobody thought of portents then. Elly was fine and healthy, unusual in no respect except that she cried with colic day and night. Even that was not unusual in our family. Becky had done exactly the same thing. There is a section in Spock on three-month colic. Our copy opens of itself to those grimy pages. Colic is a strain on everybody concerned, but it is nothing to worry about. We took turns rocking and cuddling her, my mother and I, so the family could have some peace by day and sleep by night. Elly cried and cried and lay at my breast and ate and cried again and grew. By the time she was three and a half months old the colic was largely gone, by five months she was a gay and cheerful baby, though as late as seven months she would sometimes give a sharp yelp after her milk went down to remind us of those early weeks.

One does not watch the second baby as closely as the first, and the fourth may hardly get watched at all. Nevertheless, I remember that Elly did the usual things roughly on schedule. I remember that at seven weeks she smiled, in a brief interval between screams. At two months she even smiled at her teddy bear. That seemed very advanced to us; none of the others had recognized a human surrogate so early. She reached for objects at the usual time. Photographs of her at five months show an alert, gay baby, smiling up out of her bath straight into your eyes. Memory can play tricks. My children all have the same hair and coloring, and their baby pictures are very much alike. Three years later, in the midst of Elly's dreamlike remoteness, I went over the old pictures, combing my brain for clues to when it began. I found one of a baby laughing aloud, eyes focused directly on her father's face behind the camera. I rejected it altogether. That was not Elly's empty gaze, straight through you to the wall behind. The pictures had been scrambled. That was not Elly. That had been Matt. But I was mistaken. Two years afterward, my mother produced her copy of the picture, incontrovertibly dated. That was Elly. The smiling baby had really existed. She had been different then.

I nursed Elly, as I had the others, for nine months. Her head was small and warm like the others', her body snuggled soft against mine. It broke my heart to wean her. I am a thin woman, grown from a nervous child, a nail-biter, a ring-twister. Serenity is not natural to me; I value the rare experience that brings it.

> Beloved, may your sleep be sound,
> That have found it where you fed.

The long hours spent nursing my children, relaxed, not moving, only functioning, each of us completely satisfied in the other, were to me the happiest times of their babyhood.

When I weaned her, Elly was still very much a baby. Other people's children, after six months, begin to do all sorts of things—they sit up, they crawl, they fall down, they eat pins. At an age when other people's children are pulling themselves to their feet in their playpens, mine are still flat on their backs on a blanket. I had got used to this long before Elly came. Matthew had not sat up until eight months; Becky, who had not crawled till eleven months, was seventeen months old before she stood alone, nineteen months old before she walked. Elly followed a month behind. At nine months she finally sat alone. At a year, she crawled. Months went by and she did not walk. Another family might have worried at such slow progress. We felt no reason to. Elly crawled very well once she began. It was true that even when she became mobile she seemed satisfied with very little, but what mother of four does not consider that a virtue? Does not Spock point out that babies may prefer very simple toys? She did not want to put rings on a stick, but I knew already that not all babies did. I remembered vividly that Becky had taken the educational toys that Sara had delighted in assembling, and methodically dropped the parts, one by one, down the stairs.

So when did it begin? A friend, also a mother of four, tells me she began to wonder as early as eight months, seeing Elly lying in her baby-tender, content without even a rattle in her hand. Has she hit on something significant? And there are pictures from around nine months or so (dates are vague; it did not occur to us that one day Elly would be a case-history). The friendly bubbly smile is gone, and there is only one picture in which she faces the camera. She looks serious. Had it started then? But those photographs were taken on one day. There are often days when a baby doesn't photograph well. Perhaps Elly was tired that day. If I could go back I'd know in a moment. I can never find out now.

Was it significant that as early as eight months, propped up in a chair, she showed that strange quivering tensing of all muscles in a kind of passing paroxysm—that response to intense interest or pleasure which has been with her ever since yet which no doctor has ever seen? Was it significant that as she approached a year she would not play hide-and-seek behind a diaper? If I held her on my shoulder and her father dodged up at her from behind my back, instead of discovering him, as the others had, with squeals of pleasure, she paid no attention. But children differ, and not everyone likes the same games. Elly seemed independent and cheerful. All this description is based on hindsight. We noticed nothing then.

One looks for a trauma and finds none. She was rarely sick,

never severely so. A few stopped-up noses, unaccompanied by fever. Chicken pox at six months—an unusually mild case. At seventeen months, an earache. We guessed because she whimpered and rubbed at her ear, for she was not talking. We played safe and called the doctor—for the first time in her life. She was already better when he came, leaping up and down in her crib and laughing. I remember he exclaimed, "What a lovely baby!" Yet surely it had begun by then.

She was not ill, nor was I. No one was hospitalized. We left her only once, when she was nine months old, and then only for a weekend. Nonplused, one looks for less obvious causes—events and experiences that went unnoticed at the time but that could later reveal their true significance. Once a child ran with her in her stroller, hit a bump, and pitched her out on her head. An injury? But I picked her up undazed, crying lustily, her eyes not even crossed. Then there was the trip we took in Elly's second summer, a month after her first birthday. It was a typical station-wagon safari from friend's house to friend's house. The first part of the trip had been pleasantly uneventful. We had driven to Rhode Island, stayed there a week, and were now on our way to Maine. We broke the trip in the middle, staying with a student who put up all six of us in a room of his boardinghouse. Two beds, floor covered with mattresses, Elly in her car-bed, by now too small for her. She didn't like it, and cried, and I spent most of the night rocking her, though ordinarily she was a good sleeper. Nobody slept well, and the next day's drive was one of those trivial nightmares that any family lives through on occasion. The children were intermittently crabby, we ran out of gas, we even lost a five-dollar bill out of the window. Elly was fretful from the start. She wouldn't go to sleep, and by the time we had been going half the day she was crying steadily. We arrived exhausted, and spent the next three days confined to the house by a nor'-easter as seven children who didn't know each other interacted in one not-very-large living room. Elly fretted constantly. I had never seen her like this. Then the weather lifted, she crawled outside, alone in the quiet garden, and we had no further trouble. Did it start then? Was that cramped and crowded week the beginning of her retreat?

I doubt it. Nothing so ordinary should be able to cause a major psychological disaster in a baby—not if the baby were healthy to begin with. But I record it nevertheless, as I record here everything I know of those first two years—the measles and the colic and the bump on the head and the fact that I was an intellectual mother by no means totally accepting of her feminine role, who did not at all want another baby. Out of these come the possible explanations—out of these, or out of whatever may in time be elucidated in the complex balance of a baby's metabolism or the choreography of the electrons in its brain. Every piece of potential evidence must be recorded in this account, not least the evidence that can be used against me. We need to know all we can if someone someday is to understand at last what is relevant and what is not.

So Elly grew, and though we look back and remember one incident or another, the onset of the condition was imperceptible. We perceived we had a child who, at twenty-two months, was not toilet trained—but neither were most of our neighbor's children. She did not walk, but the little boy down the street had sat contentedly in his playpen until he was two. She did not use a spoon—but she fed herself efficiently with her fingers. She spoke only a few words—but the onset of speech in children is notoriously variable, and every parent of a slow talker is aware that Einstein didn't talk until he was four. The various signs that now seem so clear then seemed easily attributable to individual differences. One should not, after all, push one's children. How many times did someone remark that of course I was so used to bright children that when I got an ordinary one I thought it was slow? Elly seemed alert, beautifully co-ordinated, and contented. We stored up the differences in our minds but we did not worry, having learned in ten years of parenthood that events usually render worries irrelevant, and that worry itself can harm a child more than most of the conditions one worries about.

Only we began gradually to be aware that we had begun to think of Elly as a "difficult" child. She had been such an easy fourteen-month-old. Since she didn't walk or even crawl upstairs it had been simple to keep track of her, although it was hardly necessary. Extreme in her caution, delicate in her judgment of levels and edges, she seldom fell and rarely hurt herself. I could be sure she would open no bottles, turn on no faucets, teeter on no high stools. And for some time, busy with my other children, I was pleased that she made so few demands on my patience. She crawled contentedly about, never very far away; she took long naps and bounced gaily in her crib when she woke up. She did not attempt to climb out, but neither had the other children at that age, and if she did not call me, I thought nothing of it. This was independence. She made few demands upon me and I made few upon her. She was so self-contained, so cheerful in her limited round of activity, that there were none of those battles of wills that take place between mothers and more active children. I began to put her on the pot at thirteen months, after breakfast, with a cookie, as I had Becky and Matt. There was some response for the first week or so, then nothing more. I let it go "until she was ready." I could afford to be relaxed, with a mother-of-four relaxation. I did not know she would not be "ready," even partially, for four more years. I made no issue over her learning to spoon-feed herself. She ate neatly, and since she took all her meals at the table with us it was easy to feed her the sloppy foods her fastidious fingers would not touch. Least of all, in our family, did it seem necessary to urge her to walk. So life with Elly was easy—until some time in the second half of her second year, when gradually we began to feel it wasn't easy any more.

Not that she had changed. She was as undemanding as ever.

But parents' expectations of a child approaching two grow more pressing. As she grew older, though we were relaxed about her talking, we expected her to understand the simple things we said to her. Yet we would ask, or forbid, offer a cookie, ask her to come or to go, and there would be no response. It was as if she had not heard us. Had it always been so?

It became increasingly difficult to leave her with baby-sitters; they expect a child nearing two to respond to simple commands. They expect a child nearing two to respond to a lot of things—a tone of voice, a smile, the sight or sound of children entering a room. Elly, contented on the floor, would not even look up.

We have photographs from this period too. One shows a plump blonde baby looking into the camera with an expression that is curiously tense. Not at all the serenity I remember, certainly, but I also remember the struggle we had to go through to get those pictures. David took them as always, and the rest of us, the children and I, put our whole effort into attracting Elly's attention and getting her to look at us. Such unusual, persistent goings-on—no wonder she looked worried. Another picture is relaxed enough—Elly limp as a rag doll in her sister's arms, her lovely face looking beyond us into space. Another is quite a success—at first glance. Elly is smiling, even laughing. But she is laughing at no one. The picture shows a forest of arms—Sara's, mine—two of us tickling her to achieve that gaiety which even in the pictures looks somehow frenetic.

Not that she never laughed spontaneously. She did, and if we could have caught it, it would have made as normal a picture as you please. But that laughter was indeed spontaneous—it welled up from nowhere, it related to no human situation. Nothing in our words or our expressions would generate it, save that wild tickling, the direct bodily invasion of her privacy. The children tried it a little, for the picture's sake, and the laughter, and the closeness to the pretty baby sister. But they tried it less and less, and at last where they were not noticed rarely intervened. She

25

did not bother them and she did not need them. On all fours, from room to room, from back yard to front, down the path, up the driveway, she followed her different drummer. I remember one sunny spring day, the yards filled with playing children, my neighbor and I standing and watching Elly as she crawled serenely away from us all. Something about her isolation—she was so tiny, and already so far away—made me say, only half joking, "There's nothing the matter with Elly. She just has a distorted sense of what's important." My neighbor laughed at the application of such inflated language to a baby. But it is I who have had the last laugh, if you could call it that.

3 · Doctors and Diagnoses

WHAT the doctor said was, "If you're not worried, I am." I do not have the novelist's ear for remembered dialogue, but some words I have not forgotten. Elly was twenty-two months old, and she was in a doctor's office for the first time in nearly a year. Only once had a doctor seen her in the interim—for the earache mentioned in the last chapter. Then, Elly had been cheerful and secure in her favorite place, her crib; he was not her regular doctor, and he had never seen her before. He had exclaimed, as recorded, that she was a lovely baby.

A house call is an unusual thing for us; we have had perhaps four in fifteen years. We are lax about doctors, having been lucky enough to be able to take health for granted. We were never ones to bother a doctor with monthly check-ups of patently healthy babies. Unlike most of our friends, we had no pediatrician. We didn't think we needed one. I had no obstetrician for Elly; I didn't think I needed one. The excellent general practitioner who delivered her saw her three or four times in her first year, checked her progress, and gave her routine injections. She had a mild eczema at thirteen months; he cleared it up with the only shot of penicillin any of my children has ever had. It was time for her vaccination, but because of the eczema the doctor suggested we defer it. Characteristically, months had gone by before we got around to taking Elly back to him. Hard to believe as that seems now, we went to get her vaccinated, not to ask about her strangeness. I was expecting nothing eventful when I carried Elly into the office and set her on the examination table. The doctor asked if she was walking. I said no, but that I wasn't worried. Becky and Matthew had both walked late, and besides, Elly was already beginning—she'd walk with me if I held her hands. I tried to show the doctor. Elly's knees buckled and she relaxed into a crawl. "Does she talk?" "A couple of words." Not suddenly, but slowly and mercifully, the realization began to take form. Any one symptom might be insignificant. Children differ. But add them up . . .

But we had not nearly reached that point, the doctor or I. It was merely that he thought she should be tested under hospital conditions. There were two obvious possibilities. One was phenylketonuria, a metabolic defect more common in blue-eyed, yellow-haired girls, causing retardation if not checked early but controllable with diet. The other was thyroid deficiency, which would explain not only the lack of speech—a slight retardation which could be caught and treated—but the delayed walking. The joint-structure is still immature from the deficiency perhaps. . . . Curiously, the nascent anxiety relaxes. The doctor has seen only this limp and passive creature on his office floor. I, who remember Elly hanging from her father's thumbs, supported only by her strong fingers, who watch her daily leaping and tumbling in her crib as on a trampoline, do not really expect to hear that there is anything the matter with Elly's joints. And of course there is not. In three days of hospital tests they find no evidence of physical deficiency at all. Our doctor watched her, checked her hearing, called in the pediatrician we hadn't thought we needed. Together they agree that she is "still within the curve of normal development." It is the pediatrician, who does not know our family, who remarks that "she seems like a child who has been raised very much alone." Considering that she has spent her short life in a house pulsing with activity, the diagnosis is already implicit in that sentence. But neither we nor the doctors know that.

I was irrationally relieved to find the tests were negative. I had never had a child in the hospital. The doctor had advised against visiting Elly; it might upset her. That first night she had been away, I had, for the first time in years, no small child to put to bed. I sat down in the living room in unaccustomed leisure, but I could not read. I put on the Brahms Requiem—the music I had chosen the night of Elly's birth to fill the time of the first slow labor pains. "Behold all flesh is as the grass and all the goodliness of men is as the flower of grass." I sat in the easy chair and listened and wept for my baby whose flesh was as a flower, who had begun her birth to this music and who might, it seemed, be something less than perfect. So much of pride had I invested in my bright and beautiful children and my great good luck. I could actually be glad when the doctors found no physical deficiency. It was as I had thought; my child was strong and well; she would walk when she was ready. Nothing was wrong with her bones or her brain. She would grow and take her place in a family lovelier than anybody else's.

It is possible to learn humility. A year later, Elly would be examined again, in a bigger hospital with more refined techniques. And this time I would wait at night and hope and nearly pray that they would find a physical deficiency—something that could be controlled with a diet or a pill. And then my baby's perfect health would be a heartbreak to me and no source of pride.

But it was not yet time for heartbreak. Elly's doctor and the consulting pediatrician had told us to wait six months before we began to worry. I remember another sentence: "I don't think you got a lemon." We heard it with gladness; in such a case one does not quarrel with phrasing. We waited and watched. Elly learned to walk shortly after she came home from the hospital, as we could have predicted. She learned new words (it was the day

after she came home that she said "scissors"). But we began to
see that she forgot the old ones, and as the months passed she
paid no more attention than before to what we said to her. If she
had come out of the hospital still within the curve of normal
development she did not long remain there. We watched, with
ever sharper and more experienced eyes. As the months passed
and Elly fell farther and farther behind we did not seek other
opinions. We were determined from the start we would not repeat the lacerating pilgrimage of other parents of the retarded
and abnormal, the disrupting and expensive treks from specialist
to specialist, city to city, trying to buy hope. Speechless,
uncomprehending, unable to care for her physical needs, Elly was
retarded in every functional way. If occasional actions suggested
intelligence, common sense told us that it must be so with all
retarded children. All parents would be tempted to magnify these
pathetic flickers into the illusion of significance.

That year of waiting was not passive. That was the year we
began the continual series of minor assaults on Elly's fortress,
the siege that is the subject of this book. But it was a year of
waiting nevertheless. Intuitively we felt it was too soon to press
for certainty about this child's condition. It was better, we
thought, to wait—better for Elly and for us all. Better, quieter,
more dignified, more normal, to carry on the life of the family
as usual than to take these ambiguous symptoms to other doctors
and bring home other ambiguous opinions. More dignified—and
also more intelligent. My husband is a physicist, and in our house
the disciplines of science are deeply felt. We guessed that doctors,
insofar as they are not magic men but scientists, work as other
scientists do, by inferences drawn from evidence. There was
little evidence here. Two doctors had found it insufficient. We
would wait until we could accumulate more.

We waited out those six months, and six months after that.
Then, reluctantly, we prepared for a second attempt at a diagnosis. Elly was not quite three.

We did not mean to shop around and we did not have to. We were lucky enough to have a close friend, himself a doctor and professor, with many connections in the research hospitals of both Boston and New York. His little boy, just Elly's age, was severely retarded both mentally and physically, though with none of Elly's mysterious remoteness. Our friend had already been through it all. His own search had made him wise. He knew what we needed: a doctor who was abreast of the most recent developments in mental and physical illness but who was above all an intelligent and warm human being. He even knew who he was. Dr. Blank was a nationally known pediatrician, a professor of pediatrics, an eminent man. There should be no temptation to appeal his decision.

We drove to Boston with Elly and stayed the night with friends. In the morning we got Elly ready to see the doctor. I dressed her up in navy-blue dotted swiss with a red sash. Pretty clothes meant nothing to Elly, but she looked charming when we took her in and that meant something to us. I do not know if it is obvious that the first visit to a doctor to consult about a mentally abnormal child is a very tense experience. This doctor was the friend of a friend; not many parents are so lucky. Yet still we were uneasy. Would it be possible to talk to this man? Would he want to listen to what we could tell him? Would he respect us that much? We imagined ourselves in his position, examining the healthy, attractive, gravely defective child of two people he did not know. He was an eminent and experienced man but he could analyze only what he saw, and in this hour before us—in any given hour—what could he see of Elly? What was there to be seen? It was highly unlikely she would exhibit one of her rare signs of intelligence right there in his office, or even speak one of her five words. More probably she would sit like a lump, as she had sat in the doctor's office a year before, and then such conclusions as he could draw would rest only on that meaningless silence and on what we could tell him. And why should he believe that?

But our luck held. Our friend had chosen well for us; we profited from his own false starts and blind alleys. Dr. Blank was a rare person, not merely knowledgeable in his profession but gifted in his understanding of people. He made it easy for us to tell him what we had learned about making contact with Elly, and using it he made of the routine physical examination an opportunity of reaching Elly as few could reach her. We suggested that he tickle her and he did. He jigged her up and down. He wasted no time with words. He had a way with children and he used it. Within ten minutes he had seen her smile and laugh—a common enough sight to us but one no doctor had ever seen before.

We relaxed. It was possible to act naturally with this kind, bright man who seemed to trust us. I began one of our games with Elly. I had brought a bag of candy to occupy her when she got restless. I took a piece out and popped it into her mouth. She did not ignore me. She did not take another for herself. Instead, she reached her own hand into the bag and fed one to *me*. Not a high degree of interpersonal activity for an hour-long session between three adults and a three-year-old child, but we were satisfied. Dr. Blank had seen Elly at her best, such as it was. What he told us we would trust.

We had asked him at the outset: "What is the very worst possibility we might have to face?" We are ready, expecting it: to be told that, like so many parents of retarded children, we have been kidding ourselves, that there is no mystery about our Elly, that her strange abilities are no more than the creations of our desperate imaginations, that she is simply a retarded child, so severely retarded that, almost three years old, she still has no comprehension of human speech.

I had no doubt of what the worst possibility would be. Off and on, over the years, I had come across a few retarded children and heard stories of others. No family is exempt—my own uncle, injured before birth when my grandmother's carriage-horses went out of control, had never learned to walk or talk. Uncle Will had died at twenty-one, still an incontinent baby, a generation before I was born. My grandmother, a strong-minded woman, had done what was very unusual at the time—after keeping him at home for years, she had put him into an institution. To spare the family, I suppose, but I think also to spare herself. She couldn't bear it. I had a horror of retardation. I assumed I could rise to most challenges if my children presented them, but I had wondered about that one. Myself proud of intellect, in my husband, in my children, in myself, I had thought that retardation was the worst thing that could happen to a baby, to a family, and to me.

But apparently this was not the worst possibility. There was another. The worst diagnosis he could give us would be a different word altogether—autism. Dr. Blank had seen other children like Elly. At Johns Hopkins, in Baltimore, the psychiatrist Leo Kanner had for twenty years been studying a strange category of children, children who were like and yet not like the psychotic, neurotic, brain-damaged, and retarded children with whom he was familiar. It was hard to say what they were. They had Elly's blank remoteness, her inability to relate to others. They had her imperviousness to speech; several of them had previously been diagnosed as deaf. They, like her, did not talk or, if they did, reeled off long formulas without communicative significance—television commercials, nursery rhymes, even lists of presidents. They had the same dexterity, the same interest in exact and delicate arrangement. They had the same unusual physical health, the same alert, attractive good looks. They even had the same intellectual parents: my husband and I, while scarcely typical of the population as a whole, were typical of the parents of autistic children.

Many psychiatrists called this condition childhood schizophrenia. But Kanner, who had many schizophrenics among his small patients, felt that this condition presented a rare but distinct syndrome. He named it Early Infantile Autism. And it was autism which Dr. Blank considered the worst possibility we had to face. The retarded child's abilities are limited, but he can progress. The autistic child's intelligence, on the contrary, may be normal or superior. There is no way of finding out. Locked in himself, secure and satisfied in his repetitive activities, he will not use it, or even display it for testing. His condition, which so mimics retardation, for practical purposes may be indistinguishable from it.

The defect seemed psychological, not physical. Yet Kanner, himself a psychiatrist, had tried the techniques of psychotherapy. He had concluded they were useless. Dr. Blank wanted to hospitalize Elly for further tests; two autistic children had recently been found suffering from an obscure metabolic defect. Such a defect, if he could find it, would be something tangible, perhaps treatable—with the techniques of the future if not of today. But if the trouble were all in Elly's small psyche then the outlook was dark indeed. There was little—Dr. Blank felt there was nothing—that professional knowledge could contribute to help her.

We took Elly home. In a month we brought her back again to Boston, for another three days in a hospital. If the trouble were psychological—I tried not to think what those hospital visits could do to Elly. So quiet, so remote—it was best to think that she, who had almost never been away from me, who had only once been away from home without me, would retreat into her self-sufficient contentment and make use of it to protect herself from this upheaval of her settled world. It was even plausible: Elly did not notice people, ergo, she would not mind the hospital. Yet I knew it was not so. During those three days a year ago she had cried, she had refused to feed herself or let the nurses feed her. She was in better contact with us now than she had been then. To abandon her again, with no explanation even possible? It broke my heart to do it. Yet it had to be done, and I was already becoming adept at putting out of my mind things that were likely to break my heart. Since Elly would never tell me how she had suffered it would be almost as if it hadn't happened. It was in any case outside the area of my control. There was no better care in the world than was to be found in the Children's Hospital. The doctors would be humane, the nurses experienced. Experienced enough to understand the needs of my wordless baby, to meet them in a way she could accept? Best not to form the question.

David and I went together to take Elly to the hospital. It is a very large building, with many wings and many floors on those wings. Or perhaps it hasn't got many wings at all, perhaps it merely seems enormous, easy to get lost in, and threatening to someone who has not the expertise of illness. I had never been in a hospital in my life except when I was perfectly well. A hospital had been a service station where I was relieved of my tonsils, and later, my babies. This hospital was different. For one thing, it was full of children, children from all over the city, the state—from all over the country children came to this famous hospital. Not one of them was perfectly well, and my Elly, cheerful in her pretty dress with no idea of what was about to happen to her, was not perfectly well either.

Elly was to be admitted at ten o'clock. There was some waiting in the lobby; she was already restless by the time we entered the elevator. There was some discussion with representatives of the administration. The ward where Elly would normally be put was full; she would have to go into another where there was more room. Occupied with Elly, we paid little attention. We had hoped to cushion our departure by making it quick and inconspicuous. Upstairs, however, it seemed there would be a considerable delay. Nobody in this ward was ready to think about Elly. Quiet and preoccupied, everyone here was obviously engaged in some serious business. We were shown into a four-bed ward, and left alone with Elly and her hospital nightgown and the small white crib we hoped a blanket and a teddy bear would convert into an acceptable home.

There was indeed room in this ward. Only one of the other beds was filled. In it lay a pale still child with sunken eyes, her curling hair a dark cloud rising off the pillow. She looked about nine. A thin tube ran from her nostril to some apparatus by the bed. Beside her sat her mother, her hair also dark and curly and her face nearly as pale. They did not speak, and when we came in they did not turn their heads.

Time passed. The crib, at 11:00 A.M., was no place for a healthy three-year-old, even for Elly. Perhaps that was progress. We tried to amuse her, at the same time remaining quiet and inconspicuous for the sake of our silent companions, but there wasn't much to do. She rocked a bit, but at length she wanted to get down from the crib. David went off to see how possible that was, and when whatever was going to happen was going to start. It turned out that it was quite possible. This was an extremely well-appointed hospital, better than I could have imagined. Here was a playroom filled with the most excellent toys, chalks, a blackboard, a television set. There was even a kitchen visible through a door. No one was ready to be occupied with Elly; they were delighted to have us take her there. We got her out of bed and set her on her feet. Her steps sounded cheerful in this strangely silent ward. And then we saw that not all the patients were confined to bed.

As we entered the hall we saw, back in the shadow, a wheel chair, and a young girl in it, eleven perhaps, or twelve, it was difficult to tell. She was not in hospital clothing but wore her own blue dress. A woman—not a hospital attendant—stood behind her. The girl gazed at us, or beyond us, from eyes that were scarcely distinguishable in the midst of the blue-black circles surrounding them. Black eyes in a face inconceivably thin, and around it the same incongruous hair, straight and pale this time, but abundant, the hair of health. And then I saw her legs. From under her starched dress they descended into her white socks, the invulnerable white socks of an ordinary eleven-year-old, which surrounded these legs of this eleven-year-old like a frill, standing alone around still frail sticks with half an inch to spare. A child's bone, I realized, has no thickness at all.

We have all seen pictures of such children, although not dressed with such decorum. We recognize them when we remember—the starved and outraged children of Buchenwald and Auschwitz. But this child was not in a death camp but a great modern hospital, there to be made well again. It crossed my mind that it would take a long time and very great skill to nourish this child back to health.

The obtuseness of the fortunate is beyond belief. It was not until we had been three hours in that hospital that we found out where we were. Of course. This was the ward for terminal cancer cases. These children were not here to be cured, they were here to die—with the best of care, hidden mercifully away from a society that has been so successful in shielding itself from the knowledge of death that two experienced adults could stare it in the face and still not know what they were seeing.

We were not smart enough to realize it for ourselves. It was from a mother in the playroom that we found out. While Elly sat and watched the meaningless shadows on the TV (there was none in our house, so the novelty was absorbing and welcome) she played a board game with her little boy. He was about seven, we thought—relaxed, outgoing, obviously extremely bright. He and his mother laughed a lot and talked to us and to the third child in the room, a three-year-old with a large plaster on his back. The seven-year-old sat in his chair and didn't get up. Aside from that he didn't seem sick. But as soon as the nurse wheeled him out for treatment his mother asked us what must have been in the minds of the other mothers too: what was Elly doing here?

Her bright little boy had leukemia. Right now he was very well, since he was having his transfusions—he had just gone for another one. He was still able to be at home; when he got too weak she brought him in for another transfusion. After a time— you couldn't know how long—she wouldn't be able to take him home again. The mothers were encouraged to spend as much time here as they could. That was why they provided the kitchen, so they could cook the things the children liked and perhaps they might eat a little . . . the toys were here if they wanted them . . . it took a long time sometimes. The girl in the wheel chair had been brought in in April with a week to live and here it was June and she was still sitting up. . . .

The bright little boy came back in again. So I had seen his future, out there in the hall.

I looked at Elly, busy doing nothing. Part of us is still a child, and thinks the universe should be fair. What had gone wrong? If Elly could not have that boy's sharp mind and bright spirit, could he not at least have the health she had no use for—health in which for the first time I felt not pride but shame?

But her health was not so easily to be given away. At last they were ready to admit her. We were sent off, and the doctors came. Dr. Blank's report, which I am glad I did not see until long after, describes her as she appeared to the eyes of science: "The record shows that she was a well-developed, healthy-appearing, blonde, blue-eyed child found hiding under a blanket and rocking in her bed. She cried during most of the examination and no words were spoken. Her head was normal in size . . . anterior fontanel closed . . . ears and eardrums entirely normal. Her pupils reacted well to light and accommodation. . . . Nose was normal, her mouth unremarkable, her tonsils moderately enlarged. She had no unusual lymph node enlargement. Heart, lungs, and abdomen were normal. . . . Examination of her cranial nerves, her deep tendon reflexes and motor and sensory reactions were all within normal limits. Her gait was normal." Hemoglobin and urine were normal. "The electroencephalogram was normal in deep sleep. Skull X-rays were unremarkable. Serum for measles antibody complement fixation test was negative."

So she was quite healthy. She had always been healthy; that last sentence meant that as far as tests could tell she had not had measles in the womb and her condition was not due to any assumed encephalitis. She was healthy now, as far as medical techniques could tell. Dr. Blank, a true man of science, made it clear that that was not very far. That he had been able to find no metabolic defect did not mean that there was none. There was no sure diagnosis, either. Elly's intelligence was still an unknown quantity; it had proved impossible to test her. Insofar as he proffered a word at all, it was autism. Mercifully, he spared us the other terms, so much more threatening—childhood psychosis, childhood schizophrenia. He knew we'd find them out soon enough. The articles to which he referred us were all studies in Kanner's syndrome. But even autism was uncertain. "In many ways she seems to be an autistic child, relating poorly to the other children. Her apparent early normal development reaching a plateau, her interest in small objects and their orderly arrangement, her failure in speech—all would fit into such a picture. On the other hand, she enjoys being played with physically, she likes to have her parents enter into the 'games' she uses, and these findings do not fit well." The tickling we had suggested, the candy she had fed me, had complicated the diagnosis. It occurred to me later that if he had seen her only as he did in the hospital, rocking under her blanket, too bruised to respond to the overtures that had worked so well in his office, his diagnosis might have been less ambiguous. How many "classic" cases of autism are diagnosed by doctors and psychiatrists who have never seen them among familiar friends in a relaxed environment?

At any rate, he had no particular advice. "Take her home," he said, "do what you've been doing . . . give her plenty of affection . . . let me know how you get along. . . ." A little shrug of helplessness, sympathy, regret. This was a good and kindly man, too intelligent and accomplished a doctor to pretend certainty where he found none. For that we admired and trusted him.

In a way it made no difference not knowing what ailed Elly. But the mind craves explanations, the will craves situations that can be faced and adjusted to. Here there was nothing to face and no plans to be made. This was not the retardation we had feared, but which we could have at least accepted as final. If we could be sure that Elly had no capacity for normal development we could accommodate ourselves to that. Perhaps, for her sake and ours, she should be sent away—like Uncle Will. But autism? What was autism? How could we adjust to an unknown? To live with autism would be like living under water. We might never come up, yet we had not the option of drowning.

In the old days I had wondered more than once if my fortune had not been too good. Half as a literary exercise, I had mused about what life had in store for me, guessed that if the poets were right there must be waiting some whips and plagues to set the balance right. After my childhood ended I had so much luck—dear husband, friends, my lot cast in pleasant places, all, somehow, summed up in my golden babies, born to comfort, cultivation, intelligence, beauty, health. It is hard not to be proud of one's luck. Hubris is part of us; knowing its name does not help one escape it. Irrationally I had felt that in some way I had deserved all I had, that I had made it happen. We deserve nothing, except to be human *comme les autres*. It is a slow lesson; the mothers in the hospital had learned it. "Call no man happy before he is dead," said Solon. The instrument chosen to humble me had the exquisite appropriateness the Greeks noted in the operation of impersonal powers like Fate—or Biology.

4 ⸱ Willed Weakness

"ON THE other hand she enjoys being played with physically, she likes to have her parents enter into the games she uses, and these findings do not fit well." We were thankful for these findings, and that they did not fit that most hopeless of possible diagnoses. It suggested that the condition was not entirely hopeless after all. It could be modified. We had modified it already. It was natural enough that Dr. Blank should think that the pathetic, rudimentary reciprocity he noted was spontaneous. Only we could know it was not. The uncertainty of his diagnosis was our best reward so far for our work with Elly.

At that time we had been at work for twelve months. For a third of her short life Elly had been under siege. As soon as she had come out of the hospital for the first time we had begun to devise our stratagems. These next chapters will describe them, and with them Elly's progress from twenty-two months, when I first began to keep a written record, until the age of four. Later development will be described in its place.

I have written already that when we brought Elly home that first time, speechless, uncomprehending, still unable to walk, we did not want to fool ourselves. The doctor had felt she was still classifiable as normal. Yet we grasped well enough that this low-grade normality was no normality at all given the environment

Elly lived in. Institutionalized babies, perhaps, or children bewildered in distracted families where speech was rudimentary and noise constant, might indeed appear like Elly and still be normal, having good reasons for the simplicity of their accomplishments. Not Elly. Who among the parents we knew had a normal child as slow as that? To dwell on Elly's alertness, to play with the idea that she was simply withholding her abilities—this seemed the most soft-headed kind of self-deception. The child was retarded—after all, the word does have a literal meaning. She was retarded in what she did. How was it possible to make a distinction between what she did and what she was? Why should we imagine that her retardation was "different"? We are proud people, and proud people do not like to feel soft-headed. So we did not want to fool ourselves.

Yet at the same time we were determined not to abandon Elly in the isolation she found so congenial. To treat so marginal a child as retarded would itself ensure that she would become so; if she were in fact retarded it would make her worse. Once I had been glad of her self-sufficiency; now I must fight it. She must be approached, played with, taken places, drawn into the family. She had liked being alone, she had spent hours in her crib, sleeping, bouncing, laughing, rocking, rocking, rocking. All that must now be at an end. Little as she appeared to want our company, she would have it. She might be content with the rise and fall of a chain; I must find better toys and try to lead her through them to more complex experiences and skills.

It would have to begin with movement and the sense of touch. Compared to touch, hearing and sight are indirect, remote, far less central to the living organism. People can exist without sight or in total deafness. They can be so preoccupied that they neither see nor hear the world around them. Touch them, however, and they will come to themselves. Touch is the most directly apprehended of the senses. The body's response to things that touch it ceases only with death.

Through sound I could achieve no contact with Elly. Her sense of sight was hardly more promising—she looked at me sometimes, more often than at anyone else, but except in exceptionally favorable situations, as when I greeted her in the morning, she ignored me too.

Unless I came very close. When I touched her, she noticed that. And although she did not seem to hear or see, her small legs and arms and fingers moved. She could inhibit her senses, but she could not entirely deny she had a body.

It was in her motion, in fact, that the discrepancy between what she did and what she gave flashes of being able to do first showed. I remember a day when a friend brought her toddler, a little older than Elly, to visit. Johnny had been walking for months. He had rushed into it, as many babies do, before he was physically ready, he had wanted to so much. He had stumbled, fallen, but he had walked. We had both laughed when, able to walk but not yet to sit down, he had collapsed from a standing position onto his bottom with a thump. Elly could stand up too. She too sat down, but it was no ungainly flop. As we watched, she lowered herself, legs gradually bending through a squat, into a sitting position, in an exhibition of controlled grace unusual in any child of that age. My friend exclaimed what we both thought: "Why Elly, you fraud!" This the child who couldn't walk? Obviously she could walk. She would walk as soon as she wanted to put one foot in front of the other. Yet it was months before she did walk.

It was the same with using her hands. She had begun to feed herself with her fingers at about fifteen months, but she did not use a spoon. We had done the usual tricks, we had kept a small spoon available, we had provided tempting foods that required it, but Elly had ignored them. One day she had finished her meal, and been lifted down out of her high chair, while the family continued eating. Suddenly Elly, hardly big enough to reach the table, grabbed a large, awkward spoon and conveyed into her mouth a large dollop of my dessert. It happened so fast we barely saw it. Then she was gone. We tried her again next day. Her hand went limp. Not only could this child not feed herself, she couldn't even hold a utensil.

There was, of course, no point in talking to her. A child who doesn't respond to "Elly, here's a cookie," will hardly understand "If you don't pick up that spoon you won't get any ice cream." Yet even pigeons can be shown that rewards are conditional upon performance; the same methods that teach rats to run mazes might have been used to get Elly to hold a spoon. Today children like her are learning, by means of the behavior modification techniques developed by psychologists like Ivar Lovaas and Frank Hewett at the University of California at Los Angeles, not only to feed themselves, but to respond to people, even to speak, as the desired behavior is analyzed into stages and every centimeter of progress rewarded to encourage the next small step towards the goal. Today these techniques are taught to parents. But when Elly was two experiments with reinforcement therapy had hardly begun. She was seven before I even heard of them.

It did not take long to learn that to put Elly into situations of extreme pressure was not only lacerating but useless. I have mentioned that she learned to crawl upstairs at seventeen months, and then forgot. After many months—it was after she came home from the first trip to the hospital—she learned again, and with some help she learned also to crawl down. But she did not learn as other children do, a skill to be extended, applied in new situations with a feeling of mastery and pleasure. She could crawl up and down our main staircase. Not our third-floor stairs, however, and not any staircase in a neighbor's house. One day—she was just past two—we carried her halfway up a friend's stairs and marooned her. I stayed at the bottom, smiling encouragement. She understood the situation at once, she who understood so little. She began to cry, with a kind of crying very rare for her, for though she might fret, or cry loudly if hurt, she did not cry much or long. This was a hard crying to listen to—lost, furious, totally committed—a crying that came up from the inside depths we never reached. We let it go on for twenty minutes. Then we carried her down. What would she have learned if we had left her there? Nothing, I think, except that we were willing to treat her with inconceivable violence. We could not have left her there. I think, I really think she was ready to stay there till she died.

But she did want to come down enough to cry about it. That itself was rare. Her detachment usually provided her with better armor. In almost all situations, the weakness of her desires was there working for her, against us. The rat wants the flavored pellet, the pigeon wants the corn. What did Elly want enough to meet any conditions for getting it? Not a cookie, not a toy, not a ride in the car. A baby who like a Zen adept acquires the knack of inhibiting its desires approaches something akin to the Zen *satori*. Serene, in perfect vegetative equilibrium, it can be content to do nothing at all. When a creature is without desires the outside world has no lever by which to tempt it into motion.

So again and again it was as if she could but wouldn't. That, of course, was the source of the doctors' uncertainty. Those vigorous legs, those exquisitely controlled fingers sifting the links of her chain became weak and useless when confronted with any imposed task. And what was an imposed task? To climb, to reach, to walk—all the activities other children spontaneously throw themselves into in their delighted desire to learn and grow. Elly seemed strong. But between her and any normal development lay this terrible weakness, a weakness that was no less real because it seemed to lie not in the muscles but in the will.

Who knows what is willed and what is not? Who boasts he can read minds—least of all a wordless baby's? In humility I can only say that Elly's weakness seemed as if it was willed, in full realization of the difficulty of believing it. It is a little too much to swallow—to accept that an infant can assess its situation—as we have all seen frightened grownups do—and decide that anything is preferable, even total withdrawal, to the risks of activity and growth. It is as if . . . *As if*. Again and again we used this formulation, as we searched out explanations of our child's strange contradictions. *As if*—yet we could not and cannot be sure. We cannot help interpreting. The words *as if* must function to remind us that we can be sure of no interpretations.

It was as if, then, Elly had realized early, earlier than it seems possible for any child to realize, that if she remained motionless, sitting on a rug in the middle of the floor, nothing could occur to threaten her, that if she attempted to do nothing, she need never fail. She did not in fact sit motionless—she was alive and healthy, her body functioned and impelled her to a fuller interaction with the world than that—but it seemed to us that this was the model of her condition. Her body was as strong as it was beautiful, but in comparison to a normal child she used it hardly at all. The first strategies of the besiegers must deal with this least abstract, most accessible of Elly's weaknesses. It was useless to assault ears that would not hear us and eyes that would not see. The first approach—the only way in—was to try to return to her her primary birthright, the use of her body.

How elevated that sounds, how elaborate and complex! Yet it is a fancy description of something most simple. There can be nothing esoteric about a mother working with a baby, trying tactfully, delicately, to encourage it to do new things. This is what all mothers learn. Everything I found to do in this abnormal, extreme situation was only an extension and intensification of things I had done with my normal babies. Such tact as I had I had learned with them. So it may be with a feeling of anticlimax that the reader moves into a description of what was actually done. It seems very simple and it was. There wasn't anything else for it to be. Even the most accomplished professional therapists of children, if we view them operationally, considering what they *do*, do something quite simple. They discover the right games to play.

Consider one of the first skills we managed to convey to her —drinking from a cup. She sat with us at the table, she fed herself, but although her cup was there before her, small and comfortably available, she never picked it up. When it was time to drink I held it up for her, as I had done ever since she was a small baby. If I put it in contact with her fingers they refused even to close around it, let alone expend the force necessary to lift it to her mouth. Months went by—she was twenty months old, two years, and still incapable of grasping the cup. Incapable at table. In her bath she had cups which she used with finesse, not only picking them up but deftly pouring water from one into the other. More months pass. It is late in November; Elly, born in July, is nearly two and a half.

One day at dinner Elly surprises us. Rapidly, decisively, she picks up a small glass of milk, pours it accurately into her applesauce. There is a precedent; the previous day I had poured milk into her applesauce for the first time, but that hardly explains it. Though man is an imitative animal, Elly does not imitate. Nevertheless, some resistance seems to be giving here; the very next day she picks up one of her bath cups and drinks from it. The day after, she picks up her cereal bowl, quickly drinks some of the milk and pours the rest on the table.

There was so little at any given time going on with Elly that it took no special acumen to note a new readiness, which could perhaps be made use of. Experience had taught me that while other babies might be encouraged if congratulated and made a fuss over, Elly would react in just the opposite way, with retreat. It worked badly when we called attention to anything Elly was doing—she always stopped doing it. *As if* she didn't want to be committed to any forward progress—*as if* she feared that any concession she made would at once be taken advantage of. I knew the new skill was best ignored, not pressed.

So I got a very tiny cup, much smaller than her small child's mug—so small, so inconspicuous that it would be hard indeed to regard it as a challenge. I filled it with Elly's favorite juice. But half full only. With her uncanny accuracy she wasn't likely to spill even a full glass, but I wanted to eliminate the slightest threat of failure. I put the cup, not on the dinner table where her ability, if displayed, would be noted and seem formally to commit her, but on a low chair. It was not yet serving time and Elly was moving about the kitchen as usual. She spotted the little cup, and when she did pick it up and drink it none of us appeared to notice. Indeed it was easy not to, she did it so fast. Above all, we did not at once set cup and juice at her place at table; we fed her her liquids exactly as before. Not for several days did I move the tiny cup from chair to table, and not for several more did the juice begin to appear in successively larger vessels. One must respect other people's concessions, and recognize that they may have cost more than may appear. Even a tiny child has face to lose, and we guessed that Elly had much invested in her disabilities, although we did not, still do not, know what it was, and is.

It was the same with introducing her to new toys—and to extend Elly's range of play seemed even more important than teaching her convenient household skills. My diary records Elly's play activities at the time she returned from the hospital:

> She is still playing primarily with rattles, which she likes to use as a tool for patting picture books. In fact exercising—joggling or rocking in chair or crib—chaining, and patting are *all* she does. She can be left alone on a bed for hours with no toys; she will not fall off or get down. Peg-in-hole toys or ring on peg she regards only as something to dismantle, the parts of which can then be used to pat or knock other surfaces.

I had tried to induce her to put rings on a stick before she went to the hospital. Had it been too soon, or had I merely not seen how it should be done? When she came back I thought harder. I got down on the floor, close beside Elly. I did not push the toy into her radius of attention. I began to play with it myself. In slow motion I put on several of the bigger, harder rings. Then I put on a smaller ring, but only halfway. Askew, yet clearly on, even Elly couldn't consider it too difficult a challenge, and what I was doing was somewhat more interesting than what she was doing, which was, as usual, nothing. I retreated a hand's breadth, and looked away. When I looked back, the ring was on the stick.

More of this, and then I could risk extending it. Perhaps Elly was ready for me actually to give her the smallest, easiest ring. I didn't put it into her hand—Elly never accepted objects as directly as that. Instead I laid it on the floor beside her hand. And she picked it up and she put it on the stick.

The next day she put all the rings on the stick, easily, neatly, as if she had always been able to. Soon—I can't remember when —she learned of herself to arrange them according to size, one of the earliest indications of something we were to become more and more familiar with, the extraordinary sense of order of the autistic child—the sense, perhaps, which made it necessary for her to adjust that first ring, left, by a lucky intuition, halfway on.

How hard it is to keep this account from taking on the tone of a success story. For what had I accomplished? In addition to book-patting, chaining, and rocking, Elly could now put rings on a stick. As if in relief at the introduction of some variety into her circumscribed activities, she did put rings on a stick—over and over and over. With each of the few activities I was able to add it was the same—received with delight at first, it was repeated and repeated and finally abandoned as if—*as if*—in boredom. She would not extend it into meaningful play, and I could find no way of helping her. Blocks were to tower, then to line up parallel, but never to build a house. Indeed at that time I had no reason to think that Elly knew what a house was, that she knew what anything was except perhaps the food she ate and the clothes she wore. It is necessary to emphasize that this account is not to be read like an account of a normal child in which the description of one activity does duty for a whole class. In describing Elly at two I do not have to select. What I tell is all there is to be told.

Yet these tiny successes accomplished something. Narrow as Elly's spectrum remained, it was less narrow than before. Each minuscule, apparently empty victory nourished something in Elly and in us. In Elly, perhaps some frail sense of adequacy, in us the necessary hope that our daughter had some mind hidden away inside her speechless incomprehension. Not too much hope —foolish hope was something against which we had to defend ourselves. Only enough to mount the next assault.

Elly grows older; she is nearing three. We have taken her on a picnic. Together we sit on a rock promontory beside a brook. I have carried her over the rough ground and the rocks; though she now walks gracefully and well, the slightest shift of a stone beneath her feet is enough to render her motionless. I drop a stone in the pool beside us—a splash, a satisfying plop, a new experience for a child almost without experience. Elly should be able to do this, I figure. The pool is right beside us. She need hardly stretch out her hand. I give her a stone. She has progressed in these months; I do not put it directly into her hand, but she takes it from my outstretched palm. She drops it in (that she would *throw* it in, with a three-year-old's abandon, is of course inconceivable). I hand her another, another. She likes this game. The stones are in a small pile close beside us. I move slightly away. With a touch, I call her attention to the pile. She wants another stone, another plop. Will she reach out her hand the six inches it must travel to pick up another stone for herself?

No, she won't. Not today. I do not press; I know the answer is final. My immobility is a mirror of hers. I have learned to wait.

The readiness expands, though far more slowly than for the slowest of normal children. Each new skill makes the next one easier, though not easy. And that is why I keep on—not so much because it makes life less burdensome if my child can feed herself and make use of rudimentary motor skills, although of course everything she can do for herself is one more thing I do not have to do. It is because each new skill must make *her* feel a little different. One works on the assumption—it must be, in fact, a faith—that the tiniest success *must* leave a trace, must move the child, however imperceptibly, toward the experience of adequacy. So, as one thinks of them, and that is very slowly, one sets up the preconditions for new successes, even if these are to be no more impressive than picking up a stone and dropping it into the water. Each new accomplishment is not only a bolstering of confidence, it is an incursion into that guarded emptiness, an enrichment of that terrible simplicity. And though Elly resists each foray, we suspect (for a long time it is no more than a suspicion) that she is glad of them. She can take no initiative toward growth, yet she is no frozen adult but a living child. We must believe she will be glad to grow.

So we keep pressing, not too much, but not too little either, in ways so simple that it seems ludicrous to record them. A few months after she is three she becomes interested in lights. She knows that light comes when one pulls a string or moves a switch. I have not taught her, nor could I; this is just the sort of thing it turns out she knows. When she wants light she moves my hand to the switch. But it is my hand that is her tool, not her own; she cannot move the switch herself. Teaching her to turn on a light is a process of choosing the easiest switch in the house. It cannot be the string, which must be pulled, nor the old-fashioned switches that require pressing, for the muscular effort required of this strong child must be imperceptible. I take her hand. With it I flick the switch. Down first, lights out, for that is easier. It takes time—how long I don't remember. At length she can do it for herself.

Though she is fascinated with water, activating a faucet is harder. Using, perhaps, her light-switch experience, she learns of herself to use the kitchen faucet, which requires only a simple push. But an ordinary faucet requires both pressure and twist. I put Elly's hand to it; wrist and fingers go limp. My whole hand covers Elly's; using hers as a tool, I turn on the faucet. This first time, and again, and again, all the force is mine. Elly likes water and she has no objection to repetition. Imperceptibly —I hope it is imperceptibly—I lighten my pressure. The small hand beneath mine is no longer quite limp. It seems that there are muscles there after all. I move my hand a quarter inch up hers as I turn the water on again. Another quarter inch. A half. Infinitely gradually I withdraw my hand, up her fingers, up her wrist. *She goes on turning on the water.* My hand moves up her arm. Finally all that is left is one finger on her shoulder, to enable her to maintain the fiction that it is I, not she, who is performing the action. We have been together over the basin a full hour. But the work is not yet over; next day we must go over the process again to re-establish the skill, but we can do it more rapidly. Then I remove my finger; my presence now is enough. The next day she does it alone, thrilled, delighted, over and over. She understands everything about the process, even things I thought too difficult to teach. She never lets the basin overflow, she never turns on the hot water. But the work is not quite done. For weeks she will require a brief retraining before every unfamiliar faucet. It is a long time before the new mastery can be fully accepted.

It is as if Elly were more comfortable with an image of herself that could not do things. Her inabilities seemed not only willed but jealously guarded. I remember her at four, after considerable progress of the kind described here, getting ready for her bath. She cannot yet undress herself, but for some weeks she has been taking off her shoes once I untied them. Today she refuses, laughing at me. (Learning to tease shows of course great progress in human contact, but that belongs in a later chapter.) I wait, resisting the temptation to assist her. The shoe is on so loosely that it falls off. Elly, who "cannot" put on her shoes, sizes up the situation. Instantly and expertly she puts the shoe back on. She was not going to take it off and she didn't!

Whatever it was that held Elly back from using her hands also inhibited her use of her body. The extreme physical caution that had made it possible for us to ignore the dangers of stairs and edges when she was small did not abate. We could only infer that she was capable of balancing and climbing like other children, as we had inferred that she could walk. For three years things on upper shelves were safe; if Elly could not reach them, she would not push over a chair and climb to get them. For more than four years she was lifted into and out of her crib. As time went on I kept the sides down and set a chair beside the bed. Elly would tentatively put her legs over the side onto the waiting chair and draw them back again. Yet we remembered a strange disturbed night a year before when the older children, left to baby-sit for an Elly who, because of guests, had been put to sleep in a playpen in an unfamiliar room, had had to call us home because Elly had gotten out three times. How had she done it? The playpen sides were higher than the crib's. Nobody knew; she hadn't, of course, performed in public. When I returned and put her back in the pen, she stayed there. Naturally; she couldn't climb, could she?

It was the same with stairs. One day in November—she was almost two and a half—she gingerly descended the stairs of a local museum, erect on her two feet. The stairs were wide and shallow, easy to manage. It was April before she walked down the taller stairs at home. Years passed, her legs got longer, but still she descended like a two-year-old, both feet touching each step. She was six before she went down like a normal child, foot below foot.

Hesitation, caution, unwillingness to interact with the physical world. These sound like the shapes of fear, and perhaps they were. Yet she did not seem afraid. It was as if she had found a way to make fear unnecessary. She did not have to be afraid; she had found a way to protect herself from the challenges of her environment. Ignore them and you will not have to avoid them. If something is there to push, do not push it. Do not pull, twist, open, lift, balance, kick, climb, throw. Attempt nothing. Then there will be no failure and you can remain serene. This was not fear in any recognizable form. If it was fear, it lay so deep it never showed itself. There was visible only a tight, closed caution. We could work on it, gradually lead her through tiny steps, each unthreatening, each well within her ability, to the experience of small successes—and hope that she would begin to acquire the ordinary child's taste for mastery of the forces of the physical world. But the process was inconceivably slow. We waited for the point when one success would generate another without our intervention, when Elly would move ahead on her own from skill to skill as other children do. But it did not come. For year upon year, the initiative remained with us.

5 ⸱ Willed Blindness

A NORMAL child develops almost automatically. It needs no officious overseers to assist it in the use of its senses. If is sufficient that it find itself in a world that can be touched, heard, seen. If babies had to be taught to reach, to focus, to listen, to interpret, the human race would never have survived. The most gifted pedagogue could hardly hope to program the speech development that takes place spontaneously in a dull normal two-year-old.

But Elly was not a normal child. She was not spastic or paralytic, yet we could not take for granted that she would use her body. It was the same with the more abstract abilities—with hearing and with sight. We could not take them for granted either. Elly was not blind, but sight is more than images on the retina. The organism must record, but it must also interpret before it can be said to see. As eighteen-month-old Elly flipped the pages of her colored picture books, what did she see? Did her mind integrate the reds and browns and blacks and blues and greys into a kitten or a car? I could not say. I could only observe that she flipped the pages rapidly, steadily, with never a pause. Once—once only—she had shown she recognized a picture, of a blue teddy bear like her own. That was at seventeen months. Months passed, one year, another, and never did Elly give another sign that she could see a picture.

Negative abilities are harder to spot in proportion as they are more abstract. With all the other things Elly did not do, it was only gradually that we began to think about how much she did not seem to see. We knew, of course, that she could look right through a person. She usually did. It was some time before we became conscious that she was blind to more than human beings. But when we began to think about it, it seemed that Elly saw little that was farther than three feet away.

I have said that she did not point. After a while, no more did we; it was impossible, by gesture and of course by speech, to get her to look at anything at a distance. The significance of this might be dubious; it was, after all, impossible without a Machiavellian strategy to get her to do anything at all. If she did not see a dog when we pointed at it there was no cause for surprise. Yet as impressions piled up, it was impossible not to be struck by her imperviousness to visual stimuli of all sorts.

A car would draw up within three feet of where she was playing. She would not look at it. A dog ran past. She seemed to register nothing. She was over three before she looked up and saw a bird. Not until she was well past four did she respond in such a way that we could be sure she had seen a cow across a highway, twenty-five feet away.

I am myopic; mine is the simple but severe nearsightedness that closes in at age six to eight, when a child begins to read. Naturally it occurred to me that Elly might be suffering from an early onset of the same thing. Without my glasses, I cannot see a cow across a road either. Yet I could not think that Elly lived in the haze that envelops me when I take my glasses off— Elly who never fumbled, never fell. She was perfectly oriented to her environment. When we went for a walk she knew every turning. I could lag behind her and she would lead me home. Unless she enjoyed some sixth sense (and I have thought of that too), she must, I reasoned, have registered the positions of trees and buildings as she passed; she must, therefore, have seen them.

We felt, moreover, that any explanation must reach beyond a single symptom. We had learned it was no lack of strength or co-ordination that prevented Elly from using her hands. We could suspect that what limited her use of her eyes was no physical disability, but the same mysterious defect of will. As she did not reach out with her body, so she did not explore with her eyes. Those who attach no significance to what they see are in their own way blind. The task we had before us was not to improve Elly's vision, but to extend the range of what she found worth looking at, to help her find meaning in what we were reasonably sure she saw.

For what Elly thought significant she seemed to see well enough. If she didn't notice dogs or cows at a distance, she didn't notice them up close either. She ignored our cat even more thoroughly than she ignored her siblings. But there were things she did not ignore—colors, abstract shapes. There was no question that she saw these.

One day—she was two years and eight months old—I was putting on her snowsuit. Ordinarily she was eager to go out, but today she acted oddly. Instead of submitting passively to being dressed, she tried to get away, and as soon as the suit was on she headed upstairs. I waited, and when she didn't return, went up and found her absorbed in a set of parquet shapes I had put out on a bureau, in hopes of getting her interested. She had caught sight of them while I was carrying her downstairs and had clearly decided she wanted to play with them. Hence the resistance and the return.

The set is of a common type, composed of diamonds, right triangles, and squares of four different colors, which may be assembled in various ways. Elly, as I watched incredulous, selected four diamonds and combined them into a larger diamond, rejecting in the process a couple of right triangles that came to hand. She did this twice more, then began on the squares, working with a concentration that is difficult to describe. For twenty minutes her whole attention was focused on the task. The abstract, meaningless shapes seemed to have intrinsic importance for her. Discriminating between them was easy. Yet this was a child of whose intelligence we were in grave doubt, whom it seemed impossible to interest in the usual toys, whose ordinary play was little more than sifting sand through her fingers or arranging blocks in parallel lines.

I put the set away when she had finished. I did not want this play to degenerate into sterile perseveration any faster than it had to. I got it out two weeks later and she arranged the pieces by color as well as by shape. A week later, on another toy, she discriminated stars, octagons, and hexagons as well. But the fine concentration was gone. This was too easy to be interesting. There seemed no place to go from here. Once she had mastered them, I could think of little to be done with shapes.

There were of course puzzles. These involved shape-discrimination, and might lead to the recognition of pictures, but so far I had had only minor success with them. Six months before— she was only a little over two—I had got out the easiest of the children's wooden puzzles. It represented Puss in Boots. There were seven wooden pieces, one for the head, one for the body, two arms, two booted legs, and a tail. Elly was able, unprompted, to put in the easier pieces, but others presented physical difficulties; to get them in she would have to adjust them slightly or exert a small physical pressure. This was too much to ask. She became frustrated and I put in the other pieces myself. She showed no sign she recognized the pieces as head or boots, or ultimately as cat.

I kept on with puzzles, off and on, but Elly rarely put in a piece herself. She would look on while I did one, without enthusiasm but with more attention than she showed most things. To involve her in the play and to test her knowledge of the puzzle I would place a piece wrong. Unerringly her hand would touch mine to indicate the correct position. By two and three-quarters, the age when she discovered the parquet blocks, she had, so to speak, a passive mastery of three puzzles at or above her age level. I suspected she could do more, but had not yet thought of a way to manage it.

It was not for some weeks that the breakthrough came. Elly was nearly three. Two weeks before, in Boston while she was hospitalized for testing, we had shopped for toys and found a very much simpler puzzle than those she was used to—only five pieces, each of which fitted unambiguously into a slot of its own. With this I hoped to tempt Elly to use those hands and eyes that could do so much more than they would—to complete a puzzle for herself.

It worked. Elly showed her usual unwillingness to pick up the pieces, but it was so easy that apparently she couldn't resist. Problems like reversal of pieces that had frustrated her in harder puzzles she solved immediately. She liked the easy puzzle. In the next couple of weeks she did it often—often enough so that I knew she would soon lose interest in it, as she had already lost interest in the others.

I put the new puzzle away, and when I brought it out again the next week I brought out the three old ones with it. I put the pile in a new place in a different room to provide a new context, since she had ceased to be interested in them in the old one. The easy puzzle was on the top. For the first time in a week she rapidly assembled and disassembled it, but she did not stop there. The cat puzzle was on the bottom of the pile. Elly got it out on her own and started to do it. She put in the easy pieces with her own hand, without hesitation. The cat's two boots, however, are similar but not interchangeable; it is easy even for an adult to confuse them. When they would not fit, Elly whimpered and took out all the pieces she had put in. I helped her with the boots, and we finished the puzzle together. When a piece resisted, I took her hand and made it pat the piece into place. The following day, while I looked on unknown to her, she found the cat puzzle and did it completely, boots and all, patting down the pieces exactly as I had shown her.

The easy puzzle was what had done the trick. Again the principle was illustrated: in teaching Elly a new skill, it was not enough to be sure it lay within her demonstrated capability. It must be well within; it must be so ridiculously simple that it could present no challenge, afford no threat, make no apparent demands on future performance. Only then would Elly dare to commit herself. I knew that. I had learned it with the spoon, the cup, the rings on a stick. But what seems clear now was groping then. I was not so different from Elly. Like her, with her, I had to learn the same things over and over again.

Now Elly could do puzzles. She could grasp a new puzzle in no time at all. Most children, doing puzzles, are guided by the picture, not by shape alone. But Elly saw the shapes so exactly that she needed nothing more to clue her. She could do a puzzle face down—picture invisible, shapes reversed. The pile grew tall. The cat was joined by a fish, an elephant, a fire engine. Elly would amuse herself by dumping out all the pieces of all the puzzles. It made a fine mess, but when we picked them up Elly could classify the pieces according to their puzzles of origin better than I. Her discrimination of shape and color was astounding. But did she see the picture itself? In assembling the cat, did she make the slightest use of the fact that the boots belonged at the bottom of the puzzle while the head belonged at the top?

Apparently she did not. Five months afterward she still could not master one piece of the simplest puzzle of all—another five-piecer we'd gotten after the success of the first. This piece represented a yellow sun, its shape and dimensions virtually identical in every direction. The only clue to its proper orientation was not its shape or color, but its painted eyes; if the piece was placed so these appeared at the top, it would fit in easily. This simple cue Elly *could not learn to recognize*. Eyes—faces—were simply not within her scheme of relevance. That piece continued to frustrate her when ostensibly far more difficult puzzles did not.

There was something frightening about those bright eyes of Elly's that discriminated minutiae we could not see, yet were blind to everything that was obvious. How could we give Elly's shapes a human meaning? Elly was three years old, and I was still trying to find out whether she recognized that a doll had a human shape. Sculpture, which reaches touch as well as sight, is one degree less abstract than painting. We sit on the floor with a small girl doll. It belongs to Elly's sisters; it has many outfits. I dress it. Elly pulls the clothes off, chooses another costume, we begin again. The game holds her interest over several weeks. Can I assume that it shows she knows the doll represents a human body? Testing, testing. In the absence of other evidence I cannot be sure. I try to put the doll into interesting situations, but of course they are not interesting to Elly. One day, however, an idea floats into my mind, which most of the time is vacant; I play "this little piggy," which Elly knows, not on Elly's toes but the doll's. Elly shows no interest, but in her bath that night I surprise her counting over the doll's toes, ending with the delighted squeal that for her signals the climax of a tickling game. It seems unmistakable that she is tickling the doll, that it is safe to conclude at last that she sees the doll has toes like her own.

I can make explicit, now, the principle that I then perceived so dimly that I made use of it only by accident: in reaching the eyes and ears of such children, and later on their minds, one must begin with sensations their bodies can recognize. From Elly's toes to the doll's. It is not for three full months that it occurs to me, as mechanically we turn the pages of *A Treasury of Art Masterpieces* (so much more interesting for mother than Little Golden Books), to play "this little piggy" on the bare toes of those Renaissance Christ-babies. Which I do. And Elly *laughs*. This is the first evidence I have had since that single time two years before, which already seems a lifetime past, that color and shape have taken on significance and that Elly can see a picture.

From her own body to the abstract representation. Later in the same month Elly becomes interested in her brother's kindergarten workbook. She turns the pages as always, looking with attention but without recognition. But now I have an inkling of how to proceed. As we pass a large, realistic picture of an ice cream cone, I take her hand and make her pat it. Next time she looks at the book there is a pause in the mechanical turning; that picture, at any rate, she sees.

This book was full of usable sights; for the picture of a school playground I made her fingers walk up the slide and go "whee" down, I made them ride the seesaw and the swings. I no longer wondered about her comprehension; her delight left no doubt of it. When we came to that picture, if I omitted to move her hand Elly herself put my hand on hers, silently requesting me to make her fingers walk up the slide. She would not go so far as to move that hand herself. But there was no doubt that she was happy at this new extension of her world.

Yet that did not mean she was ready to pursue it on her own. She continued to look at the bulk of her picture books exactly as before. It seemed that each new picture, like each new switch and faucet, must be a separate conquest. One day, two weeks later, as we looked at a picture of a small girl, Elly took my hand in the peremptory way that meant "Do something." I assumed she meant, as often, "It's time to turn the page," but that did not satisfy her. Instead she made my hand take hers and pat the picture. She was asking me to do for her what she could not yet do for herself. She wanted me to make her see. Progress indeed. But I could not help noticing that she did not seem to care whether she touched the girl, or the blank space around her.

I did not do at this time what it seems obvious I should have done—plan out a program. I am not good at that, and besides, I had only the vaguest notion of where we were headed. I had no idea how powerful the tool we were working on would turn out to be, that within a year I would be communicating with Elly through pictures in ways I could not yet do in words. Perhaps it was as well—a glimpsed goal might have imparted a sense of urgency that would have done no good to either of us. At any rate, I kept on almost at random, using the materials the household threw into my hands. I took from women's magazines bright pictures of familiar food, cut them out, and to bridge the gap between representation and experience conveyed them to Elly's mouth and my own. One day I found a picture of a diminutive Ritz cracker, no more than a quarter-inch in diameter, so small I doubted she could recognize it. I cut it out and gave it to her. She knew what it was, all right. She put it in her mouth and ate it.

But the forward movement was slow, with setbacks. The cutting play, which began as a way of drawing her attention to pictures, degenerated, like other hopeful starts, into sterile repetition. Though Elly would bring me the scissors, she would not cut herself. Her fingers went all floppy when introduced into the implement. But if I said, "Put your hand on mine," she would take part in the cutting to that extent (and understand the command even though in her bath she could not distinguish between a request for a hand or a foot). However, she now paid no attention to the pictures I cut out. What she wanted was the magazine cut into strips—letterpress, pictures, it made no difference. It seemed a deliberate retreat from the meaning she had seemed to welcome three months before. Yet she did see more than she had, if one could find ways of getting her to admit it.

She liked pictures of cars and did not mind me cutting them out. She had little interest in food pictures now, and she did not ordinarily respond to human figures or faces. One day, however —who knows why?—she took some interest in the large, colored face of an adolescent on the cover of a magazine, and allowed me to cut it out. She then wanted the next page and seemed pleased when I cut out the face of a little girl. A car came next, and after that she became set on the repetitive strip cutting. I acquiesced, but after several pages, encouraged by the unusual tolerance she had shown already that day, I attempted to guide the scissors round a human figure. Elly resisted, became angry. She made that inarticulate noise like a creaky door, the protest of the dumb, that to this day exposes my nerves as on an operating table. When I continued (for one can cut in silence whatever the state of one's nerves), she crumpled the picture and threw it away. I went back to strips, then tried another figure with the same result. I then found a handsome car, and tried cutting *it* in strips. She resisted; she was as unwilling to have the car treated as invisible as she had been to have me pay attention to the human forms.

I treated the next cars respectfully and passed over several faces. I cut the requisite strips, but only from the edge of the page, deliberately avoiding the picture. At length came a very large and blurry black-and-white photo of a child's face. Elly asked for a strip from this page; she may well not have recognized it for what it was. The face extended almost to the margin; a strip of the requisite width would have cut it. I made a compromise strip, slightly curved around cheek and hair. Elly accepted it, though without interest.

Then more strips and more. Both of us are reacting mechanically now. My mind is elsewhere; who knows where hers is? There comes a photo of a man. I say, "It's a daddy with glasses," not with any hope of comprehension, idly. It's best to say something every now and then. You never can tell . . . I begin to cut—not a strip but the outline. She does not object.

Suddenly (did she understand me?) she notices the glasses, which are like mine, laughs, brings her face close to mine, hugs me. I laugh and squeeze her and continue cutting out the face, she laughing as I work. Laughing again, she picks up the picture and brings it to her face as if to kiss (she has never kissed). The triumphs are as mysterious as the failures. Laughing, we take the face upstairs when she goes for her nap.

The next month I thought of something else that I could do. I began to cut out pictures I drew myself. This gave me considerably more flexibility. I had no longer to depend on what magazines offered me. I could make pictures that would embody my guesses, uncertain though they were, of what would be significant to Elly. I made a cardboard baby with movable arms and legs attached with paper fasteners. Elly watched passively but absorbedly as the baby took shape—as I worked my incredulous ears even heard her *say* "bay-bay." But she soon lost interest; when I tried to clothe it with paper clothes she threw them away, casually but definitely. I drew our house and cut a door she could open and shut. She liked that, although she had never before responded to a picture of a house. I made an Elly-figure dressed in Elly-clothes, and she seemed unusually interested, by which I mean that she held it and stared at it awhile before putting it down. She dropped a father-figure on the floor. She did not even let me get beyond the outline of the head of what was to have been a mother-figure. Slow down, slow down, don't push, always allow the one step back for the two steps forward. "Learn to labor and to wait."

I had not thought of it, but as I drew more I began to realize that part of the power of this technique lay in the fact that drawing is a process and takes place in time. A completed picture is seen all at once. A picture that someone is drawing focuses the attention by the very gradualness with which it takes form. The process is dramatic, it involves suspense. The head first, then arms, body, eyes, nose, mouth—not always in the same order. Each is an event. What is coming next? I drew slowly but without pause. Initially I drew careful, realistic outlines; I didn't expect that Elly would recognize a representation that was merely schematic. When I cut pictures, Elly had merely looked. She *watched* when I drew. Her attention was a strange thing and a precious one—long for her own concerns, for other peoples' evanescent or nonexistent. A dropped pencil might forfeit it. Sometimes, when I knew she was watching and the paper lay between us so that the figure I drew right side up would be upside down for her, I would try to draw upside down rather than change my position and risk losing her. It was June. Elly was almost four. More than half a year had passed since she had first seen the babies' toes in the *Treasury of Art Masterpieces*. Yet she had no word for any part of the body. How much did she really know, I wondered, about this most basic factor in her experience? One day I was drawing with her, idly, nothing new in mind. As I often did now, I started the figure of a child, beginning with the feet. I drew toes, feet, legs, underpants. But this time it occurred to me that I might make use of the drawing process itself; I could find out what Elly would do if I did not complete the figure. If I stopped drawing now, perhaps I could inveigle Elly into replacing her passive attention with active collaboration.

I relaxed my hand. It lay limp on the paper, pencil in still fingers. I waited. A moment passed, and Elly pushed my hand to keep on drawing. I completed the trunk and stopped. Elly started me on an arm; I stopped when it was done. Elly touched my hand and I was beginning the second arm when I felt her correct me. She was no longer passively accepting, she had her own idea. She wanted the head next. I drew it, stopped at the neck, and prompted by Elly drew the second arm. The figure was complete, and I had determined that Elly, who had only recently learned to see a picture, knew as much as any child her age about how the human body should be visually represented.

But all this time it was I who was drawing, who was active, at work. Surely it would be better if Elly drew herself? That was very difficult to accomplish. Drawing meant pressure, meant holding pencil, crayon, brush, and Elly had no strength in her hands for that. I have told in Chapter I of the circles she crayoned when she was two and a half, and how she abandoned them. She abandoned crayons altogether—if one was successfully put into her fingers, the line she made was almost too faint to see. After those first miraculous circles and crosses there were no more drawings of any kind for almost a year, until Elly was a little over three.

An unusually active and imaginative baby-sitter had kept her while I was out, and instead of standing by while Elly did nothing, she had tried to engage her attention. I had told her that Elly recognized shapes, and Jill had taken paper and crayons and drawn her a sheet of triangles. She drew thirty of them before Elly herself made a faint, wavering, but unmistakable triangle. How did it happen? I was not there to see. But it was a doubly remarkable occurrence. Those circles and x's of the past had been made, not in immediate imitation of a model someone had just drawn, but after a long delay. They appeared unexpectedly the next day or the next week, affording evidence, to the hopefully inclined, of intelligence, but also of that strange remoteness, the denial of interpersonal contact. The child would draw a circle, but it must not be an imitation of someone else's circle; it must come out of nowhere. These frail triangles were different. They acknowledged not only hidden capabilities of eye and hand and brain, but a personal contact as well. The intensity and interest of this young girl had got through to Elly, who usually looked right through a stranger.

Perhaps she was reacting as normal children so often react—they are able to do for a stranger what they will not do for a parent, knowing it need not commit them. I acted as if that were the explanation, whether it was or not. I let it rest. Not until two days later did I get out paper and paint. Paint and brush might be harder to control than crayon, but Elly had no difficulty with control. The advantage of paint was that it required no pressure. Elly could be as weak as she liked and still make a mark.

This time Elly reproduced a triangle as soon as I made the model. (There are normal three-year-old children who cannot copy a triangle, but I did not know that then.) During the next three months it was possible to get her to draw, at intervals. Always it was drawing; fastidious Elly never used paint as paint, never splashed, spread, or mixed it on the paper. She who could match colors spontaneously showed no interest in using them. Her drawings were monochrome—whatever color she started with she stuck to. Magic marker came on the market that year and Elly soon preferred that, which requires no more pressure than paint and is easier to manipulate. For the weakness was still extremely prominent—it was about this time, after all, that I was working with her on flicking switches.

Elly drew rapidly and uninterruptedly, working for about twenty minutes at a time. (I noticed that, of course; attention-span is one sign of intelligence.) She drew x's, dots, lines, circles, triangles. She never scribbled at random, or even freely. Each line seemed weirdly deliberate, the product of a decision. I learned to take away one sheet as soon as she had drawn on it and substitute another; if I left a sheet in front of her, circles and triangles would disappear, carefully obliterated beneath a cloud of dots applied in close pointillism. Again, always, it was as if she did not want to commit herself—to assume the responsibility that admitting her new skill would imply.

Little of what Elly drew was spontaneous. They were copies of figures we had made. We made figures rather than pictures, since Elly at this time (about three and a quarter) had not yet recognized a picture. Seen without the significance we give them, letters are only figures. Somebody—I perhaps, perhaps one of the children—wrote Elly's name in block capitals with the paints. The next time Elly drew, she made a rickety E. As of old, the act was delayed. She still retained her extraordinary ability to register impressions and bring them out, unpracticed and unchanged, after an indefinite interval. About a week later she added an L—this three-year-old child who could neither speak nor comprehend.

It was very encouraging while it lasted. But by the time two and a half months had passed, with perhaps ten drawing sessions in that time, Elly's interest was waning. It was harder to get her to draw herself, although I have a sheet of rectangles that she drew using my inert hand as a tool. Three months after her first triangles I made another set and tried to get her to draw some. She wouldn't. When I tried the old trick of leaving one incomplete, the line she provided to finish it was more frail and wavering than the first ones had been. I took her hand and made it draw a pattern of cross-bars. This was new and interesting, and after two or three sheets of it her own will took over and she drew some on her own. The last two times she drew, it was she, not I, who decided on a drawing session; she astonished and delighted me by getting out marker and paper herself. Then too, she put each sheet aside as she finished it, instead of going on to blot out the figures with marking. It was a fitting valedictory. Not for six months would she voluntarily take up brush, marker, crayon, or pencil. Once only, in that period, I got marks on paper out of Elly. I spent five minutes slowly painting bars and circles before she took my hand and, using it as her tool, made two parallel lines, an E, and two L's. I gave her the brush. She made a final E alone and would make no more.

I let it go. It didn't seem worth it. There were other things we could do together, more than there had been—puzzles, pictures, even a little music. Accept the retreat which qualifies each advance. Hope that instead of denying the advance it somehow secures it. Put the paints and markers away—for a long time, this time, so that when they appear again they will seem interesting and quite new. But even so, when Elly, nearly four, did at length employ her hand to make a mark again, it was with neither paint nor marker, but in a totally new situation and one that bears thinking about. Taken to her father's office, Elly used chalk and blackboard for the first time. She found it a uniquely satisfying medium. Anything she drew could be immediately erased, denied, canceled, made as if it had never been.

Elly could deny her abilities to herself. But we knew now at least a little of what she could do. She could use her body and her hands. She could draw. More important, she could see— not only shapes and objects, but people, and not only these themselves but pictured representations of them. It was that much more than we had known two years before. We would have to be content with it.

6 · Willed Deafness

ELLY's inabilities, physical and visual, were evident to us. But once she had learned to walk they were not conspicuous to others. Only those who observed carefully would notice the blindness behind the apparent alertness, the passivity behind the deftness and apparent vigor. As Elly grew beyond two, to most people who knew her the significant thing was not that she did not push or reach or climb, not that she did not look at things, but that she did not talk. When a child reaches two and a half, and three, and four, mouthing no more than a few unintelligible syllables, it is this that tends to seem primary—especially if the child appears alert and attractive. It is natural to wonder if there has been some specific damage to the speech centers of the brain.

To us who knew her well, however, this was only the visible part of the iceberg. A speech disorder? Anyone who had lived with her must have felt it was much more far-reaching than that. Even if one did focus solely on the failure of speech, what seemed significant was not so much that she didn't talk as that she didn't understand, and not so much that she didn't understand as that she didn't seem to hear you at all.

It is not uncommon for autistic children to be diagnosed initially as deaf. Surrounded by mystery, one is always trying out hypotheses. Retardation? The child seems sharp when it wants

71

to be. Deafness would explain almost everything—Elly's failure of speech, her failure of comprehension, even her withdrawal, which would be natural if she lived in a silent world. She not only did not respond to speech; more often than not, she did not respond to sound either. I remember her sitting on the lawn one day, her back to the driveway. An astonishing thing was happening; one would think any small child would notice it. Our neighbors had a chimney fire. Up our small court came a genuine red fire engine, making the usual amount of fire-engine noise. I remember that Elly did not even look up. So cautious in everything involving direct bodily danger, for years she paid no attention to the sound of the car motors which could bring her the greatest danger of all. The signals came from outside herself, they did not impinge directly on her body, so she ignored them as if they did not exist.

Yet, like all the other hypotheses, deafness did not seem to fit all the facts. For those few signals that she had invested with significance, her hearing could be preternaturally acute. For some reason she disliked the dishwasher; if it was in operation she would not even remain on the same floor. Naturally we avoided turning it on in her presence, but that was not enough. Elly could hear the sound of the switch through a closed door. A little click, and she would already be on her way upstairs.

Once—Elly was not yet three—as we all sat at table, talking, eating, a dog barked outside. No one registered it, of course; the general noise level was high. Five minutes later, when our quiet Elly suddenly barked, we remembered it in our laughter.

But things like that did not happen often. Written down, they take on significance we dared not give them as we lived through a tangle of events, many of which pointed in the opposite direction. As we looked for evidence that Elly could hear, far more significant than such rare occurrences was the fact that Elly did, on occasion, speak. Now and then—sometimes three or four times in a day—Elly did say a word. The words indicated her imperviousness was not absolute. They had to come from some-where. Deaf children have no way of acquiring words.

We had not even had to wait particularly long for Elly's first word. She had said "teddy" at fourteen months, as normal as you please. A month or so and she said "mama." The next month, "dada." Another month, another word. It takes some time to realize that the new word is not added to the old words but sub stituted for them; that at any given time she has a one-word vocabulary. It takes time, too, to realize how strange it is that though she may say "teddy," and right in her bear's presence so you know it is no accident, she shows no sign of comprehension if you say "teddy" to her. A normal child's passive or recognition vocabulary is larger—even much larger—than the vocabulary it can itself make use of. One is unprepared for the phenomenon of a child whose active vocabulary is pitifully small, but whose passive vocabulary is smaller still.

Elly was twenty-two months old, fresh from her first hospital examination, when I began to keep the record of her speech which forms the basis of this chapter. My rule was to enter a word only after Elly had used it at least three times in a convincing context; the single exception I made was for that strange, unmistakable, one-shot "scissors." It was not hard to be accurate, there was so little to record. By the time she was two years old, Elly had spoken six different words—those mentioned above, "walk-walk," "no-no," and her own name. Of these, however, she gave signs of understanding only two. She would turn in response to "Elly," and she would stop what she was doing if you said "no-no." She intermittently responded to "come," though she did not say it. That was all. A six-month puppy can do as much.

Not that she was silent. The house was full of her cheerful sounds, the musical ba-bas and ah-ah-ahs of a normal baby. Lying in bed in the leisurely mornings the summer she was two, I listened to her pronounce her name. "El-ly," she said, "El-ly"—

73

laughing, chuckling, over and over again. The sounds, even the consonants, were exquisitely clear. I'm glad I got the chance to hear her. For a month or so she said it. Then she ceased completely. It was two years at least until she spoke her name again. When she did, it was so indistinct as to be virtually unintelligible. Even today she does not say it as clearly as she did those summer mornings six years ago.

There was another peculiarity of her language that went far beyond its sparseness. Elly spoke words, though not often. But she did not use them to communicate. She had no idea of language as a tool that could cause things to happen. By the time she was two and a half, there were several more words to add to the record. A few were simple nouns like "book," "pin," and "milk." Others were sounds referring to activities, like the "there she is!" intonation with which she responded to the peekaboo game in which I had finally succeeded in interesting her. But not one of these words was ever *used*, as distinguished from merely spoken. If Elly saw me, she might or might not say "mama." She would never use the name to call me. She might possibly say "teddy" if he appeared. She would never ask for him by name.

This was of course related to the fact that there was so little she wanted to ask for. If it's all one to you whether mama comes or not, you aren't likely to call her. If you don't want teddy enough to reach for him with your own hand, you will hardly ask for him with a word. But even when she did begin to acknowledge desires—she was reaching two and a half—she did not communicate them by speech. She had other methods. If the object was near, she would take your hand and use it as a tool. If it was more remote, she would push or lead you to it. There were some foods she liked better than others, but she was no more likely to learn the words for them than for objects that had no interest for her. In fact, though food was one of the few things she might want, she had no word for any food but milk, which she had no particular desire for. Language, for Elly, was so nonfunctional that I often felt that what was inexplicable was not why she didn't have more words but why she had as many as she did.

For where could these words have come from? If you said words, she did not appear to hear them. She never repeated any sound after you said it—the easiest way of acquiring new words. If you said one of her own words to her, she did not understand it. Yet if she had not at some time heard it with understanding, she would not have acquired it at all. Each of Elly's words started in the public domain. Yet it was as if as soon as she acquired it, it became her own and nobody else's. Words are channels of communication, but Elly's words were things-in-themselves that led to nowhere and nobody.

So there she was. Two, two and a half, three. Every couple of months she'd say a word she'd never said before. By the time she was three my list was up to twenty. But of those twenty, in the entire month before her third birthday she spoke only five. Most of them were out of use for months at a time and several, like the clear and frequent "Elly," had been abandoned altogether.

Where did they go? Some simply disappeared. Elly learned "milk" and "pin" at two and lost them by two and a half. She was five before she said them again and when she did they seemed entirely fresh acquisitions. Some seemed rather to go underground. "Ball" had a strange and suggestive history. Acquired around two, the word went into almost immediate retirement. It emerged once, six months later. Two months after that she said it three times in a single week. Another six months and she said it again. It was never triggered by our familiar household balls. Elly said it once when she saw a small, entirely deflated white rubber football—an object it took real perspicuity for a two-year-old to identify as a ball at all. (Ten minutes later, shown an ordinary ball, she said nothing.) She said it once when I tossed a perforated plastic golf-ball into her bath. The word

75

existed deep inside, apparently. But only an unusual stimulus could call it out.

Other children's vocabularies build and proliferate, like their bodily skills. They add one word to another, then begin to combine them. Elly did not. For years every expansion of her vocabulary was matched by a contraction. Most often the old word would simply be gone. But sometimes it was possible actually to observe the process. I was present when Elly acquired the word "eye," and I watched it degenerate and disappear.

She was three when she acquired it. Although bodily sensations were her main avenue to the world, it was her only word for a part of the body. (She was over four before she acquired another.) She learned it in what were for her unusual circumstances—not from me but from a friend, and not from a real eye, but from a large and striking stylized eye on a bathing cap. She repeated it next day in a new and correct context and kept it current for some time, saying it for approval several times a day. (By three she had progressed enough to be able to enjoy approval.) I tried to keep meaning in the word by showing eyes on dolls, pictures, and people, and Elly enjoyed this. She had an "eye" game; she would take off my glasses, say "eye," and laugh. I could even ask "Where's doggy's eye?" and get an answer, though previously all "where" questions had been answered like "Where's your belly button?"—by a delighted revelation of that intrinsically comic spot. But repetition has its dangers, as I had already seen in Elly's block play. Within a month the word was already losing meaning; it was becoming an approval-winning trick. Two months later it was entirely out of use and Elly showed no signs of comprehending it when spoken.

At three years and ten months, a year after Dr. Blank had first seen her, I reported to him, "words still come and go; no real change from a year ago. About 5–6 in use in any one week." For her fourth birthday I made a complete vocabulary review, checking over my records of every word I had ever heard her speak, the date of its acquisition, and the frequency of its use. The total was 31. This is the summary I made then.

Of the 31 words she has used in context in her four years of life it would not cause me surprise if she today spoke any one of 12 or 13. Others would be cause for a special entry here. Among these would be #27, 28, and 29 in order of acquisition, so recent use does *not* save from oblivion.

In her own speech, then, Elly, in four years, had made hardly any progress. The vocabulary pool she drew from was larger, but she used no more words, no more often, than she had a year before. About comprehension, however, we could be a little more cheerful. Elly regularly said words and abandoned them, but once she began to understand something we said to her she tended to hold on to it. There was a slow but steady increase in what she understood and would respond to. At two she would turn when we said "Elly" and crawl when we said "come." By two and a quarter she seemed to know the meaning of "Let's walk-walk up"—or "down." At two and a half she responded correctly to "give me the [pins/book/brush]." But in all these cases it seemed likely that, while appearing to respond to words, she was in fact responding to something else—to the nonverbal cues afforded by the situation. When I said "come" I held out my arms. My hand outstretched accompanied "give me." It was not until she was three years and two months old that I could record in my notebook: "Response to 'come,' 'let's go walk-walk,' 'climb up in your chair' now perfectly sure *even if* I am out of sight while speaking (*i.e.* it is not a situational cue)." By the time six more months had passed I could add "Shut the door," "Come get your diapers," "Let's go outside," and "Let's go riding in the car." The expansion continued; two months later I could report to Dr. Blank that she

understands a perceptibly greater range of commands and suggestions of the "put your foot in," "climb up in your chair" variety. These

77

are all quite long; she seems to respond to them as complete tone patterns rather than separate words. She will, for example, respond to "Come on, let's go upstairs and have your bath," but shows no comprehension of much easier sentences made with words within her current vocabulary like, say, "Butter, Elly?" These words she understands only when *she* says them.

What she understood was in fact a limited range of routine, expected commands. I tried once—not then, but six months later—to make a game where the commands required a flexible response: "Put the bean in my pocket," "Put the marble in my hand." It was too soon. I got no comprehension at all.

Yet there was progress. We allowed ourselves a little encouragement. Comprehension—even routine comprehension—seemed to us, at this point, infinitely more significant than actual speech, since comprehension was the strongest sign that Elly could give that she was in contact with other human beings. It is possible to speak without contact; the very word "autistic" points to this, and speech can be autistic. But comprehension is contact itself. For the time being we could be comfortable with the slow increase in what Elly seemed to hear—if the word "comfortable" could ever fit our underwater existence. For speech itself, we would have to wait.

And all this time, what were we *doing*? Not very much, in fact. Such techniques as we evolved were hardly worthy of the name. But few and obvious as they were, they were all that Elly was ready for, which was lucky for us. We too needed time to learn how to help Elly give meaning to sound.

Again and always, it helped that we had had other children. More often, parents of autistic children are less lucky; the disorder seems, like many others, to pick out the first-born. But we had watched three different children learn to talk in their three differing ways, and we had learned how to talk to little children. Little normal children, that is—obviously it could not be the same for Elly, who heard almost nothing that we said. But it could not be so very different either—after all, the range of what one can reasonably say to very small children is not great. With Elly the range was all downward towards zero. Yet it was plain that it must never reach there. We must not chatter to Elly, for a constant background of noise is more easily ignored than single, occasional sounds—and to Elly, all speech was noise. But whether or not she seemed to hear us, we must talk.

We tried to talk simply and directly, waiting, if possible, until Elly was already looking in our direction. We spoke as clearly as we could. We avoided long sentences. We used her own vocabulary as far as possible, little as she appeared to comprehend it. We tried not to use more than one term for the same thing. We were faithful in naming objects that Elly used or played with or merely focused on, at the moment of focus, although months turned into years and she acquired only a pathetic fraction of the hundreds we named. Deliberately, we introduced our games and activities by words; in fact, at four, the bulk of her thirty-one-word "vocabulary" consisted not of simple object-words, but stock responses to familiar activities, like the noise she made for "there she is" in peekaboo, or the "whee" as she went down the slide. We experimented with varying loudness and softness—a loud sound, close by, was somewhat more likely to attract her attention, and besides, there lingered in our minds some apprehension of deafness, partial if not complete. Later on, when she began to lower her defenses, we were to find she could respond to a whisper, but in the early years we were careful to keep our speech direct and clearly audible.

We learned that along with loudness, a certain kind of benevolent aggressiveness was unexpectedly effective with Elly. We learned it from others; it was not at first natural to us. Besides, it seems at first blush less threatening to a reserved child to treat it with reserve. The summer Elly was three, however, our old friend the doctor came with his wife to visit us, the doctor mentioned in Chapter 3, who had the retarded son and who had sent us to Dr. Blank. Of course Fred and Joann looked at Elly with special interest. Joann, I knew, had made heroic, unceasing efforts to help her son—to crawl, to walk, to manipulate, to think. I can imagine what pain it must have been to her to see Elly in her poise and health and to think of her bumbling George, the same age to the month. While Joann watched, Elly did a puzzle she had never seen before; dextrously, immediately, she put all the pieces into place, scarcely glancing at them as she did so. Then she dumped them all out and put the puzzle together again—blank side up, with only the shapes to guide her. Joann, remembering George's pathetic attempts to put a peg in a hole, thought she was seeing something miraculous. She could not believe there was anything really wrong.

But what is "really"? "You have to admit," I said, "that if she can do things like that, it's striking that she doesn't understand anything you say." And of course she had shown no signs she knew Joann was in the room. She heard me rarely enough; she almost never seemed to hear a stranger.

But Joann was no ordinary stranger. She knew things I did not—the techniques she had had to find to break through to her sluggish, defective little son, who was apparently so different from our deft Elly. Joann was highly colored, gay, vivid, aggressive, larger than life. She shouted at Elly—not words, but nonsense syllables: Ba-ba! La-la! And Elly heard her. Instead of shrinking, as perhaps should have been expected, she looked at her and laughed. Months after, she was still saying "La-la!"

But speech is not the only kind of meaningful sound. There is also music. One of the best arguments against genuine deafness in Elly was that early on she had shown signs that she could hear music. The ninth entry on her vocabulary list (age two) was a word only by courtesy. It was a sound, and it had a consistent referent, but it was in fact an imitation of music. When I sat down at the piano, Elly would say "daddle-addle-addle" and move my hand to C#. It was by that that I understood her; I would not otherwise have caught on to the idea that "daddle-addle-addle" represented the two repeated notes in the left-hand part of Mozart's C-major Sonata, the almost-trill that provides the background when the second theme comes in. But as so often with Elly, nothing came of this early response. She abandoned the word and lost interest in the music, to which she had in any case been attracted not by the pretty theme but by the repetitive notes. Nor did she take an interest in anything else I played. It was not until the summer she was three, a full year later, that I noticed any response to music again.

As with Joann's syllables, this was something she did not learn from me. Though I sang to her regularly, and though some of her own sounds were not unmusical, she had never herself sung any tune I could recognize. But on a visit to friends—it lasted a week and was a distinct break in Elly's usual routine—their teenage daughter sang to Elly "Row, row, row your boat." She made of it a rocking, pushing game that pleased Elly, who continued to sing it for a few weeks after her return home. She sang it all the way through—we could even recognize the word "row." Then it joined Mozart in limbo. We still sang it, of course, and rocked and played the game, but as far as Elly was concerned it was gone.

We got a folk-song record that fall, simple, direct songs a child would enjoy, and Elly seemed to like it well enough. We played it often; it had about twelve songs on it. That January, when she was three and a half, I thought—I was almost sure—I heard her singing one of them, a Scottish folk song, "Three Craws Sat Upon a Wall." To reinforce and encourage, I began softly to sing along with her. I should have known better; I knew well enough from other experience how important it was not to seem to notice when Elly made a step forward. Elly stopped at once as I began to sing.

But my helpful meddling had delayed her singing, not destroyed it. After six weeks she sang it again all through, I not being so foolish a second time. A new readiness was on its way. By March of that year she was singing five distinct songs, including one tune she had invented, and she had reactivated "Row, row." She sang them well. Even her first "Row, row" six months before had been as good as the best of her siblings at her age; now, as she sang more freely, her intervals grew exact, her rhythm perfect. And as a year earlier she had begun to acknowledge the simple desire for food, now she found a way to acknowledge a more subtle one. Not by speaking, of course, or by singing herself—instead she would put a gentle hand on my lips to indicate she wanted me to sing. Which was progress as thrilling as the song itself.

We had kept in touch with Dr. Blank. That spring he suggested we get Elly a record-player, a 45-r.p.m. with a thick spindle a small child could handle easily. Of course that was not necessary: the first day we got the machine, a conventional one, Elly changed the records alone and meticulously returned each record to its proper album, keeping track of them, I suppose, by the colors of the labels and the configurations of printing they bore. I had intended to wait until next day to show her how to switch the machine off and on. After all, Elly had mastered the light-switch only recently, and one could not expect her to learn much at a time. But while I was still downstairs I heard the record-player going up in Elly's room and found she had needed no teaching. As so often, it seemed a question of values—what she thought important, she was able to learn as fast as any normal child.

That year, music was important. In part her experience of it was discouraging; it had that same obsessive character that we had observed take over all her new skills. She played *The Three-Penny Opera* every day for two solid months; I was thankful she had picked music that could wear well. But the obsessiveness was not everything. We soon realized that her new ability to sing was not one more repetitive and closed autistic activity. It was providing an unexpected avenue to communication.

We had laid the groundwork for this a year before, quite without knowing it. My husband and I both sing readily. We have always sung to our children. We sang to Elly—more, perhaps, because we talked less. We have always made up little songs to fit recurring situations; like many parents, we had a good-night song, and others of which we were scarcely conscious. One of these was a car song; to the simplest of tunes, we sang

> Riding in the car
> Riding in the car
> Elly and her mama
> Go riding in the car.

In this little verse, we could substitute for "mama" the name of any member of the family who happened to be along, and we imagined that this might help Elly learn them, although she gave no sign that this hope was anything but empty. But one never knows what buildings will rise on one's foundations. Elly was nearly five before she learned anyone's name, but "Riding in the car" was one of her first songs. Surprisingly, she sang it first not when riding in the car, but one day after I had merely spoken the words. This was the beginning of a curious and encouraging development: what we came to call Elly's leitmotifs. We became aware that this strange child who could not take in the simplest word could absorb a tune and make it do duty for an idea.

Tunes became words for Elly. "Ring around a rosy" was the first. She was three and three quarters that spring, and she had been playing the game for many months. Now her new musical alertness picked up the tune. As soon as it did, she extended it spontaneously to a picture of children in a ring, then to a garland of flowers, and finally to the unadorned figure of a circle. The song—shortened to its first few notes—for more than a year remained her word for "circle" and the cluster of ideas around it, functioning far more reliably than any of her actual words.

Other leitmotifs followed. "Happy birthday" equaled cake and, by extension, candles and fire. "Rockabye baby" went for any rocking motion. The ascending and descending notes of the scale indicated stairs. We found we could increase our communication with her by ourselves suggesting new leitmotifs. She could pick these up easily, as she had never been able to pick up words, and she retained them. "London Bridge" became a bridge motif; the dwarfs' song from *Snow White* did duty for "dig." We noticed that though she now sang many songs freely, she never sang her leitmotifs at random or for their own sake as songs. Nor did she sing them musically, like the others, but rapidly, schematically, *functionally*—only just well enough for them to do their job of communication. Music was serving as her avenue to words, for of course inside each leitmotif was a germ that was wholly verbal. She had first responded with the car tune when I had spoken, not sung, the words. The one musical motif whose verbal content seemed totally to lack connection with its characteristic situation turned out, when at last we understood it, to illustrate the verbal content of Elly's music more strikingly than any of the others. For years we did not guess why Elly, at four, had sung "Alouette" when we combed her hair after washing. It was not until she was over six, and speaking much more freely, that we discovered the connection: "Alouette" equaled "all wet" —words which at four she had neither said nor appeared to understand. Clearly, however, she had registered the sounds, and made through music a connection which she was unable or unwilling to make verbally.

And through music I could sometimes gain an insight into her mind that I could not as yet get through words. I transcribe one remarkable event as I recorded it in my diary at the time. It breaks the chronology a little, but not much: Elly was four and a half.

Today I *heard* Elly thinking. It was exactly as Wagner uses his leitmotifs; Brunnhilde is singing, and beneath her voice can be heard in the orchestra the Valhalla motif and we know she is *thinking* of Valhalla though she is singing of something quite different.

Elly and I were walking on the college grounds. We arrived on the bicycle and left it parked against a shed. We walked some way and started to return. As we passed a branch-off in the path that would have led back to the bicycle, I decided to prolong the walk by going a different, slightly longer way. As we passed the branch-off, Elly murmured (to herself, not me) a bar or so of "Riding on the bike." She was, I feel sure, wondering about how we'd get back to the bike by this new path. I told her we'd find the bike in a minute and she continued cheerfully on, seeming to have understood. A few minutes later she asked the first question in her four and a half years: as we walked and made a turning, she said (*not* sang) an unformed series of sounds clearly in the *rhythm* of "Riding on the bike," and ending in a pronounced rising intonation such as I had never heard her use. It was as if she had asked me when we would arrive at the bike. I told her again we'd soon be at the bike and she remained cheerful until we were.

Only those who have lived with a walled personality can realize the impact of such an expansion of the possibilities of communication, rudimentary as it may seem (and rudimentary as it remained, month after month). It was as if the barrier that Elly maintained against words had been lowered for music. This mattered. For what had we to work with but the faith (like many faiths, it was at first no more than a hope) that the lowering of any one barrier must help with all the others?

It was little enough. Of all Elly's inabilities, the hardest to affect was the inability to speak and comprehend. We could progress slowly toward bodily adequacy and specific skills. We could work to expand visual perception. But auditory communication was more important than these. Speech is an open gate. The personality who cannot speak is in prison, the personality who will not lives in a walled fortress. Who knows which is which, or if there is really any difference—at two, at three, at four years old?

We could work on other things, but speech was crucial. It was, in the current state of knowledge, the only indicator of the future. Kanner had written that if autistic children did not develop useful speech by the age of five the prognosis for them was very bad. We did not have to be told what "very bad" was; we knew that a significant proportion of Kanner's cases had been institutionalized as functional idiots. Obviously we must not think statistically when the number of recorded cases was so few. Obviously—even more obviously—it could do no good to think in terms of deadlines. It could do harm. Yet deep in our minds, as far back as we could push it, remained the number five.

7 · Willed Isolation

As I describe, I articulate. I divide into parts, I imply relationships, I put one thing first and not another. I cannot avoid doing
this; I must articulate to write things down at all. I must analyze,
and as I analyze I falsify. Experience as analyzed is no longer experience as lived. Weakness, blindness, deafness, isolation: I have
divided one thing four ways, but it is still one thing. This chapter
will deal explicitly with Elly's remoteness and the methods we
devised for affecting it, but it is a new chapter, not a new subject. Elly's inability to relate—to use the psychological jargon I
have had to learn the knack of—has been implicit in all the
phenomena I have described so far. If I say Elly was reluctant to
use her hands, or if I say she used other people's hands as tools
without regard to their existence as human beings, I am giving
two alternative descriptions, but of a reality that was not divided but single. Elly did not see, but most of what she did not
see was people. She did not hear, but most of what she did not
hear was people's voices, most of what she did not understand
was their words and their concerns. She did not speak; it would
have been extraordinary if she had. A child reluctant to use even
her hands as a tool is hardly likely to trouble to acquire the master
tool of speech, which has its inception in an acknowledgment of
other people—of need, of contact, of interdependence.

Of all Elly's inabilities, which should be taken as primary? Should we do what seems natural and emphasize the most striking symptom, the isolation-in-self which gives the autistic condition its very name? Or do the phenomena call for deeper scrutiny? Should we posit some defect profounder than all these which would explain them all—some inability of the brain, perhaps, to decode its perceptions or render them usable? Might the new individual, faced with a world in which an unreadable welter of impressions obscures even the distinction between objects and human beings, wall itself up as a defense against the anarchy outside? Psychologists formulate the question in their own language: which is primary, disorder of affect—roughly, feeling or emotion—or dysfunction of cognition? But even for psychologists the answer is years away.

It is fortunate, then, that one needs no answer in order to go to work. Which is primary? It is an analytical question. In the living whole, nothing comes first. Work done on any one of Elly's inabilities affected the others. Every game we played, every exercise we devised to extend Elly's use of her body, her eyes, her ears, her voice, her mind, worked in addition to breach that jealously guarded isolation which for those who lived with her remained the most obvious and the most terrible aspect of her condition.

Other children are paralyzed, deaf, dumb—not in effect merely, but in very truth. But these children feel, react, relate. Whatever their disabilities, some force within them drives them outside the wall raised by their handicap to make contact with the world. If blind, they explore with their fingers, if dumb, they grab for what they want or push out some inarticulate cry. What is one to think, feel, and do when confronted by a two-year-old —one's own—who makes no exploration or approach, who expresses neither hostility nor anger, and who wants nothing?

The autistic child is complete in itself. Its every action—or inaction—functions to keep it that way. Elly's consciousness seemed empty, her responses simple or nonexistent, her activities rudimentary. Yet as we lived with her at that time of her most extreme withdrawal, what impressed us was not, as one might expect, the inadequacy of this child, but rather the extraordinary degree to which her environment was within her control. Having found ways to keep her world one that she could cope with, she was the most undisturbed of "disturbed children." A normal two-year-old experiences in a day more of anxiety and frustration than came to Elly in a week.

Elly's inabilities operated to tailor the environment to her needs. If you decide, at eighteen months, to spend the rest of your life sitting in the middle of the rug, who has problems? Certainly not you. When you take the risk of getting up, walking, wanting things, attaching yourself to people, exploring the world and acting in it—in short, assuming your humanity—*then* you have problems. As we all have. Perhaps we are naïve to be surprised at Elly. Perhaps we should rather be surprised that the normal baby creature meets this tough world with such ready welcome.

But surely we are talking metaphor, not fact. At thirteen, fifteen, eighteen months, what could Elly have *decided*? To speak of a baby's decision is preposterous. Yet as we lived with our baby, month after month, it seemed as if—*as if*—some such decision had been made.

Much later, when we began to know enough about our own situation to look beyond it, I found the exhaustive book we had needed so long. It hadn't been written when our trouble came upon us. The field is as new as that. Elly was six when Bernard Rimland's *Infantile Autism* * was published; we did not come upon it for several months. We read in it with wonder of child after child who could have been Elly herself. One of them, I

* *Infantile Autism: The Syndrome and Its Implications for a Neural Theory of Behavior*, Appleton-Century-Crofts, 1964.

remember, would eat ice cream with pleasure when placed in its mouth, but would make no effort to get it. It seemed to me that this could stand as the model of autism. It is this phenomenon that any explanation of the condition must elucidate, and this that any treatment must try to change.

Those who pay homage to an ideal of total self-sufficiency have never seen the thing itself. That secret smile may be the Buddha's, but it is monstrous seen on a baby's face. To conquer craving is indeed to conquer pain, but humanity goes with it. That Elly wanted nothing was worst of all. That was where we started.

It was bad, too, when she began—rarely at first, then more often—to want something, and to take your arm and throw it toward the object of desire. But it was better.

As weeks passed, the peremptory grab gave place to a touch of feathery delicacy, a pressure exquisitely adjusted to attain no more and no less than the required response. This was easier to take. We could interpret this new gentleness as an emergent consciousness of people and their feelings. That was an encouraging way to look at it. But it was equally explainable as an application of a principle of which Elly had an intuitive grasp, the Principle of Least Effort. A mere touch, now, was enough to bring Elly what she wished. But that we were attuned to Elly did not necessarily mean that she was attuned to us. The rude touch and the gentle one were equally detached.

Another mother, writing of another such little girl,* has called her "the child in the glass ball." What is the task of those who try to touch the untouchable, to reach those who have found reasons to keep themselves separate? How is one to render the world desirable to those who do not desire it? One holds out a flower, a soft doll, an orange candy. One points at a bird. All are ignored, this time and the next and the next. How does one con-

* Karin Junker, *The Child in the Glass Ball*, Abingdon Press, 1964.

vey that touch and sight and sound promise pleasure, that the world rewards those who interest themselves in its varied faces? How—most lacerating question of all—does one reach that walled entelechy with news that people exist, that they are warm and loving and have need of each other?

One is mounting an invasion. Invasion is not easy. There are scruples, especially for those who themselves appreciate the mechanisms of reserve, control, and self-defense. There are risks —that one will press too hard and injure the creature one is trying to help, or that one will find oneself insufficiently armored against the steady unresponsiveness which it is so natural to interpret as rejection. It is not easy to push one's way in where there is every reason to believe one is neither needed nor wanted, or to remain confident that what one is offering is worth having.

It is fortunate, then, that the actuality of what one is doing is so very simple, simple enough so that one passes through the structures of one's hesitations to remind oneself that there is no point in getting so elaborate about it, because all one is doing is playing with a baby.

All one is doing is lying down on the floor beside her as she sits absorbed in one of her inconsequential activities, so that one's eyes will be on her level when she looks up, one's hand ready to make some small change in the pattern, to which she may respond but probably will not. Or one is standing by her crib, that symbol of her withdrawal, at once a certain refuge and a delightful toy. Into the crib she can retreat. Once there it becomes an extension of her body; she can bounce in it, leap, sometimes a foot into the air, and as she tires, rock and rock and rock until she falls asleep. Inside the crib her guard relaxes; she is at home. The crib is a model of her citadel. The crib is a good place to play games, the simple games the other babies liked. One makes an animal of one's hand, for instance. Thumb and three fingers walk along the crib side; the middle finger, extended in front, quivers, sniffing its way. Safe behind her fence, Elly looks on with interest. The animal runs, stops, runs again. As Elly's attention fades it scampers, along a bridge made by one's other arm, right to Elly's shoulder to tickle her neck, and Elly laughs. She likes that game, which is her father's specialty. Soon she is extending her own arm for the animal to walk up. She puts out her foot for "this little piggy," her hand for "round and round the garden." Each game ends with a tickle and a laughing squeal. Now walled Elly sounds like any other baby. But with any other baby the games grow, change, lead somewhere. These are good games and we enjoy them. While we play them, Elly seems to be in contact. But when we stop she moves into herself again. She accepts the stimulation, but when it is withdrawn she does not miss it. Where do we go from here? One cannot tickle all day long.

Elly is prone on the floor, legs frogged out on either side of her. She is under a blanket and so invisible, but I know the position and the steady rhythm that goes with it. She is rapt, removed, she needs me not at all. I crouch beside her, ready to enter her world in a way she can appreciate if she will and ignore if she wants to. My finger goes under the blanket, then my hand. No response. My head follows. Elly knows I am there. There are two of us now, withdrawn from the world but near each other. It is very inward, warm and dark—a physical expression for undemanding intimacy. There is nothing difficult here—nothing to do, nothing to say. The only thing you need is time and the willingness to spend a lot of it with your head under a blanket.

It became possible to make a game out of raising the edge of the blanket. By the time she was two we could get her to play the peekaboo game whose absence we had noticed at ten months, and she even made a little "there-she-is" noise to go with it. As time went on we moved forward, but not far. She began to welcome me into her enclosures. At three and a half she even developed on her own a new discovery game—herself closed in a closet, I to open the door. Better yet, both of us sit quiet in the dark closet, door pulled to, she and I, close together, everything else shut out. We still do that sometimes, even today.

One curious fact helped us as we worked. We saw it happen more than once; something of it has been described in the previous chapter, with Joann. But it had happened before; some big, loud, friendly daddy of a man, passing through town, would visit us, take a look at our pretty baby, and knowing nothing about her to make him wary, would sweep her off the floor, hug and tickle and toss her while she squealed and chuckled with the most ordinary baby delight. During one such visit I watched, incredulous, as Elly—impervious Elly—got up off the floor, went over to the stranger, and crawled onto his lap. A year and a half later, at the time of her second hospital examination, we remembered his magic and took Elly to visit. But he had lost it. He knew now that something was wrong with her and he treated her as any intelligent and sensitive person would—delicately, tentatively, cautiously. Elly never even saw him.

What could we make of this fact—that Elly could be reached by the exactly the sort of crude initiative that one would think would most repel her? Invasions are mounted on faith. We have not been people to whom faith came naturally, and there was little here for faith to work on. It helped us, then, in our continual assaults upon Elly's sheer walls to remember that we had seen her welcome invasion. It sustained us to think that though she could not take the initiative she was glad when initiative was taken. Every time we forced ourselves to force her privacy, taking her hand (as she took ours), lifting it, manipulating her fingers so stubbornly left limp, it helped to think that there was perhaps a friend in the citadel, a fifth column unable to assist us yet hoping for our victory.

There could be no more important help. Of course we had learned for ourselves already that Elly liked to be touched, stimulated, occupied—that she was bored inside her serenity. But what one has learned for oneself is a frail reed if no one strengthens it from outside. Watching the rare people who succeeded with Elly, however temporary all such successes were, we were strengthened in our knowledge of what was necessary if we were to succeed.

What we learned is what actors know—actors and good teachers: that if there is a distance between you and another, whether an audience or a single child, it is you who must make the effort to reach out. You must throw a bridge over the distance, and the only material for that bridge is the force of your personality, such force as you can give it. You must project. You must project in ways that may seem exaggerated or unnatural or artificial to you if you are not an actor already, but you cannot mind that. You must become an actor, if an actor is a person who knows more ways of projecting than most people. You will learn to use loudness and softness, sound and silence, emphasis, change of pace, gesture. And since the distance you are trying to bridge is not, like the actor's, physical, you can learn to project in ways he cannot. You can surprise by approach, you can fix attention by a dynamics of touch as varied as that of voice. There are many ways; you find them when you look for them. But somehow you send your personality out beyond yourself, into the waiting vacuum. You will be making a fool of yourself. But you cannot mind that either. Sooner than you think, you will get used to looking up at a visitor from the inside of a cardboard carton.

It is seduction, make no mistake about it. You are setting out, with every charm you own, unasked and uninvited, to make another person love you. If what you do is to be more than seduction, you must assume the responsibilities of love. You must accept the fact that love binds. You must imply no promise you do not mean to fulfill. You cannot entice her out and then just not be there. You must be ready to see dependence modify isolation, and to find that one does not drive out the other.

Naturally enough, most of Elly's games were played with me.

Brother and sisters, and most of all her father, were more gifted players than I, but they were away much of the day. I was the steady companion, and in my first year of work she grew more and more dependent on me. There were no more long naps; no longer did she crawl alone in the yard. First it was I who was where she was; then she began to follow me until it was a rare thing for us to be in different rooms. She actually became intolerant of other children's sharing her play with me, or her long walks. I watched the dependence grow with mixed feelings, but joy kept uppermost. This was after all what we wanted—that she should be able to relate to another person. She was still all too capable of detachment. If other children were not present to share my attention she could still cheerfully ignore me altogether. I could leave the house and she would take no notice. I could return after a day's absence and though I might spend several minutes talking to father or sister as Elly, her back to me, played on the floor, the sound of my voice would not make her turn round.

She grew slowly more aware of others. But most of the time it was I who was alone with her as the hours passed in the quiet house. It was an environment devoid of events unless I generated them—especially in the long, enclosed Northern winters when few small children can stay outside for long, least of all Elly, who unassisted would throw no snowball, climb into no swing, slide on no sled. Yet though Elly was content to do nothing, she was glad to be occupied. She could not play herself, but she welcomed someone who would play for her.

Most of our play has been described already. But there was one kind of activity which I have not described because it was not a matter of specific skills: our play with toy animals and with dolls. I hoped that doll play might promise a way to bring Elly into the social world of which she seemed unconscious.

The nursery of a fourth child contains quantities of substitute people, some soft, some fluffy, some rubbery, some realistic with

95

nylon hair and eyes that shut. Over the years they have acquired personalities and names. Elly had her own as well as the castoffs of her sisters and brother; she had been a tiny baby when she first smiled at her blue teddy, new then, and "teddy" had been her first word. The single picture she had recognized in three and a half years had been of a blue teddy. She would play with her teddy, freely and often, jumping with him in her crib, throwing him on the floor, cheerfully, casually, with no more sign of feeling for him as a surrogate human (or, indeed, animal) than she had for the real humans (and animals) who surrounded her. I could elicit a friendly laugh by adapting the hand-animal game to doll or teddy—Teddy would walk-walk-walk-go-see-the-baby, and "walk," abstracted from this game, was one of her earliest words. But the initiative was all mine. Moreover I could find nothing better for the teddy to do than walk. It seemed she could understand only the crudest actions attributable to a teddy, and ones that directly approached her. She did not dress or undress him, or put him into situations mimicking those observed in the family, or respond when I did so. Not surprising, certainly; since she herself imitated nothing that anyone said or did, one would hardly expect her to imitate at one remove. It was the more remarkable, then, the day (she was not quite two and a half) that decisively she took her teddy, set him in a chair next to a row of other dolls, and looked up at me and smiled the way any small child does when it has done something clever. It was one of those swallows that we became familiar with—the kind that do not make a summer. "Unprecedented," my diary notes. Unprecedented, it set no precedent. Like the single time she swept up after me, the single time she fed her doll, it led nowhere.

Where all progress was slow, progress with dolls was almost imperceptible. Elly was almost three when I succeeded in interesting her in a small baby doll. "Interest" is perhaps too strong a word; she would look on while I dressed it and she would condescend herself to pull the clothes off (still too weak to unsnap the snaps) and choose another costume. It was a step beyond "walk-walk," and time for one, just recently she had considerably diluted the social relevance I had hoped for in that game by taking some new and delightful colored shapes and making *them* walk toward her.

The dressing game proceeded mechanically, the clothes chosen at random, put on, taken off. That was all there was to it. This was not surprising; in spite of her exact color discrimination, Elly took no interest whatever in her own clothes. Two months passed and we were still playing the game every night at bedtime. Even Elly could get bored—she was now cutting short the number of costumes—but my attempts to vary the game or to extend it to mimic social situations met with no success. Yet there appeared to be some small carry-over; it was at this time that she understood when I played "this little piggy" with another doll's toes. She took a liking to two tiny teddies, small enough to fit in the chairs of our dollhouse. She enjoyed it when I put them at the doll table, and when I set out tiny plates and silver for them, Elly clearly recognized the situation; she took the half-inch doll-knife and attempted to cut their food. Very encouraging, but another dead end. A person trained to it might have seen further ways to connect with the social world so closed to Elly. Or perhaps even a trained person would have found no more to be done with it than that.

Another month passed. We dressed and undressed the doll at bedtime, but attempts to interest Elly in putting the doll to bed met with complete failure. A trained person might be surprised at how slowly an untrained one thinks: it was not until I saw a doll's crib at a friend's house that it occurred to me that crib-centered Elly might recognize its function better than that of the conventional beds our dolls slept in.

I borrowed the crib and took it home. The effect on Elly was immediate. She caught sight of it while being diapered for bed; as soon as she was dressed she climbed down, went over to it, and put her own foot in. We sat down by it and were dressing dolls as usual when Elly got up, went over to her own crib, in which she had already placed a book—a normal part of her nighttime preparations—removed the book and brought it over to the doll crib. She tried to put it in—unsuccessfully, since it was twice as big as the crib. I got her a miniature book but she laid it aside. The crib was no toy to Elly. It was not a representation of the business of life, but part of it. She played a little more with the doll clothes, then once more put her foot into the little crib. It is difficult for a three-year-old child to climb into a crib nine inches long, but Elly tried; holding out her hand for support she actually stood in it.

Little interest as Elly had shown before in toy representations of reality, she had never before confused them with reality itself. She had not tried to sit in the doll chairs or try on the doll costumes or eat the doll food. The crib was different, though I did not understand why, and do not. Perhaps it spoke to that deepest part of Elly—the whatever-it-was that craved enclosure. At any rate, it seemed to me that we were in a sensitive area and that I should go slow. I kept on dressing the baby doll—the game was into its fourth month—but I let two weeks go by before I put the doll into the crib.

Elly paid no apparent attention. She had made no further attempts to get in the crib herself and seemed now to take it for granted. But a readiness was silently building. Four days passed, each of which I ended by putting the doll in the crib. The fifth evening Elly decisively went and got the old doll bed from the cupboard where it was kept. Ignoring the crib, which was in plain sight, she crouched over the bed, attempting to get in it. The crib, perhaps, had brought it to her attention, but I suppose she had always known what it was for. Accident plays a large part in progress; it happened that the wooden frame of the bed was old and partly broken, and I took it away for repair without objection from Elly. The mattress remained. Idly, I placed the doll pillow on it, and the small quilt. To my surprise, Elly at once took another quilt and carefully put it in position on the first one, adjusting it to perfect congruence and smoothing it down with satisfaction. Encouraged, I put the baby doll on the pallet she had prepared, only to find to my astonishment a small teddy already hidden under the quilt. This time there was real comprehension and admitted pleasure. Elly laughed, patted the quilt, and even said "ni'-ni'"—her twenty-first word. We put her into her crib in triumph.

I cannot overemphasize the gradualness of this process. It was as if we were trying to conceal, Elly and I, even from ourselves the direction in which we were moving. What was too much to accept in the crib could be accepted in the bed, and perhaps even better in the dismantled mattress on the floor, for when the bed returned, repaired, Elly would not allow the mattress to be put back. Twice in one week Elly made up the pallet on the floor. But we seemed no nearer the proper use of the crib, though Elly was if anything more fascinated by it than she had been. She carried it about with her. She carefully collected all the tiny doll shoes and put them in it. She filled it with animal crackers. But if I put a doll or an animal in she removed it at once in her characteristic businesslike manner. It was as if—*as if*—she knew quite well what we were getting at, but, as one of her baby-sitters had expressed it, "She won't give you the satisfaction."

How to proceed? It was impossible to predict the ploys that could slip through that massive resistance—impossible for me, though someone trained to the work or more naturally gifted in the nursery might have been able to formulate a plan for progress. We lurched forward by accident. One day, weeks later, an idea came out of the nowhere where all my ideas come from. It came to me to put in the crib a doll that was too large for it. Its head stuck out at an uncomfortable slant; the whole set-up was clearly disproportionate, wrong. Elly saw the doll and as usual auto-matically removed it. But in a few minutes she returned. She looked straight into my face and laughed, and put the doll back in the crib—not the baby doll or the little teddies that fitted so nicely, but this outsize interloper that clearly didn't belong there. For this doll she got blanket, spread, and pillow, laughing like anything, happy and delighted—as was I. Finally, laughing even more (the joke's on you, I won't give you the satisfaction) she dismantled the whole business.

This was the culmination of a process that, from the time she first caught sight of the crib, had taken fifty-seven days.

"She doesn't want to give you the satisfaction." The baby-sitter had noticed that Elly would sing, unnoticed, in the back seat of the car, but would stop if you looked at her. We had all noticed that when she heard a new tune she almost never sang it immediately afterward. However difficult the intervals, however tricky the rhythm, she did not need to repeat it to fix it in her memory. Days afterward, sometimes weeks, unpracticed but perfect, the tune would appear. Yet she seemed completely to lose her ability to render a tune on the rare occasions when she requested one. She would stand by the piano, her voice moving vaguely up and down; she would put my hand on the keys and I would not know what to play. I recalled the way we had learned to ignore, not congratulate, when she first held spoon and cup. I remembered the circles she drew, but only the day after I had drawn them. I began to think about imitation. "Imitating is innate in men from childhood. Men differ from other animals in that they are the most imitative, and their first learning is produced through imitation. Again, all men delight in imitations." What had Aristotle ever remarked that was more just, more obvious than this? But my child did not imitate. What was there involved in the process of imitation from which Elly held herself back? It seemed clear that she *could* imitate—the few words, the tunes, the figures, the rare activity were proof of that. Why wouldn't she? What is the difference between copying a circle immediately after your mother has drawn one for you, and reproducing it after a day or a week has gone by?

The obvious difference is that the latter is much harder to do. Many children could not do it at all; it was remarkable that Elly could, not that she did not do it often. The time to imitate an action is immediately after it has taken place. Elly was handicapping herself by this delay. What function could the time lag serve?

It could, it seemed to me, function to preserve isolation. If you draw a circle immediately after someone, you are acknowledging that the two of you are in contact. Someone sends, you receive. If you wait, the connection is successfully obscured. Your action can seem to come from yourself alone.

I began to focus on the problem of imitation, but it was a long time before I thought of anything to do about it. When I did it was not much—nothing more than that I should do what she would not. If she would not imitate me, we would make the current flow the other way. *I* would imitate her.

I began the fall that she was three. There seemed to be a general readiness to move forward—the first exercises in picture recognition began then, the work on switches and faucets, the play with dolls. Elly was not silent. Her words were rare, but she often made noises—ordinary, relaxed baby sounds. These I imitated as closely as I could, not systematically but on occasion.

I had been doing this about four months when one day Elly happened to make five little sounds, ending with a rising intonation—ah-ah-ah-ah-AH! That was easy to imitate, and I did so. But this time, unlike all the others, Elly imitated me again. I imitated her back. She laughed. I tried two more sounds, choosing the explosive ba-ba and la-la she had learned from Joann and never forgotten. She imitated them at once. I then risked all and said "eye," the word she'd learned so well and then abandoned. She repeated that too, full of gaiety and amusement.

We were in contact—not by means of touch, which is hard to

ignore, but by sound, which is easy. It seemed a great leap forward, but by now we knew that Elly did not proceed by leaps. We kept the game going, and Elly continued to enjoy it. She herself made more complex sounds, almost as if she liked to hear me imitate them. She imitated more nonsense syllables. But she did not say "eye" again. Nor, after that first day, could I bring her through noises to any other words, either abandoned or in current use.

But all this—head under the blanket, doll play, practice in imitation—was for one purpose: to bring her into contact with people. The evidences of progress were small, but they were beginning to accumulate. In the weeks before her third birthday, all these things happened. In the course of a tickling game, *she* poked *me* with her finger, to her great amusement. (It did not happen again for six months.) She fed me a candy, as she did a little later at Dr. Blank's, putting it into my mouth herself, not merely pushing my hand to do the work. When an elderly gentleman had held her hand and tickled it, she held out her hand to invite him to begin again. She even clowned a little for him, as a normal baby would. One memorable afternoon she spontaneously hugged her sister. Three or four times she pushed the children, not with the detached don't-bother-me attitude we were used to, but with the first anger and hostility she had ever shown. It may seem strange to mark down anger as a sign of progress, but it too is a way of relating. It is better than indifference.

Yet it poses problems, especially when it occurs, not at home with one's own children, where it can be mediated and explained, but with others.

From the very beginning I had gone out of my way to introduce Elly into social situations—to take her to stores and into crowds and to friends' houses, particularly if they had children. It seemed the obvious thing to do, and it had not been difficult. Elly was too withdrawn to cause any trouble. She sat and walked about and sometimes played with unfamiliar toys, while I visited and hoped that her mere presence in a social milieu was doing her some good. But as Elly came a little way out of herself, her progress presented difficulties. On one such visit she actually noticed a friend's baby; instead of looking straight through him as she had done before, she gave him a block. We were delighted, of course. But were we to be delighted when later, without provocation, Elly pushed him over with unmistakable hostility? I could welcome hostility in theory, but in practice, if we were to continue to go into society I could not encourage it. I had to say no-no and slap her hand. A week later when the same baby pushed her she did not push back. She slapped her own hand instead. From that time on she paid no further attention to babies.

Yet there was a general forward motion that helped us bear setbacks. As Elly approached four she abandoned doll play altogether and resisted all attempts to lure her back to it. But other things took its place. The new ability to joke and tease did not disappear. She spilled water on me on purpose, and laughed. She turned the light off while we sat at supper. Teasing is not an autistic activity.

We were able to establish a few reciprocal games—ones in which Elly too must play her part. Elly, who six months before would lackadaisically roll a ball back to you from twelve inches away, would now retrieve it with enthusiasm if you threw it several yards. Out on the wide college lawns, I could now do as I had delighted to do with the other children—crouch down and hold out my arms while a small, laughing creature came running from fifty feet away to end in my embrace. At two, Elly had played ring-around-the-rosy with me alone, for I could take both hands and make her dance; at three she would accept other members of the family in the circle; eight months later she included strangers—indeed, she accosted passers-by and peremptorily forced them to join the game. It was no longer difficult to introduce her to baby-sitters. I would place her in her swing, station the new girl to face her, and myself stand behind and push. The repeated, predictable approach and retreat seemed to operate as a model of a manageable human relationship, one from which she could always withdraw, as the swing would always swing back. For years I made sure that there was always someone in front of her when she swung. I looked for activities that could be made reciprocal. Elly looked on while I made beds. She liked to see me cover the pillows; she would motion me to pick them up. It was not hard, it turned out, to move her hands and so teach her to pick the pillows up herself and bring them to me—a beginning of training in giving which inside a year would make it possible for me to say "bring me" and expect a response. Everything worked together. Speech, comprehension, use of the hands, social relationships developed inseparably. Everything fed into everything else. As time went on, Elly remained strange. In some ways she got stranger. But she lived more nearly among us than ever before.

One day, the month she was four, her brother flopped down on a bed. Elly—who had not put a doll to bed for six full months—gently covered him over with a blanket. My eyes filled. That was what all that had been for.

A few weeks later we were back at the drawing work. I made a circle and gave the crayon to Elly. With faint yet certain strokes she put four marks inside it: eyes, nose, mouth. Casually yet unmistakably she made a body and scratched in arms and legs. Elly, whose eyes six months before could not see pictures, whose hands had been too weak to press down a crayon, had drawn, not a triangle or an E, but a human being.

She drew another the next day, this time supplying the circular head herself. She drew it in the sandpile with a stick; she scratched it out at once. I would wait many months before Elly drew again. But I could remember this.

8 ⋅ In the Family

THIS, then, was Elly, from babyhood until she was four. This is
what she did and what we did with her. I have put down almost
everything. So empty are the days of an autistic child that it is
possible in a hundred or so pages to set out nearly the full content of the most concentrated and fertile years of a normal
child's experience. In the midst of our noisy, active household
here was this cipher, this little island of detached simplicity,
living its life, and we with our lives to live around it.

I knew the question so well: "But isn't it hard on the other
children?" It is hard on the other children. In the first bad
years it was very hard indeed. "Why doesn't Elly talk?" "I was
younger than that when I talked, wasn't I?" "Is Elly going to
be retarded?" It is hard for children to sense that something is
wrong and have no inkling of what it is, not even the security of
a name to give it. Why didn't Elly talk? We could not give them
answers we did not have ourselves.

It was hard to be looked through by the pretty baby they were
so ready to play with and love. It was hard for a little boy six and
little girls nine and ten to put all their minds to choosing a
Christmas present for their two-year-old sister's first real Christmas and know that in all probability she wouldn't look at it or
them. It was hard to learn to be aggressive and yet not too

aggressive, to know when to tickle and when to stop. Sara, whose baby Elly had been from birth, had a kind of self-confidence stemming from this special relationship. She was also the eldest, a poised, omnicompetent child. It was easier for her to take the initiative than for the less assertive Rebecca, or for Matthew, who was not so far out of babyhood himself. Sara could get Elly to look at her. She was a good tickler, a good picker-upper. The younger children found it harder to press in where they were not wanted. So Elly noticed Sara more than she noticed them. But she did not notice any of them much. To take the initiative and be rebuffed is terribly painful. In differing degrees all shared that pain.

But children get used to being ignored—they have plenty of other things on their minds besides whether their baby sister is interested in them. If Elly gave nothing, she demanded nothing. She did not occupy a very important position in their lives. It seemed to us that for the time being this was as it should be. If she ignored them, they could ignore her too. Our task at this point was to see that the few ways in which she impinged on them should be, if not actually pleasant, at least neutral. Later they would have to learn to accept the inconvenience and embarrassment that any abnormal child brings. Acceptance would grow of itself as Elly and they grew together. But we could act now to minimize inconvenience and embarrassment.

We had decided—or, rather, we had never questioned—that Elly was to live with us, to benefit, we hoped, from surroundings of warmth and love. From that choice, certain things must follow.

If love was to be her therapy, it must be possible to find her lovable. At first we might be able to do no more than ensure that she not be hatable. That would be a beginning; for the children's sakes, our sakes, and her own, we must do what we could to make sure of that. No one can be expected to love a child whatever it does, least of all its brothers and sisters.

If Elly was to live with us, we could not allow her to be

destructive, dirty, or repellent in her personal habits. The children's possessions, and ours, must be safe. We must be able to take her to restaurants and public places. The family had enough to bear from Elly without having in addition to be ashamed of her behavior or appearance.

It was our good luck that Elly was pretty. Or perhaps it was more than luck; physical attractiveness, like good health, is one of the inexplicable items in the syndrome of infantile autism, and this makes the family's burden lighter. The world is unfair, and in a pretty child people will overlook a great deal. We kept Elly's yellow hair washed and brushed (against considerable opposition), her nose and mouth wiped, her fingers unsticky. We saw to it that her clothes were attractive. When she spilled food down the front (less often, as I have said, than normal children) we sponged or changed her dress. There was no danger of conveying an exaggerated fastidiousness to Elly. She was fastidious already. Perhaps it would have more "natural" or "healthy" if she had been relaxed enough to like being dirty, but she did not. It might be a sign of her pathology, but since it made things easier we might as well be glad of it.

Behavior, however, was harder to control. Yet some sort of control was a necessity.

It is not easy to discipline an abnormal child. The difficulty lies not so much in the child itself as in one's own reluctance to be harsh with the handicapped. It is not easy to punish a child who does not hear what you say for a transgression whose nature you have no reason to believe she can understand. You cannot say that Sara will be sad if Elly tears her book (Elly was six before she began to understand what "sad" meant). You cannot even say that if Elly tears books Mama will have to take the books away. You cannot say that if Elly pours her bathwater on the floor it will soak down and leak through the ceiling below. You cannot say anything, because the child understands only action, and not much of that. She understands only what touches her presently, physically. She sets no store by things, so you cannot discipline her by deprivation or by reward. What remains is the traditional method of discipline—the use of force.

I need not explain to modern readers that for our generation of parents force was not the method of choice. To impose one's will on a normal child by force is distasteful enough (though at times, as our generation of parents at length found out, quick force is less damaging to all concerned than indulgence or elaborate moral suasion). To use force on an abnormal child seems too brutal to contemplate. I do not know whether I could have contemplated it, and I'm not sure I could have done it. By good luck I did not have to. It happened that the major work of disciplining Elly was done before we knew there was anything the matter.

Until she was twenty-two months old, after all, we thought Elly a normal, though increasingly obtuse and stubborn child. She responded to no prohibitions or commands; when she was doing something anti-social it was almost impossible to get her to stop. She simply paid no attention to what we did or said. Amused at first, I would become irritated, then infuriated at behavior which looked in every way like willful disobedience. Why would she go on drenching the floor with bathwater when again and again I asked her not to? The other children hadn't been like that, even when they were smaller. Why wouldn't this one listen to her mother?

I grew more angry than I have ever been with a child—so angry that I cannot recall it without shame. In my anger, I slapped my little girl's naked flesh again and again, until I could see the redness on her skin and she was screaming with pain and shock. I screamed myself. "No, no, no, NO!" I don't know how often I did this—three or four occasions, perhaps, no more. Then it was no longer necessary. Elly understood nothing else, but she understood "no, no." I rarely had even to slap her hand, never to hit her hard. I did not have to scream. The words were enough.

And of course almost as soon as she understood the words, I came to understand that she might not have been able to help the behavior for which I had punished her. Everything was different after she came home from the hospital. It was years before I could get really angry with her again. Of course I felt guilt for those rages that only Elly and I had witnessed. (I would have been ashamed for the older children to see me behave so.) It was a bitter thing for me to reflect that in two years the only verbal contact I had achieved with my baby was the word "no." I am a verbal person; for me, words have tremendous significance. It seemed to me that that *no* might impose its minus sign upon a whole universe.

I was wrong. That guilt was unnecessary and after a time I ceased to feel it. It was not only a matter of realizing that it was better for Elly herself that she now responded reliably to "no, no." I had known that to begin with. I had to go further, to realize that in a child so out of touch with others, any contact is better than no contact at all. Would that I could have reached Elly first with "I love you," or with "yes" (though to be realistic one should remember that the nature of the world is such that "no" is an essential word and "yes" is not, and that most children learn it first). The important thing was that I reached her. Perhaps nothing less than that storm of force and emotion was necessary to break through the wall. If so, I am glad it came when it did; six months later it would have been impossible for me to feel that anger.

I should have had to fake it, then. I am convinced of that. And that would have been exceedingly difficult, though much less is impossible than one at first believes.* Violent anger is better felt than faked. But it is necessary, if it is the only way of con-

---

* Therapists in California were having their first success in dealing with severely autistic children by treatment in which violence and punishment played an important part. See *Life*, May 7, 1965, for a contemporary account of the work of Dr. Ivor Lovaas. — CCP. 1981

veying to a child that there are limits to what it can do and that someone cares enough to set them. I am no longer sorry that I used force against Elly. Those who know the story of Annie Sullivan know that she had to use more force than I before she could work her miracle and reach the waiting child inside the lonely little wild animal that was Helen Keller. And the little animal, through force as well as love, in some sense knew that this was the first person who cared enough about their relationship to find a way to make it work.

I found that Elly *wanted* discipline. When she tore a book or penciled a wall I began to notice that if I overlooked the transgression she would take my hand and use it to slap her own. As she approached three she made a game of it (I need not re-emphasize how unusual it was for Elly to invent any kind of game). With no provocation at all she would herself say "no, no," take my hand, make me slap hers, and laugh her head off. This was in contrast to the infrequent occasions when I really slapped her for a real transgression; she did not laugh then, even though it was usually, now, no more than a symbolic tap. The punishment game made me feel better about the real punishments. I came to see that discipline, too, is a kind of communication. Negative though it is, it sets up a relationship of mutual expectation. I was trying to find reciprocal games; Elly showed me that this was one. If you do this, then I do that. A normal child needs this assurance of order and predictability, but it can survive without it. For an abnormal child whose abnormality lies in lack of contact, it is more important.

For a child suffering from the specific autistic syndrome it is essential. All observers of such children have been struck by their extraordinary investment in order, their urge to set objects in arbitrary but exact and recurrent arrangements, their capacity to note and be disturbed by the most minor displacements. An autistic child may carry on inconsolably if its milk is offered before rather than after its dessert, or if a missing block makes completion of a design impossible. It was this interest in order that suggested autism to Dr. Blank when he first saw Elly. Such children, then, might be expected to have a more than usual need for an orderly social environment. What will distress them and fill them with anxiety is not the arbitrariness or unfairness of a punishment. For them, since they have no comprehension of social causes, all events are equally arbitrary and fairness has no meaning. What is difficult to bear is, rather, inconsistency, deviation from that expected pattern of events which is their only surety in an incomprehensible world. A normal child can take it if behavior that yesterday brought punishment today gets off scot-free; it may sense the reason and will very probably enjoy the fact. An autistic child will not; it will suffer, wordlessly, in the same way it suffers when something is out of place. We are told to be consistent with all our children, and we try to be. But laziness or inattention often intervene or special circumstances arise and the expected consequences do not follow. The autistic child cannot appreciate the circumstances or its good luck, and shows its anxiety by an uncharacteristic turbulence. Many parents who have lived through Dr. Spock's great revolution in child care have seen the results of dogmatic permissiveness and have come to feel, as Dr. Spock himself has, that to indulge a child is to do it no special favor.* Normal children, however, can survive permissiveness, as they can survive most things. For an autistic child, the indulgence, hesitation, and softness that are so naturally called forth by its condition must be avoided at whatever cost. They will not help the child or its family, but do serious injury to them both.

Not that Elly's life was hemmed in by prohibitions. It did not have to be. She did very little, and very little of that needed to be controlled. She was not destructive but passive, not aggressive

* Those who take the trouble to compare the 1957 edition of *The Pocket Book of Baby and Child Care* with the first one will discover that Dr. Spock in it revolutionized his revolution.

but withdrawn. This made our work easier. What touched her own safety directly she herself looked out for. Because of her pathological caution there was no need to forbid edges or heights. She opened no bottles, allowed nothing unfamiliar past her lips. Danger from traffic was something else; as I had no need to teach Elly physical caution in running or climbing, so I had for years no hope of teaching her to look out for the danger of an oncoming car. I looked out for her myself and thanked heaven we lived on a cul-de-sac.

There were only a few things we had to be strict about, so we could come down hard on those. For the rest, she could do as she liked. Since she could understand so few prohibitions— at this time, in fact, I do not think she *understood* any—we were glad to keep them to a minimum. They concerned almost exclusively damage to other people's property—extended to her own if the situations were too similar to expect her to distinguish them; for example, she was not allowed to tear her own books or any others. I did not, in these early years, say or suggest "no, no" for a whole range of behavior that might well have been limited. I let her eat snow. I let her splash through puddles. She was an unusually healthy child and I had worse things to worry about. I let her soil herself, though to keep her socially acceptable I moved fast to clean her up. I let her make puddles on the floor; by the time she was four her natural fastidiousness allowed her to make very few. I did not try to force her to the pot, guessing it would be useless. Characteristically, she developed her own strange controls; by the time she was four she was holding her urine all day, to empty it into her bath. It seemed to cause her no discomfort; after a while it caused me none.

I did not try to modify such behavior because it did not seem important to me. What was important to me might have seemed equally unimportant to another mother: it was important to me that Elly should not disturb me at night or wake me early in the morning. Since this is not something one can effect with hand-slapping and "no-no," I made use of every expedient I could think of. I put animal crackers in her bed for her to find when she waked up. Later (for she was four before she climbed out of bed and five before she opened her door) I went to the length of locking our bedroom door when she got into a spell of waking us at six-thirty. Not that I approved of locking a little child out; I did not, and least of all Elly, whom I had spent years teaching to want my company. The point is something else; it goes beyond what specific behavior should or, ideally, should not be limited, or what methods are justifiable in limiting it. The important thing is not what the child should be allowed to do, but, rather, what you can stand. For beyond the importance to the child of any specific prohibition, even if it affects such potentially sensitive areas as toilet training or exclusion, is that which is of the most crucial importance of all: that the people who live with the child must not be pushed beyond what they can endure. People can stand most things if they have to, but no one can stand everything. Other mothers might have got up cheerfully with the child at 6:00 A.M. and balked at the puddles. If so, they should have done what they had to and gone guilt free. What is important for the child is not that it be liberally treated in this or that aspect of its behavior, but that its mother and its family do not fall apart. If they go under, the child goes too. For every family the last straw will be different. Whatever it is, from smearing food to being followed into the bathroom, it must be eliminated, firmly and with no sense of guilt. That is what discipline is for. Any child would sense the firmness and find security in it. An autistic child will go further and, once the firmness of the limit is appreciated, will welcome it as an essential part of its routine.

No more is being said here than that if an abnormal child is to be helped in the family, by mother, father, other children—then mother, father, and other children must be considered as well as the abnormal child. As most families are set up, it will be the mother who does most of the considering, and one of the things she must consider is how much she can stand. It may be a great deal, but she must not take on everything in a misguided spirit of self-sacrifice, since if she cracks no one will be helped at all. She must assess how much the rest of the family can stand, too, before they begin to feel that this burden is more than they can bear. What I had to do was to keep Elly and her problems as peripheral as I could to the major concerns of my husband and my children.

I even had to keep her, in some sense, peripheral to my own. Not that this was possible in the hours and days at home with Elly, shifting puzzle pieces, sitting in closets, lying under quilts. As long as I was at home, even while she was asleep, Elly was in my mind. I do not know what would have happened to me and to us if I had followed the rigid conception of my duty that I had had when I became pregnant again with this fourth child. I had thought that because I must give no less to this one than to the others I would put off my re-entry into the world for another six years—until she was ready for school. I would see about going back to teaching then. Luck, however, was with me here, as in other things. Circumstances changed my mind for me.

It was true luck, not intelligent decision-making. Elly was just two; we had entered the six-month period of watching and waiting to see if she would catch up with normal children. We were anxious, but not yet sick at heart. It was summer, and I read in the paper that a community college would open in a city twenty miles from our small town, to be the first in a projected network of two-year colleges which would bring higher education in our state within reach of every student who could use it. In all the thinking I had done about returning to teaching the stumbling block had been how and where. My husband's all-male college would not employ me even if I were qualified, which I was not. I had no teacher's certificate, so I could not teach in the public schools. There was a private school nearby; now and then they needed a teacher of elementary Latin. I was ready to teach grammar to thirteen-year-olds (I was ready to do almost anything). But as I read of the new college I realized how glad I would be not to have to. My teaching experience, such as it had been, had not been with privileged younger adolescents in a sheltered school, but with freshmen in a teacher's college and a state university. They had ranged in age from eighteen to twenty-seven, for I had been privileged to teach among the great wave of veterans who flooded the colleges after World War II, and in my first class there had been only two students who were younger than I. Such a background, I thought, might be usable in the new college. I had been twelve years at home, my time spent largely in the company of young children and of other mothers absorbed in their care. I knew these years had scarcely added to my professional adequacy or my ability to function outside my home. A place like this, however, would perhaps not find it easy to recruit teachers. I could drive over for an interview and still not risk much. I would merely fill out an application and get my name in their files. I could come to terms with my hesitations gradually. It was already the middle of August; the college was to open in September. They couldn't still be hiring faculty at this date. Even if they took me, I could hardly begin teaching before next year.

But I walked right off the street into a job.

Had I waited that extra year I might not have taken it. I would have known then how far Elly was from normality and how much she needed me and I might not yet have known how important it was for us all that I too should have some place of refuge and refreshment. I might have thought out the wrong decision instead of falling into the right one. I was indeed lucky. My new job took me away from home only for a few hours three times a week, but it was so hard, so various, so demanding and absorbing that for that time at least it kept my mind from trouble. I do not think anything else could have. The job held me together.

It does so still. Though I shall have little to say about it, it should be thought of as a major element in this story.

It meant, of course, that I must get part-time help with Elly. I had no access to skilled professionals; my houseworker had known Elly from birth and she took over while I was away. My salary just covered hers. Elly required, after all, very little. She was gently and warmly cared for while I was away; her father made a point of coming home for lunch to make sure that all was well. Her quiet life was even quieter with me gone. It occurred to me that she might suffer from the lack of stimulation. But I also thought it possible that she could use these periods of lying fallow—a comforting rationalization which I now think may very well have been true. In any case we thought it good that she be in regular, comfortable contact with someone besides me.

So began the series of mother's-helpers who helped Elly, helped me, and helped us all. There was no rapid turnover. We did not often make use of other sitters; sitters who were not disconcerted by Elly were not easy to find. I had the same houseworker for two years, and then a series of girls who lived with us. I chose them as carefully as I could, for they were to be not only helpers but temporary sisters and daughters. They must be flexible and intelligent. Fitting into a new family is not easy, even if your job is not the all-demanding one of loving and teaching an autistic child. But a sensitive and enthusiastic young girl can bring a great deal to that job—far more, on occasion, than an emotionally exhausted mother. Our first new daughter came to live with us when Elly was four, and she has proved no temporary acquisition. Four years later she is our daughter still and Elly's best-loved friend. A complete story would describe her devotion and the techniques she and her successors developed, along with mine. But I suspect that she will write her own book one day. Until then I can only pay her, and those who came after her, this brief tribute. They gave with open hand to Elly and to our family all that was in them to give.

Elly benefited immeasurably from the variety they brought into her constricted and empty world. The quilt and the closet and the quiet games with me gave Elly much that she needed, and for a time perhaps all that she could take. But they could not be enough. The size of our family was our good luck too. She needed—and as she grew better she began to be able to use—the varied eventfulness a big family provided. The door would open and the children would come home from school with a tickle for Elly, or new books and balls that she could play with. In the summer they would run on the lawn with their friends, six or more of them, and Elly, though in no real contact with them, would run up and down in the same direction. Each individual in the household treated her a little differently. I was good at the passive plugging, the long pull. Her father gave something quite different; his flair was for jokes and excitement, the fertile and unexpected, for games I would never have thought of or would not risk trying. As Elly improved she could use the occasional practice in coping with the spontaneous and unlooked for, the occasional departure from routine which, if all else remained secure and orderly, even she could begin to enjoy. The young mother's-helpers did things we didn't. As Elly passed four she went with them to movies and parties and hamburger joints and was introduced to young men with beards and guitars. (Some of the young men recognized in Elly the classic cop-out. They said they wished they could be like her, and my heart constricted.) The differences in treatment were good for Elly, now she was bigger. It was still true that in most things we adapted ourselves to Elly, but Elly in a number of things was learning to adapt to us. She accepted that though Mother does it this way, with Jill it might be otherwise. I had to peel Elly's apples; Jill did not. Rosemary asked her to put on her own pants and she did. She accepted these variations as she would not have accepted variations in my behavior; even autistic children at length appreciate that different people do different things.

The socialist motto held good in our little collective; from each according to his ability. I was fortunate indeed in my family and in the job which had forced me to make my family bigger. We were a turbulent group when you got us all at home at once; sometimes I grew tired with the complications of our interrelationships. But we impinged upon Elly's simplicity with what she needed as much as she needed retreat and quiet communion —with stimulation, random elements, and the varied shapes of love.

The helper-sisters took some of the burden off the children, as they were meant to. I wanted the children to help with Elly, but while they were still children themselves I did not want the help to be felt as work. The best thing they could do for Elly, as she entered the world by slow degrees, was to be children with her, to play naturally and with enjoyment the games that came to me, at forty, with such difficulty and awkwardness. They carried her about, dressed her in clothes from the dress-up chest, rode her in the wagon, chased her on the grass. I tried to ask of them only such contributions as they could enjoy making. If they were to accept Elly, I must be careful that the necessity of "taking care of her" did not continually pull them away from things they'd rather be doing. And I tried everything I could think of to help them come to terms with the uncertainties and mysteries of her condition. I pointed out each extraordinary accomplishment which leavened the general blankness, and soon the children began to notice them themselves. It was her brother who saw her paint the letter E; her sister who, eating Cheerios as Elly fed them to her one at a time, realized from the little grunt she made for each that she was counting. I used any ploy that came to hand. Elly brought sweets into our previously cavity-conscious household; I made sure that the children knew to whom they owed their cookies and candy. I even stooped to making use of intellectual snobbery, a commodity which with us is usually in long supply. After we were given the term "infantile autism," we were careful to let the children know that Elly wasn't an ordinary retarded child (as if any child were "ordinary") but was suffering from a rare and interesting syndrome that had only recently been discovered. They deserved any satisfaction they could squeeze from that thought.

Another approach we used was, characteristically, verbal. We continued to refer to Elly as "the baby" or by babyish pet names long after the time for it was past. It helped us all if we could find ways of forgetting that this baby was three now, and four, and five, and six. The words helped keep our expectations babyish; they hazed over the discrepancy, more evident each month for all her progress, between what she was and what she should be. Elly herself helped out by keeping her fairy charm. It would have been harder if she hadn't stayed small and delicate and easy to sweep into the air. But even as she grew more responsive her chuckles and smiles, the quality of her enjoyment, had the transparency of a young baby's, not the complexity of a child's.

Of course as she grew more responsive the children's task grew easier. "Elly hugged me this afternoon!" "Elly fed me Cheerios and she was *counting!*" They could take real pleasure in her as she began to tease and chuckle and look straight into their faces. They could take real pride in the knowledge that they had a share in her progress.

Because there could be no help for Elly in a home heavy with anxiety or hushed with the gravity of her condition. The only home that could do her any good was the cheerful, natural place we had lived in before she came. Of all the necessities of Elly's condition, we came to feel that the most imperious was the necessity of gaiety.

They call it play therapy, after all, and play must be a gay thing. It won't work if you do it grimly, gritting your teeth and letting yourself and everyone around you know that you are making an effort of will. We tried to act as if our lengthening baby were a normal child between one and two years old, and to enjoy her as if our pretense were true. We sang all the old baby songs, and invented new rhymes about how silly she was. They couldn't hurt Elly, and they comforted us. For Elly could not be helped with tears or long faces or self-sacrificing martyrdom. Knowing that children soak up their parents' attitudes, we schooled ourselves as best we could never to treat what had hit us as a tragedy or a visitation, so that the children would not feel it so. To regard our common task not as a burden but as a privilege was wishful thinking at first, but it helped it become one. It worked for us as well as for the children. The front we kept up for them sustained us too, until the assumed attitude became (almost) the real.

Almost. I will fool no one by making it sound too easy. We kept our act up well with the children, but now and then, alone with Elly, it did not work so well. One was not always gay then. But curiously, because Elly was what she was, it did not matter much. Certainly it was important to be positive and cheerful when one was in contact with Elly. But most of the time one was *not* in contact; that was the whole point. The sensitivity to mood a normal child is said to exhibit was simply not there. So when she was looking beyond one or absorbed in her chain one could slump into passivity—stare into space oneself, weep if one needed to, even, occasionally, cry out. She would not take note— which might or might not make one feel better.

And we need not pretend that for the children either we succeeded in making every rough place smooth. I remember one awful week when Elly's routine had been uncertain and disrupted. She was anxious and fretful and we could not calm her. We were in a strange house, cooped up together by bad weather; everyone was on edge. One of the children cried out, with tearing intensity, "We ought to send her away! She ought to be in an institution!" The words came from the gentlest of the three— the one who never seemed to ask for anything for herself.

No such words had ever been spoken before. There was little to answer, and yet one had to say something. I said the obvious— that we all felt that way sometimes and that it would always be

something we could do but that now after we'd all worked so
hard and she'd begun to love us a little we could imagine what it
would be like to visit her in an institution and to find she'd forgotten it all and didn't even recognize us. I don't know if it was
the right thing to say. No one has ever mentioned it again.

Elly has lived with us and the experience has been kept manageable. It's well to claim no more. One day, perhaps, my children
will tell someone else of suffering I did not guess. But we have
managed. As the children have grown older—the eldest is
ready for college now—they have not tried to hide Elly or dis-
sociate themselves from her. At home and at school they seem
comfortable about themselves and her. They take her about with
them without embarrassment. Their friends come to the house,
and they show off her weird abilities with some pride. And I am
not really surprised. If I had any faith in all this business it was
that we had good children, that they could help Elly, and help
us, and help themselves through helping. We were uneasy over
many things as Elly grew, but over this one thing we were profoundly at ease. We never thought that it could injure our children to discover that there was a real world in which all were not
fortunate, and where those who were had obligations to those
who were not. I have written already that they had grown up in
an ideal place, if an ideal place is one which is free from insecurity and danger. It should be clear by now that I am by no
means sure that it is. James wrote years ago of the need to find
the moral equivalent of war; I think we may also have, today,
a need to find the moral equivalent of poverty, of illness, of sor-
row in the privileged enclaves from which we have almost excluded them. At any rate, I have never been sorry that our children had this trouble in the midst of all their good fortune. Our
ancestors would have said that we all have our cross to bear. Our
vocabulary is different, but the meaning is precious and should
not be lost. The children have not grown up poorer for having
Elly in their family. I think they feel this to some degree even
now. Later they will know it.

9 ⸱ The Professionals

ELLY was past three and a half before we took her to a psychiatrist. Dr. Blank, of course, could easily have referred us to one, probably in his own building. Instead, he told us that Kanner, himself of course a child psychiatrist, had tried the techniques of psychotherapy on autistic children and found them useless. In the current state of knowledge there was nothing that medicine or psychiatry could do. We should continue as we had been doing and keep him informed. And for six months this is what we did.

But we did not live in an intellectual vacuum. In New York or Boston it would have happened sooner, but even in a small college town the invisible presence of Psychiatry began to press upon us. Somebody knew of Dr. Blank; his reputation as a pediatrician was excellent, but his anti-psychiatric bias was well known. Somebody else was troubled because "no one was working with Elly." Somebody else asked if she would not be better off in a residential school, where they could give her the kind of care she needed. We were lucky; our friends were civilized and tactful. Nobody said the harsh things they could have. But the implications were there. I could not answer them. I could not say that Elly, in the give and take of a family we had struggled hard to keep cheerful and normal, was getting far more of what she needed than she could in a residential school, in the mournful company of others like herself. I could not answer that *I* was working with Elly, hours every day with no traumatizing terminations of treatment when the therapist took a vacation. I was not yet sophisticated enough to realize that I was working under unusually favorable conditions, since my contact with the patient centered around the especially sensitive experiences of awaking, feeding, and putting to bed and it was easy to arrange that her major gratifications came from a single operative (me). I could not speak such heretical thoughts; I could do no more than allow them to hover at the edges of my mind. I might think in my tougher moments that the things I did were no odder than the things the psychiatrists did in the two books of case histories that interested friends had lent me—indeed they seemed very similar. But these moments were succeeded by others, in which I feared that as soon as a real psychiatrist learned about our games he would recognize them for what they were—a mother fooling around, lucky if in her inexperience and deep involvement she merely escaped doing harm.

For how likely was it that she could escape it? Alone, without professional guidance, what possible qualifications could a mother have for working with her psychotic child herself?

It is necessary now to introduce this word, and with it the subject of nomenclature. For we were finding out that there was no agreement on the right label for Elly. "Autistic" meant to Dr. Blank, and now to us, the sum of the specific elements of Kanner's syndrome, all of which appeared in Elly. To many others, however, the word still held its broad root meaning of "totally self-absorbed." This was the way the celebrated Bruno Bettelheim seemed to use the term, and he applied it freely to children who by Kanner's criteria did not seem autistic at all.*

---

* "Joey, a Mechanical Boy," *Scientific American*, March, 1959. Dr. Bettelheim describes Joey at even greater length in *The Empty Fortress* (Free Press, 1967), where his impressive recovery is presented as typical of the possibilities for autistic children.

He also used, as did many others, another term: childhood schizophrenia. This seemed to apply not only to Elly and her kind—if she had a kind—but to a wider range of children who exhibited a few of Elly's symptoms with many others of their own. We began to be aware that there were rival ways of classifying—that professional psychiatrists could argue whether Kanner's syndrome was a distinct condition, a sub-species of childhood schizophrenia, or synonymous with it. Some begged the question by calling it "atypical development." Some denied it existed at all. Yet all these were at least in agreement that the condition should be classified as mental illness or psychosis. A smaller group of observers, including the Dutch psychiatrist Van Krevelen, considered it the result not so much of illness as of a constitutional defect, to be classified not under schizophrenia but under oligophrenia, or feeble-mindedness. This minority opinion, however, hardly penetrated to us—it was only faintly suggested in the reprints Dr. Blank had referred us to. The weight of American opinion was overwhelmingly in favor of describing the condition as a psychosis. The application of that word to Elly had been ratified by the most objective of agencies, our insurance company. The expense of Elly's hospital diagnoses had been, in part, covered by insurance because her trouble was no mere behavior difficulty, not even a neurosis, but a genuine psychosis. Elly had met the standards; the form had it down in black and white. For what it was worth, Elly was psychotic. And no one was working with her but her mother.

The situation was preposterous on its face. The very dentist, when I brought in a terrified Elly for an open cavity, suggested that she would be easier to manage if someone else accompanied her. (Someone else did and she wasn't.) Everyone knows—I know myself—that the mother may be the last person who can handle a child. And this popular wisdom is today massively reinforced by professional opinion. The last people who ought to be able to work with a "disturbed" child are its parents, for who, after all, disturbed it? The disturbance, after all, did not come out of nowhere. Nobody could be expected to believe that.

Babies, we are told, are infinitely vulnerable. Before they can sit or crawl they may feel the coldness of rejection. Their parents may injure them by neglect; they may injure them by fulfilling their needs too quickly.* A child's first years are all-important—psychologists tell us this in many ways in many places, and if we do not read psychology we get their message from the mass media, vulgarized but not essentially falsified. Dr. Spock is a psychiatrist, and he has tried to tell us that babies are tough, but we have been rendered too nervous to listen. We hear on every hand that what we do in the first months of life—it may be six, or twelve, or twenty-four—may mark our child forever. Who are we to qualify this account of our responsibility? Even the parents of normal children move with a certain knowledgeable edginess. What goes through the minds of parents who know they have a child whose development has gone wrong? Bettelheim writes that parental rejection is an element in the genesis of every case of childhood schizophrenia he has seen.† Beata Rank sets out as her "main hypothesis" that "the atypical child has suffered gross emotional deprivation," and adds that "the younger the child, the more necessary is it for us to modify the mother's personality." ‡ Even the wise and humane Erikson, though he remarks that the rejecting mother is the "occupational prejudice" of child psychiatrists, reiterates in the same

* Morrow and Loomis, describing a psychotic child (in many ways similar to Elly) remembered by its parents as an infant who was "not demanding," add that "one may assume that this recollection reflects the likelihood that his demands were not appropriately met. By excessive anticipation of his needs, the parents denied him the right to demand." ("Symbiotic Aspects of a Seven-Year-Old Psychotic," in Gerald Caplan, editor, *Emotional Problems of Early Childhood*, Basic Books, 1955.)

† Letter, *Scientific American*, May, 1959.

‡ "Intensive Study and Treatment of Pre-school Children Who Show Marked Personality Deviations, or 'Atypical Development,' and their Parents," in Caplan, *op. cit.*

study that a "history of maternal estrangement may be found in *every* [italics mine] history of infantile schizophrenia." *

In this respect it made little difference whether what ailed Elly was called schizophrenia or autism. Kanner's original hypothesis was consistent with the psychiatric consensus. He considered that the parents must play a large part in the genesis of infantile autism. Certainly (like Erikson) he took account of a possible constitutional predisposition in the child; he reported that many autistic children (unlike Elly) were manifestly unresponsive from earliest infancy. But in his discussion of etiology he devoted far more attention to the role of the parents. In the process he discovered some curious facts, facts that, since they in some sense affected how we thought of ourselves as we lived with our situation, it is necessary to summarize here.

I have already said that my husband and I are typical of the parents of autistic children. I must now make clear what this entails. Early in his work Kanner was struck, not only with how similar one autistic child was to another, but at the unexpected similarity of their parents. The fathers of the first eleven cases Kanner saw included four psychiatrists, one lawyer, one chemist, one plant pathologist, one professor of forestry, one advertising man, one engineer, and one successful businessman. Of the eleven mothers, nine were college graduates. Hardly an average group, one would think; yet as Kanner collected more cases he found that the pattern varied very little. Almost without exception, the parents of his autistic patients seemed unusual both in their intellectuality and in their professional achievement. Naturally it occurred to him that he might simply be registering characteristics shared by all the parents who brought patients to an outstanding child psychiatrist at a famous research center. Accordingly, he checked his impressions. He took out the file

* "Early Ego Failure: Jean," in *Childhood and Society*, W. W. Norton, 1950, pp. 197f. Jean sounds extraordinarily like a case of Kanner's syndrome. She responded fitfully to Erikson's therapy but did not recover.

of each of his autistic patients, and the file directly next to it in his cabinet. These control files represented a random cross-section of his practice—children suffering from the full variety of conditions a modern child psychiatrist sees. Kanner compared the two sets of parents. He found that statistics bore out his impressions. The "autistic" parents, as a group and individually, had more years of education and significantly higher professional competence. Moreover, they differed in another particular, especially from the parents of schizophrenic children. The incidence of recorded mental illness among them and even among their families, was unusually low. Whereas schizophrenic patients had in their families more mental illness than is found in the population as a whole, the autistic patients had less.

Kanner began to study more closely the parents who had produced, out of such apparently strong material, such pathetically deviant children. He began to dissolve the idea of "professional achievement" into the less measurable characteristics which make achievement possible. He found in these parents, in addition to intelligence, an unusual degree of energy and persistence, as well as a capacity to control both events and their reactions to them. As he observed them in his interviews, where they might be expected to be under considerable stress, he found them a very reserved group. The capacity of these parents for detachment and objectivity seemed to him extraordinary. It is not surprising that he was led to try to relate these unique group characteristics to the unique condition he was trying to understand.

If a group of parents differed from the average as extremely as these seemed to, was it not likely that they had treated their children differently? The combination of drive and detachment may augur well for success in a profession; it is not so well regarded as a qualification for bringing up a child. To Kanner, these parents seemed *too* detached, *too* controlled. They seemed, in sum, a cold lot—"detached, humorless perfectionists, more at home in the world of abstractions than among people, dealing with their fellow-men on the basis of what one might call a mechanization of human relationships."* One of them, a prominent surgeon, even affirmed in response to Kanner's question that he wouldn't recognize his children if he met them on the street. Kanner came to think of the group as "refrigerator parents" — "able to get together just long enough to produce a child." There were exceptions — about ten per cent of the group seemed warm and responsive. And of course the deleterious effects of their personalities were not universal; virtually all the autistic children's siblings were normal, and indeed except in the case of identical twins autism rarely visits the same family twice. But in general the profile seemed clear enough.

When my husband and I read these characteristics in Dr. Blank's reprints we did not find it hard to recognize ourselves. Objectively we belonged in the group; we had a Ph.D. and an M.A., and the nearest we had come, before Elly, to mental illness was a single great-uncle who had spent a few years in a sanitarium. Subjectively we felt, both of us, the acute shyness that defended itself as reserve. We both knew what it was like to cross the street to avoid an acquaintance seen fifty feet away— not because of any anticipated unpleasantness, merely because one is not always able to sustain the effort of finding something to say. We were both capable of detachment; sustained thought is rather difficult without it. We had both been bred to self-control, and perhaps born to it. Four times I had discovered that one of the difficulties of having a baby is that nurses won't give you so much as a sedative if you can't scream. We were well suited, my husband and I. These characteristics had brought us together and kept us close. They had served us well. Most of them had

* L. Kanner and L. Eisenberg, "Notes on the Follow-up Studies of Autistic Children," in *Psychopathology of Childhood,* P. H. Hoch and J. Zubin, editors, Grune and Stratton, 1955.

seemed to be strengths. We saw them now transmuted into pathology.

Time had taught us, we thought, to live with our shyness, to fight it, increasingly to transcend it. But it is easy to deceive oneself; psychologists know that. Consider—as I considered—this sketch of the mothers of "atypical" children as I read it in one of the books my solicitous friends lent me:

On the surface these mothers may give the impression of being well-adjusted; not too rarely they are highly intellectual, prominent people. Close investigation reveals that the majority of them are immature and narcissistic with precarious social contact . . . who have struggled heroically to build and maintain the image they have created of a fine woman, wife, and mother. The nearer to perfection the success of their efforts, the stronger their belief in magic and their own magic (impenetrable defenses). . . . In spite of the outward appearance of self-assurance or worldliness, there is inner isolation. This type of mother tends to function on two levels: the surface level in contact with the outside world is a thin crust only, overlaying a strong tendency to detachment. When this dual level of functioning is a constant way of living, it bespeaks a serious disturbance.

The article then got down to cases.

The picture which Mrs. I. had of herself and which she successfully communicated to the world was that of a well-educated, vigorous, charming woman with many abilities and a host of satisfying interests. She had in fact obtained a graduate degree and had achieved success in her professional career. . . . The personality behind this façade was gradually revealed to us during the course of Mrs. I.'s therapy. We came to see her as a very isolated person who tries to combat her perception of her own emptiness and her tendency toward withdrawal by precipitating herself into constant activity and excitement.[*]

I would have been obtuse indeed not to reflect that the therapists who on close investigation had revealed the reality below

* Rank, *op. cit.*

Mrs. I.'s façade might uncover something very similar below mine. These were threatening ideas to confront. Yet somehow they did not take hold.

It is hard to see why we were not crushed with guilt. Not long ago, in a television program on autism, I heard a distinguished psychiatrist say that "of course, all the parents feel guilt." Even a close friend, a psychologist herself, once suggested I should have an analysis "to work my guilt-feelings through," and I don't think she believed me when I told her I never had any. I should have. Even if I had not been a typical autistic parent, I had been far from welcoming my pregnancy with Elly. I knew that and so did my friend. It would have made good Freudian sense for me to fear, as I slowly awoke to the severity of Elly's condition, that she rejected human beings because her mother had rejected her.

The dogma that all parents of the psychotic must suffer guilt-feelings is well based. Popularized psychology has encouraged a high level of free-floating anxiety even in the parents of normal children. The situation is made worse by the fact that a disproportionate number of abnormal children in general, and of autistic children in particular, are first children. Their apparent rejection of love is more terrifying because their parents have no experience of the affection of normal children; their bewildering behavior is, to uncertain and inexperienced mothers and fathers, more bewildering still. It would be hard indeed, in today's climate of opinion, for the parents of a seriously deviant first-born child not to feel they were in some way responsible.

But we were lucky; we had Sara, Becky, and Matt. Responsive as well as intelligent, they functioned well in school, in the neighborhood, and at home. If it is fair to lay failure at the parents' door, as much should be done for success. It was of course possible that our success, like Mrs. I.'s, could be dismissed as a façade, its hollowness shown up at last by this small, atypical baby. Occasionally, in nightmare descents into compulsive objectivity (after all, objectivity was part of our syndrome) we might see it that way. But these nightmares could not stand the light of day. A look at our children would dispel them. We were proud of them. We had done a good job with them. We knew it, and knew that others knew it. This knowledge and this pride sustained us as we read the formulations of the Bettelheims of this world—this, and a certain natural skepticism which had been with us even before Elly made us need it. No scientist's household, after all, can fail to be familiar with the great procession of plausible hypotheses that have yet proved incomplete or false. My husband's discipline, and common sense itself, warned constantly of the dangers in the premature formation of hypotheses; for his graduating seniors he had copied down the great cautionary words with which Newton closed his *Principia:* "The true reason of these properties . . . I have not yet been able to deduce from the phenomena, and I frame no hypotheses. For whatever is not deduced from the phenomena is to be called a hypothesis, and hypotheses, either of metaphysics or of physics, of occult qualities or of mechanics, have no place in experimental philosophy."

"*Hypotheses non fingo.*" Everything works together, though we do not always see it. This was doubtless one of the reasons why, among all the things we had read, we had read so little psychology.

So even as we began, slowly and reluctantly, to read a little more, we were not disposed to blame ourselves. Now, when I have talked to other parents of autistic children, I know what agony we were spared. We knew we had been the same kind of parents to Elly as we had been to the others. I knew I had been the same kind of mother. Elly had been warmed, cuddled, tickled, and loved. Experience with three children had taught me that the mind-reading powers of babies are greatly exaggerated. I knew that Elly had never guessed that (like so many mothers of normal children) I had not really needed another baby.

But I had had another baby and the baby needed help and so did we. We had sought expert medical advice and taken it. Yet how can one be sure one has done all one can? There are so many possibilities of help. An acquaintance stopped me in a supermarket; she knew of a man in Philadelphia who prayed with the parents of abnormal children and had remarkable success. A good friend wrote of a friend of hers, a theosophist and clairvoyante who was working with doctors in New York; she read auras. Later, others recommended the work of the Rehabilitation Institute in Philadelphia; no one understood how, but by a demanding program of physical therapy it was apparently possible to restore a large measure of function to the brain-damaged of all ages. Perhaps Elly could crawl her way to health. It is not with irony that I record these suggestions. Irony comes easier when you're not in trouble. I have Catholic friends who pray for Elly, and I, who cannot pray myself, can use their prayers. If the friend who read auras had lived within convenient distance I might well have taken Elly to visit; I knew already that some individuals had powers with Elly that seemed near-magical. In a desperate case one thinks carefully before one rejects any course of action that responsible people think holds out some hope.

Many responsible people thought Elly should have psychiatric attention. One of our dearest friends actually knew a psychiatrist at a renowned children's institute; they cared enough about us to discuss Elly's case with her and tell us what she said. Extraordinary things, it seemed, were being done with children like Elly, especially if you got them young enough. Time was passing. Elly was three and a half. Every month counted. We listened, and knew that we could never justify it to ourselves if we did not find out what possibilities psychiatry held for her. In the climate we lived in we could get by without crawling, or auras, or prayer. It was clear, however, that whatever Dr.

Blank said or Kanner reported, if we did not try psychiatry we would never be able to feel we had done all we could for Elly.

Once the decision was taken I was eager. I would no longer have to work alone. Desperately I needed helpers; at last I would have them. As I told my psychologist friend, "After a while my mind just gets exhausted. There are times when I can't think of anything new at all. They have so much experience—they know so many play techniques they could show me—"

"Oh, I don't think they'd do *that*," she answered. Later I remembered those words.

We wrote Dr. Blank. Noncommittally he agreed. I suppose he knew that the intellectual parents of a strange baby would not long be allowed to accept the irrelevance of psychiatry. We got in touch with the renowned children's institute, in a city not impossibly far from our home. In treatment and research it was one of the most active in the country. We wanted the best. This was another decision we did not intend to appeal.

So began an experience as penetrating as our sojourn in the cancer ward, and more far-reaching in its effects.

The Institute's approach was reassuring in its thoroughness. For a proper diagnosis, Elly should be observed over a ten-day period, and both my husband and I should be interviewed at length. For us to get away for so long was not going to be easy. The interviews would have to be scheduled in the short period between teaching semesters, and well in advance so we could get my mother to come stay with the other children. Knowing this, we had got in touch with the Institute early in December.

They were very understanding; they would get in touch with us to give us an appointment soon, very soon. We need not contact them. And then it began. We waited, with increasing anxiety, as December stretched into January and our semester break drew nearer. If we missed this chance we would have to wait four more months, and did not every month count? No letter came. It was six weeks before we were frightened enough to telephone. We got our appointments on three days' notice. Luckily my mother was coming on the chance, or we could not have got away.

We were learning what we could never have guessed; that the Institute, although theoretically aware that human beings exist in social contexts and that family life is complicated, was not interested in visualizing any detail of the life that went on outside their large, comfortable building. They had no concern with the difficulties of providing for our children in the longest absence from home we had ever had. They had scarcely more interest in what we were to do with Elly during our first interview. We learned with some astonishment that we were not to bring her. Not to bring her? Where could we leave her? Surely at so well staffed an institution there were people with whom she could stay while my husband and I were interviewed? Apparently not. It was not their practice to allow parents to bring the child at the first interview. Luckily we were staying with kind friends who knew Elly a little; we could leave her with them without too much uneasiness. But we wondered about the other desperate parents who had brought children here from all over the country. Did they all have friends who were capable of baby-sitting for small psychotics?

But we were reassured all over again as we walked in the door of the Institute, a huge old house in a run-down section, shabby and pleasant and not at all slick. We waited with a group of mothers whose children were in therapy upstairs. "It's all very well for *them*," one said, "but I wonder if they know what it's like, never to even be able to go to the toilet without him in there with me." We've come to the right place, I thought. These people are in the same boat with us, and if this place is helping them it's where we belong.

My husband and I separated for our interviews. It was not their practice to interview parents together, where they could supplement, support, and correct each other. My interviews were with the social worker, his with the psychiatrist. So it began.

The social worker explained first what the procedure would be: three interviews for Elly with the psychiatrist, the same one who was seeing her father, an intelligence test, a session in the diagnostic nursery school, and a neurological examination. We would have to discuss what time would be best for the electroencephalogram.

"The electroencephalogram?" I remembered the disoriented baby, hair still coated with jelly, I had taken home from the hospital eight months before. Must Elly go through that again? "But she's *had* an electroencephalogram! She's had a lot of tests, she was in Children's Hospital for three days. Wasn't it down in her history?"

Elly need not, then, repeat the electroencephalogram. But it was not their practice, she explained, to look at the history until they themselves had assessed the case. They had their own methods of finding out what they needed to know.

These methods are familiar enough, I found later, to those who know something of analysts and social workers. We, however, were quite unprepared. The situation seemed normal enough— two people alone in a room, one seeking information and help, the other able to give it. As teachers and as people, my husband and I were familiar with both positions. In spite of our shyness— perhaps, rather, because of it—we had learned much about bridging the gulfs between people. We were consequently slow to realize that the whole method of these interviews was so to set them up as to eliminate any possibility of a natural relationship between the two people in the room. The method was simple but rigid. We were not there to consult but to talk—to talk steadily, without guidance, without response, to an almost totally

135

passive listener who was studiously careful to betray no reaction and volunteer no comment.

In the best of circumstances one cannot talk naturally to a listener who makes no response. And these were not the best of circumstances. We were conscious that we were not ourselves. With our children, sick and well, we were firm and confident because we knew that our confidence was their security. Not here, though. Here we were on trial. Nothing had to be said about parental responsibility for infantile psychosis. I record it to the Institute's credit that nothing *was* said. But the thought hung heavy. I tried to bring it out into the open. I imagined they knew of the paper I have quoted at such length earlier in this chapter; timidly I mentioned it. At least we could find out where we were. The response was admirably controlled. "You've read that, have you?" was all the social worker said.

One could not talk naturally, yet so much depended on what the silent listener would think. In the absence of feedback, I tried to talk in the way that would be most helpful to Elly—to play it their way, insofar as I could figure it out, to be reasonable and obedient, to make sure that in the limited time available they got the information they needed.

My family, my pregnancy, Elly's whole life—how could I get it all in? I began to take out the material I had brought—the photographs that showed the progress of the condition from babyhood, the notebooks recording skills, vocabulary, the games we played, their purposes and their results. "I began keeping these as soon as we suspected . . . they're quite detailed . . . they tell about the work I do with Elly . . . if you could look them over you could ask me questions and we could go on from there. . . ."

But of course the words trailed weakly off. It was not their practice. . . . I put my records away.

Obediently, I talked. I have a good memory, I am experienced in the stages of child development, and Elly's growth had engaged all my attention. I tried to cram in all the interviewer could have read in the notebooks, afraid some significant fact would be left out. I began at the beginning—the unexpected pregnancy, the depression, everything they might be expected to find usable. It was not for me to impose my standards of relevance on the material. It took me time really to take in the ground rules; I thought they wanted me to be informative, and I kept trying to make it personal, trying—it was one of *their* words—to relate. It's not normal for me to talk very long without some stab at a joke. Jokes relieve tension, they help make strangers friends. The social worker received my jokes with Oriental calm—the same calm with which she received everything I said, whether I told of anxiety, satisfaction, or pain. Only once did I jolt her. In describing Elly, I happened to use the word "autistic." Instantly, sharply, she asked, "Where did you get that word?" "Dr. Blank," I said, "you know, the referring physician. . . ." "We don't use that word here," said the social worker.

In another room, my husband was also trying to convey helpful, relevant information. Like me, he asked questions at first. There were so many mysteries about Elly. These people had seen so many children, they could tell us so much. But every question was courteously fielded; we would be able to ask that at the final interview. We stopped asking questions almost as soon as we stopped making jokes.

They were now ready to see Elly. Since it was not until late in her third interview that she was ready to remain alone with the psychiatrist, I was able to watch him with her. His behavior was communicative if he was not. I watched him operate with clay, lollipops, the dollhouse. Elly took up the pieces of doll furniture one by one and methodically impressed a leg or an edge into the clay. She picked up the little toilet. I felt the quality of his attention sharpen, but she merely used it, like the other pieces, to imprint the clay. The psychiatrist spoke little;

when he did, it was a gentle, reiterated, positive statement: "Clay [lollipops/puzzles/dollhouses] can be *fun*." I understood, I thought, why he said that, though I could not ask him. One day, perhaps, Elly would be able to take that meaning in.

I learned from his cautious, indirect approaches; I learned more from observing Elly among other strange children in the diagnostic nursery school. There was a huge mirror on the wall. I thought I guessed why, and made a note to get Elly a mirror on our return. I was fascinated by the IQ test. The tester did not quite manage to conceal her surprise when this uncomprehending child, who had no conception what the verbal part of the test was about and fretted because she could not pull the objects she was supposed to identify off the cards to which they were attached, still strung the beads, stacked the blocks in order of size, and slapped the stars and crescents of the twelve-piece formboard into place as rapidly as an adult. This was progress. At the hospital it had been impossible to test her at all. And I enjoyed the session with the neurologist; it was like being back among human beings again. She answered questions, we joked, laughed. I suppose she, a physician, had not been trained in the couchside manner. It was all right for her to relate.

So it was over. On the whole we had been impressed, especially by their skill with Elly, who at the end of her final session with the psychiatrist had gravely tried to follow him upstairs. I was not reassured when the very last day the social worker could still ask me "Does she ever smile?" But that was my fault. I knew that their gentle caution had missed Elly's gay side; I had wanted desperately for them to see us romping together, to watch her delight in "this little piggy," her laughter when her father threw her into the air. Every day I had determined to ask if they would watch us play. One day I even came in an old pair of pants; in our gayest game, I would lie on my back and lift her with my feet, high into the air. But they never learned the reason for my odd costume; I played no games with Elly there. Surrounded by that cool detachment, I just couldn't. So we took Elly home, there to wait for them to schedule the climactic final interview when all their observations would be synthesized and presented to us and where at last we could ask questions.

We waited. Again we watched every mail. (Every month counts.) We waited one and a half months. Finally the notification came and we traveled back to the city to hear the verdict.

This is what they had to say about Elly. It is not a summary of what they said. It is *all* they said, although the psychiatrist, a hesitant, rather inarticulate elderly man, took considerably more time to say it than it takes to write it here:

1. Elly needed psychotherapy.

2. She had performed above her age-level on the part of the IQ test she could do, and it was their belief that she had no mental deficiency.

3. "She has many fears."

That is what they had made of all that information. We had been afraid we would not be able to tell them enough about Elly. Our fears were groundless. They were based on a misunderstanding of the purpose of the interviews. We had thought, naïvely, that these were a means of conveying information about Elly from us to the psychiatric team to aid in diagnosis. But since no use was made of the information, their actual purpose must have been something else. Those trained in psychology will perhaps know what it was. I can only conjecture. Perhaps it was to get us to reveal ourselves as people and parents. Perhaps not. For nothing was said about that either, for good or ill.

Of course we asked questions. We had been told we could. But no question we could think of could get the psychiatrist to add anything to those statements. He did not say she was like any child he had seen before. He did not say she was unlike any child he had seen before. We had hoped he would speak from his vast experience of abnormal children, but when we asked about other children at the Institute he suggested, vaguely, that every child was different. . . . He would give the condition no name, suggest not even a possible range of prognoses. I asked if there was any reading I could do. Case histories? I had gotten some ideas from them already. Hesitant before, he was suddenly firm. Case histories would be bad for us. I tried again. I had been impressed by the nursery school. There were, perhaps, books on nursery-school techniques for disturbed children? "Disturbed children? It was hard . . . very hard . . . in fact it was very hard even to bring up *normal* children," said the psychiatrist to the mother of four.

What, then, were we to do with Elly? If we lived in the city, he said, Elly would obviously be a case for the Institute. But we did not live in the city, and there was no child psychiatrist within many miles of our small town. He could, perhaps, give us professional advice on psychiatric facilities in our part of the state. Well, there was a place only thirty miles or so from you, very well thought of, good people there. . . . I knew already that they did not take pre-school patients, but he did not. We got again the feeling that the world outside the Institute did not exist at all.

Once or twice, by asking a question he did not expect, we got him to say something unplanned and significant. We were going on sabbatical leave; we had planned to take it in England. Should we take it instead in this city, where Elly could have treatment? Again he was firm; we should not disrupt the family's plans for a process that might appear to yield nothing and breed resentment of Elly—for "we don't work miracles, you know." We salted that away. Elly had no mental deficiency, and she was not yet four. Yet a year's psychotherapy might sink without a trace. So it was as bad as that.

At one point he mentioned my notebooks. "We read them," he said. We waited for some comment on all that work. "They were very interesting," he remarked.

The interview lasted only forty minutes. We were still trying to find the magic questions when it ended. But there was no more time. We had had it.

We walked slowly down the steps of the homelike building that had turned out to be a model of Kafka's Castle. We had come prepared for bad news; we had expected to leave shaken and upset and drive back immediately. Instead we could only laugh helplessly, and went and spent a lovely afternoon in a museum.* It was only gradually that we began to feel angry and resentful, to react as intelligent adults, not as obedient children in the hands of those wiser than we. Our powers of indignation reawakened—indignation at this pleasant, passive, blandly inconsiderate institution, at their incredibly casual scheduling, which multiplied difficulties and intensified anxiety, at the attractive, softly smiling social worker whom the passage of time had made forget the number of my children, at the cloudy, gently evasive old man who would tell us nothing unless we surprised him into it. We fed information into that computer for ten days. And when finally we were allowed to press the button, the light didn't even go on.

Yet we were not where we had been. Elly needed psychotherapy. We must try to get it for her. There was no children's specialist near us, but there was a state child-guidance clinic in the next town. Should I contact them? The Institute definitely thought I should.

I did, prudently waiting a month (though every month counted) to allow the Institute to respond to my request to forward their report on Elly. I arrived for the intake interview; the clinic had received nothing. Two months later I made a progress report for Dr. Blank, who had not seen Elly for a year. Of course, I remarked, this was only a supplement to the Institute's

* Elly's father adds: "A museum was a natural choice. An artist communicates with us, even over time, by being very careful and loving and honest, by revealing all he knows."

report, which was by now in his hands. But it wasn't, and for a very good reason. It wasn't written yet. It was not put on paper until six months after Elly's last interview, and then only after I appealed in desperation to the Institute's director.

And yet when I compare our experience with others I see that again we were lucky. They treated us well, according to their lights. I was accused neither of rejecting my child nor of a symbiotic relationship. The director of a clinic for autistic children, part of a huge medical center, has written that one of his greatest problems in treatment is the resistance parents make to the idea that they cause the disease. We might have gone there.

We got off easy. The professionals had neither praised nor blamed us and they had done their best to say nothing discouraging about Elly. They had said nothing terrible to us at all. Yet we emerged damaged, hurt, and frightened. We had gone in with expectations that, to those with no experience of the field, will not seem unreasonable. We expected to talk with wise and sympathetic people—wise because of a wide experience with sick children, sympathetic because it was their vocation to help those in trouble. We too had experience with a sick child, intense and prolonged if not wide, and we had been trying with every resource we possessed to help those in trouble—our baby, our normal children, ourselves. We were amateurs. They were professionals. But we had, we thought, a common task. Unconsciously we expected to be welcomed, not as patients, but as collaborators in the work of restoring this small, flawed spirit. We were doing something terribly hard, and we had been doing it quite alone. We had learned all we could from the biography of Annie Sullivan. We wanted information and techniques. We wanted sympathy—not the soppy kind; we were grown-up adults—but some evidence of fellow feeling, which ordinary doctors give readily enough. And—was it so unreasonable?—we wanted a little reassurance, a little recognition, a little praise. It never occurred to us that these expectations were naïve, that the gulf between parent and ministering institution must deliberately be kept un-bridgeable by any of the ordinary techniques of interpersonal re-lations. It should have been easy, after all, to say it: "Look, you're a professional. I need references, I need to find out about play therapy, I need to know all I can about children like Elly, because whoever else may or may not work with her, her main psycho-therapist is me."

But of course it was not easy but impossible. Their system made it so. Autistic was not a word they used. They were wise to avoid it, it fitted them so closely. We knew that impervious-ness, that terrible silence, those eyes that turn away. And this was the most frightening discovery of all: that we could make better progress against the walls around Elly than we could in reaching these people.

Comfortable, well-educated members of the upper middle class ordinarily escape the experience of depersonalization, of utter helplessness in institutional hands, of reduction to the status of children to whom situations are mediated, not explained. Like so much that hurts, the experience is deeply educational. We know now in our skins that the most threatening of all attacks is the attack on the sense of personal worth, that the harshest of all deprivations is the deprivation of respect. We know now, I think, how the slum mother feels as the welfare worker comes round the corner. It takes, one would think, so little knowledge of psychology to put oneself in someone else's place.

The failure of the Institute was not a failure of knowledge. Ultimately they produced, though not for our eyes, a reasonably detailed report, far fuller than the three oracular utterances they had trusted us to hear. Their failure was one of imagination. For all their silent attention they were not able to imagine the thoughts and feelings of my husband and me.

I think I can guess how we appeared to them—highly intel-lectual, cool, controlled, well-informed, prime examples of Kan-ner's parents. We *were* controlled; we had no alternative. Refrigerator professionals create refrigerator parents, if the parents are strong enough to keep command of themselves at all. I had gone in in a highly emotional state, ready to tremble, to weep, to dissolve in gratitude. Received not even with reproaches but with no reaction at all, I of course dried up my emotions at once and met professionalism with professionalism. The type of personality Kanner observed, with its control, its reserve, its capacity for detachment, may seem invulnerable. A wise healer of souls will realize that it is for that very reason particularly vulnerable. In the light of my new experience I remembered the tale of the father who admitted he would not recognize his own children on the street, and I wondered if this classic reaction had not in fact been the irony of an unhappy man whose response was simply to shrug his shoulders and fall in with the hypothesis of the doctor who could misunderstand him so utterly as to dare ask him such a question.

A book should be a silent dialogue; the reader, I hope, is ready to burst out in exclamation (if he has not already done so): "But all psychiatrists aren't like this!"

I know it. I have told this story in such detail because many are, and of these many are good ones. But such was our good fortune that before the next eight months were past we had found out that they need not be. When, in its place, I record our next experience with psychiatry, it will be in a very different tone. Elly's next examination was in England, at the world-famous Hampstead Clinic. The Institute had suggested it as soon as they had learned we were going abroad. They had said they would send us the address, though they hadn't done it. When we saw Dr. Blank again we mentioned their suggestion. His face lighted. "Yes," he said. "Take her there. As a rule, as you know, I don't have high expectations of psychotherapy. But Anna Freud is different. I'll write her for you. Anna Freud—whatever language you speak, she will speak it too."

10 ⸳ To Retrieve the Past

ELLY's fourth birthday was as uneventful as all the rest, except that it took place in a household marshaling itself for a major removal. Two days later we were to fly to England.

For weeks trunks and suitcases had been accumulating in the halls. Elly played unconcernedly around them. Most of our conversation dealt with England and what we would find there. Elly did not hear it. Her father had been gone a month. Elly did not notice his absence. We made no special effort to prepare her for the trip. I knew no way to do it, no words to do it in. Nor did it seem necessary. I had some minor misgivings about the effect of the move, but no more, really, than today's mother, well schooled in up-to-date anxieties, has about the effect of a new house on any young child. Elly showed no unusual attachment to places, and she had been away before. We had never tried to shelter her or hide her. She had always come with us when we visited; we had stayed with her overnight, a week, ten days, in many different houses. No new surroundings had ever upset her. Why should they? Her strange imperviousness protected her. Only a very few aspects of the environment seemed important to Elly, after all. It was not hard to keep them constant. A few special foods, a few routines that could not bear changing—and everywhere she went, we made sure there was a crib, to become her new citadel. Recently, in one of her frequent shifts, in which overnight a new routine would become a settled habit, she had taken to wanting a spread draped over her bed. Enclosed on all four sides and above, it made a fine redoubt. Ordinarily I would have tried to limit or modify such a tangible symbol of withdrawal, but now I fostered it. It would be handy for the coming move, for converting the unfamiliar atmosphere of a new house and country into the unchanging ambiance of Elly's inner world.

The logistics of the trip were minutely worked out. Every stage was planned to minimize disruption, hesitation, delay—the normal hazards of travel. It had become second nature to think ahead, so that movement could be sure and firm, environment smooth and orderly. The reason that my husband had gone before us was to find and make ready a house for seven—the six of us and Jill, the young girl who was to help out; a house which, whatever chaos it might otherwise present, must provide in good order a separate room and a crib for Elly.

Kind friends drove us one hundred and eighty miles to meet the transatlantic plane. We flew alone; the girl was not expected for another month. The trip went well. Elly let no unfamiliar substance pass her lips, but it was possible this once to give her a pill, artfully concealed in a Hershey kiss, and under her spread, dramamined and doped, she accepted the unfamiliar bedding down beside me in the plane seat. The three older children rose to the occasion, cheerfully enjoyed their dinners, brought me what I needed so I never had to leave Elly's side. No plans miscarried; no emergencies arose. David was at London Airport to meet us and decanted us into a rented car. Ten hours after we left Boston we arrived in the new English house, where Elly, exhausted like the rest of us from the strange night which had lasted only five hours as we flew against the earth's rotation, settled serenely into the old white iron hospital crib that David had picked up secondhand. The slot was still there at the foot to hold the fever chart—for Elly, whose illness was so deep and who never had a fever.

The pink spread worked its magic. Nothing had changed. Elly settled in the new crib and began to rock, back and forth, back and forth. At home she had moved her crib all round the room with her rocking; finally we had nailed strips of wood on the floor and boxed it in. It made more noise here, very much more. The floor shook with the impact of the iron. Soon, however, Elly was asleep and the crashing stopped.

Things went well for the next week. There was the usual chaos of unpacking and settling in, and the beginning of a long apprenticeship in a difficult and unrewarding art—shopping in England. There was no one, as yet, to leave Elly with, so she came with me as she had at home. The new sights and sounds brought no visible reaction. She seemed undisturbed.

There were minor difficulties. The Danish salami looked Italian but didn't taste it, and Elly refused it. There were no hot dogs. She would not drink the delicious English apple juice. The foods Elly would taste were as rigidly self-limited as all the other elements of her world and the elimination of any of them was immediately felt. She had drunk no milk for months; with apple juice gone, she was down to water. But she had turned against foods before and it had passed. Lean, pale, she was tough and resistant, ineluctably healthy. Elly was adjusting to England at least as well as we were. We felt we had come off very well.

Then one day she was healthy no longer. Suddenly, without warning, she whimpered, vomited, relaxed, and in ten minutes vomited again. No one is surprised, though, when a small child throws up, especially after a change of food and water. I patted her, sat by her crib, and waited. Not long; almost at once she was gagging and coughing, her empty stomach convulsed, trying to bring up what was by now only saliva and a little bile. It passed and she lay down exhausted.

This went on for five days. Elly ate nothing and drank nothing.

At first she played a little between attacks, but soon she was too weak for that. She had no reserves of fat. Her flesh melted before our eyes. Her new lightness as I lifted her took my breath away. Under her pale skin her ribs and joints showed like those of the children on famine posters. Oddly enough, she did not take refuge in her crib. It was, perhaps, her rigid sense of propriety that told her that she could not spend the day in a place reserved for sleep. Instead, like the old Prince Bolkonski, gathering her weakness for the effort, she would drag herself from one room to another, there to collapse on bed or rug, passive until the fit seized her and she threw up again.

Strangers in a strange land, we didn't even have our National Health cards. But though we as yet had no official existence, the doctor came an hour after we called him. In blessed England, the land of socialized medicine and impersonal bureaucratic care, the doctor came daily, unasked, as a matter of course. But the affliction was as mysterious to him as to us. Elly had no fever, no looseness of the bowels, no signs of infection—only the continued, meaningless revolt of the empty stomach, preceded by the same whimpering and followed by the exhausted resignation of the mute. The doctor feared dehydration, but she would not lick the sweets he gave her and refused the water. Without words there was no way to explain to her that she was sick, that water would make her better. A child without speech is as unreachable as a sick animal. I forced a spoonful of water down to be vomited up again, and waited. These were quiet days and I could work on the house. Elly made no demands and there was nothing to do for her.

On the sixth day the vomiting stopped. Elly drank half a glass of water and ate a lollipop. (It hadn't been easy to find it. Later on she ate British sweets readily enough, but at first they were the wrong shape.) She sat up. Next day we carried her downstairs to the kitchen. Shakily but without hesitation she led me to the refrigerator. She took my hand and put it on the door handle.

When I had opened the door she took my wrist with her firm, feathery touch and moved it to take out an egg.

Elly had not had an egg for more than two years—half her lifetime. Eggs were not on her list of edible substances. As far as I knew she knew nothing about them, for cooking, like so much else that was human, did not interest her—she watched it, if at all, with unseeing eyes. I took out the egg in some astonishment. To the innocent eye it is by no means obvious that an egg is food; someone who had never seen one would find it scarcely more promising than an oyster. But Elly, it developed, knew all about this egg, including how she wanted it cooked (scrambled) and what pan to use, all of which she indicated with her delicate light grip. She requested six eggs in the hour, and she spent the next week sitting in the kitchen, eating eggs by dozens. She couldn't, of course, have chosen a better convalescent food. In a week she was well.

But she was curiously changed. There was, for one thing, no more need to worry about how to muffle the crashing of her crib. For years that rhythmic rocking had been a part of Elly; in a life of limited activities it was, if nothing else, one of the few things she did. She had been too weak to rock during her illness. She never rocked again.

She was cheerful enough inside. But though at home she had ranged the neighborhood, barefoot through the roughest brush, now she would not voluntarily set foot outside the house. Active as ever indoors, her movements out of doors were no longer free and open; she did not run or jump, but squatted in one place and dug in the sand or played with pebbles—and that only as long as someone stayed with her. She would no longer walk with us on our small excursions round the neighborhood. We would coax her along a few steps—only a few, for she would whimper and then, if we persisted, cry. We would carry her for twenty feet or so, put her down, and coax a few more steps out of her, and thus, picking her up and putting her down, maintain the fiction of a walk. It was only a fiction. But we dared not let her seem to herself to succeed in regressing to her babyhood.

These changes were permanent. Although we were able, with tact and care and many weeks, to get her to walk normally again, not once while we were in England did she step over the threshold of her own accord, and even since we have returned to her familiar ranging-grounds here at home, she has not moved alone out of sight of the house.

We began to wonder about the meaning of that sudden illness that had no ascertainable cause, only consequences. Could this be what a traumatic experience was—mysterious phrase, plucked out of the sophisticated air we breathe, not really understood? Was the trip a psychic trauma, unexpressed and for Elly inexpressible, internalized, and manifesting itself the only way it could, in physical symptoms? Elly had seemed to take the move serenely. But we had failed to imagine what it must be like for a child of four to leave her home behind without a word of explanation. For a week or so it seems a visit like any other. But as the days pass and there is no return, it becomes plain that home has simply disappeared—been annihilated, swallowed up and gone. Without speech, the child can ask no questions, give no form to anxiety. No explanation can reach her, even if one should be offered. She has no hint that home still exists, that it was abandoned for a reason, that one day she will return there. A single inexplicable convulsion has overnight abolished her physical world. For, lacking words, remote from people, her world was above all the physically known—toys, furniture, houses, streets. When these disappeared, for all she knew forever, who can know how much seemed to disappear with them? To what degree was her own frail selfhood locked into those vanished rooms? Did they express in space, in the only way she could appreciate, the sense of time, the continuity of personality, the past?

Such questions have no answers, and we never found out the

nature of that unique illness. But if we had waited for sure knowledge to determine our actions with Elly, we would have never acted at all. In a few months we would be moving again, to yet another house; we would spend the summer in Austria before we made our way back to America to show Elly that home was not forever lost. How could I prepare her? Though Elly was acquiring single words, little by little, as the months passed, they were all simple nouns. There were none in which I could discuss with her such subtleties as place and time and cause— no "when," no "back," "again," or "soon"; no "go," no "because"; no "Austria," "England," or "America"; not even "home." Without words, how can one convey a shared recognition of what is not present to the senses? Does one discuss past and future with a cat?

It was at this time that I began to simmer in my mind the problem of giving Elly a usable memory.

The operative word was *usable*. We knew she had a memory, and no ordinary one. We had become accustomed to its prodigies. One day, when she was a little over two years old, without speech, without comprehension, with no apparent capacity to attend to her surroundings, she had disappeared. This was unprecedented. She was a baby; she had been walking only three months; she had never gone anywhere alone. Where to look, when no direction was more likely than another? Then I remembered that the day before I had taken her, in her stroller (she was not yet a steady walking companion), a new way downtown, via the parking lot near her father's office. She had been so enchanted with the stripes and arrows painted on the surfacing that I had taken her out of the stroller and let her crawl about on them. It was a frail clue, but there was no other. Without expectations, I began by looking there. I found her absorbed, on hands and knees, circling the one-way arrow, her tiny body less conspicuous to an oncoming car than a dog's would have been.

To reach that parking lot she had to cross three large back-
yards and two streets, to ignore two possible turnings and make
a third. On foot, she had followed a route she had traversed only
once before, and then not under her own power. She had moved
fast; though it seemed longer, from the time I missed her to the
time I found her was only a few minutes. A remarkable performance for any two-year-old; it is hard to convey its impact
coming from a child who seems not to see, to hear, or to register
impressions—who for days at a time shows none of the common
signs of intelligence at all. I tested her. A mother with an abnormal baby is always testing. On our walks I would deliberately
lag behind and let her lead me home. She never hesitated, never
took a wrong turn. A single visit and her knowledge was in-
fallible. What's more, it needed no reinforcement; at three and a
half she led me behind a screen of trees to find a house she had
visited once only, and that six months before. After eight
months, on her second visit to the Hampstead Clinic, she led us
unerringly to Number 21 Maresfield Gardens, one of an endless
row of identical houses—and those who know England know
that row houses in England are more identical than anywhere
else in the world. I had become so dulled to this capacity that
only the most extraordinary instances startled me. I took it so
much for granted that I was surprised when the bright, verbal
children of my neighbor failed to remember the location of
every room in my house. Elly needed no second lessons.

Elly knew the whereabouts of every cookie shelf in every
supermarket in the North Berkshire area of Massachusetts. There
was not a location, not an orientation in her world that she did
not have memorized. I knew, then, that I would not have to create
a memory. She remembered her room, her house, her neighborhood, her town. The experiences I wanted to make available
were not lost; inaccessible to words, they must be there.

How certain that sounds! The certainty is false. With Elly
I was never sure even of what I knew I knew. That she re-

Above left: At seventeen months, Elly sits in her mother's lap as her sister leans toward her. She is in no contact with either. *Right:* Her expression is more concentrated but more tense; the photographer (her father) has succeeded in attracting her attention. *Below:* About two-and-a-half. Elly selects a crayon with delicate precision. Six months later she seemed incapable of using crayons at all.

Both pages: Elly as she appeared at the end of the eight-and-a-half-year period described in the original text of *The Siege.*

Above: Writing practice with her father. *United Press International Photo.*
Right: Learning fractions. Quivering with excitement, Elly makes one of the curious gestures characteristic of autism. *United Press International Photo.*

Left: Doing things to-
gether: making Jell-O with
her sister. *United Press
International Photo. Be-
low:* Cheerily she climbs
the slide. Later, mysteriously, she refused to climb
any ladder. *United Press
International Photo.*

Figure in a doorway. Significantly, Elly drew this open door during a period when she would remain only in a room whose door was closed (see page 238). Age five.

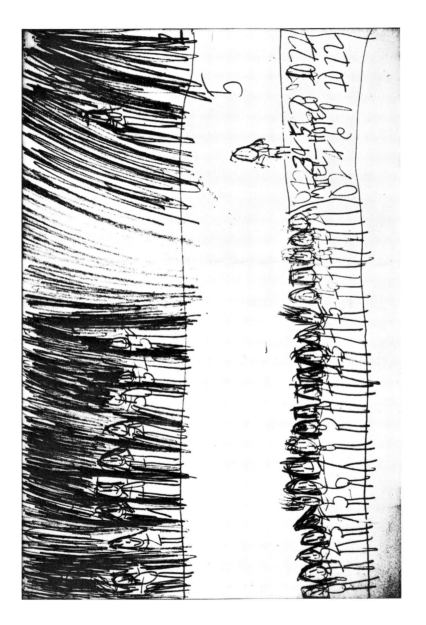

The "number people," comparable to those described on page 249. Age nine.

THE LITTLE IMITATION
PERSON IS ON
THE PORCH.

1

THE LITTLE IMITATION
PERSON IS AT
THE DOOR.

2

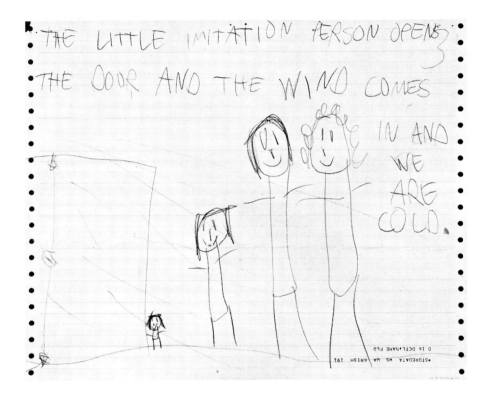

Both pages: The "little imitation people" who inhabit the household (see page 296). The series illustrates Elly's logical, sequential thought processes. Age eleven.

membered home might be an intellectual certainty, but the emotions counsel differently. These show you not the child you construct out of your rational knowledge of what she has occasionally done, sometimes seemed to know, but the child you see every day who does little and knows nothing. It is this child, wrapped in veils and mists, that one is working with; the mind inside it, however impressive it appears when all the instances are put together, seems at any given moment a figment, a creation of the wishes. The child has memories of home and we can unlock them? What optimism! The child is complete and untouchable, and has no past at all.

Yet I began to think what I could do. Elly had a puzzle. It represented a large house, with four oversize windows in each of which a smaller puzzle could be assembled, the sub-puzzle showing four appropriate rooms and their furniture—kitchen, living room, bedroom, bath. Simple nursery ideas are hard to come by if you aren't trained to the work. I had looked at that puzzle for weeks before it occurred to me: I would draw our house at home on a large sheet of paper, and see if through pictures I could bring Elly's memories out where they could be shared.

Together, as so many times before, we sat on the floor. I drew the house. Elly watched with quiet attention; her empty stare was growing rarer now. It had not, of course, occurred to me to bring a photograph. Uncertainly I reconstructed the façade in my memory, so much less sure than Elly's. What was the pitch of the roof? Should I make the chimney visible? What was the orientation of the windows and their relative size? While I thought, I had to be drawing, steadily and confidently even if incorrectly. Elly was watching and I must not dissipate her attention by fumbles. I had no time, even if I had had the skill, to make a convincing architectural rendering. I settled for a schematic roof and the right number of windows and put my best efforts on the porch, which I *did* remember. Three steps, two columns (Doric), a plain pediment, a door with four panels, a mail-basket. I drew the shrubs and flowers. I made it spring and drew daffodils, a word which Elly knew. Elly watched with non-committal interest. Following the lead of her puzzle, I started to fill in the downstairs window with the furniture of our living room—chairs, coffee table, couch. The window grew crowded, perspective was abandoned. I didn't know whether Elly saw pic-ture-perspective anyhow. Why should she? People in the Middle Ages didn't. At last, deep inside the room, floating above the other furniture, I drew the record-player—the sliding doors, the turntable, the tone-arm, the needle, the record itself. Now Elly was more than attentive. Tense and excited, she began to jump up and down, her sign for approval and delight. She got down again and put her finger on the crude circle that represented the turntable and moved it round and round. Then she began to sing. At first I scarcely recognized the song, it was so many months since I had heard it—the song "Instead Of," from *The Three-Penny Opera*.

It was almost a year since Elly had heard that music. She had been obsessed with it; for two months and more she had asked for the record every day. Then, like so many other things, she had abandoned it altogether. No one had sung it since. We had left the record behind in America, and there it remained and the music with it, dissolved, extinguished, part of the irrecoverable past. But it was not wholly irrecoverable. We had recaptured a minute part of it. We could find more.

Many of the things I drew evoked no reaction. Oddly enough, Elly showed little interest in her crib, however lovingly detailed the drawing. Instead it was the rocking chair that excited her, and again it was music that let me know she shared my memory, for as I drew she began to sing the melody of "Rockabye Baby," which she had first learned as I rocked her, so many times, in that very chair in her old room at home.

After that, I knew the way. Elly was happy when I drew a separate large rocker outside the house, and a mother with glasses to sit in it, and an Elly with straight hair and bangs to put in the mother's arms. I would not only retrieve the house; I would try to put into it the human relationships, which Elly had tried so successfully to deny. I made crude portraits of the family, a face at each window, a figure standing at the door, and although Elly's real interest was still in the house and furniture, the details of the bathtub and washbasin, she accepted the figures with placid attentiveness. We drew often, several times a week, and time passed.

We left England, put the Microbus and our eight selves (my mother had joined us) into the Channel plane, then into a train for Munich, then into the car for the ultimate destination, St. Gilgen, an hour beyond Salzburg. Austria's mountains and the unreal blue lakes were paradise for us after the flats of the English university town, but I had never seen any signs that Elly cared for scenery. How would the new upheaval affect her? As we settled into yet another orientation of rooms and fixtures, we watched Elly for any signs of shock. Would she be sick again? stop walking? refuse to go outside?

The day after we arrived I started drawing. I drew the house in England (prepared for this, I could do a reasonably accurate job). I drew the bus with our eight heads looking out. I made the little plane with its open maw, and the bus going in. I made us all go in the door, and Elly recognized herself and jumped and squealed. I made the train with the eight heads at the windows, and Elly, who had never responded to a picture of a train before, was beside herself with delight. I made the Wagon-Lit, three beds, one above the other, and me and Elly's grandmother and Elly each in one. Elly's eyes shone, she laughed, she said "choo-choo," and she had to have all the pictures again, people and things—all summer long.

She was never sick again. She was perfectly natural outdoors. We had a wonderful summer, and at the end of it, just in time for the ten-day trek to Le Havre, Elly began spontaneously to use the pot. All of which, like all negative evidence, proves nothing. We might have had no trouble in any case. I do not know. But the human being is human in that he has a usable past. All human societies are built upon it; in even the most primitive cultures the poets and artists, the keepers of the memory, have an essential place. To be fully human, a child needs a past to which it has access. Even now, Elly and I have not reached a level of verbalization which would enable us to say "Do you remember?" But one of her favorite pastimes is to watch while I draw her three houses—one in Austria, one in England, one in America. There are six pictures, for she insists on front and rear views, appropriate furnishings visible at each window. She can put in words now questions which before went unformed: "Becky's bed?" "Daddy's bed?" "St. Gilgen house?" Austria is almost four years behind us, already growing dim. Recently, however, I thought of a new possibility: I added a rough rendition of the lovely onion dome of St. Gilgen, saying to Elly, "downtown." Each onion dome has its own individuality; only charity would have recognized this one. But Elly did. She squealed "St. Gilgen *church!*" and I had to add, that very minute, the appropriate churches to accompany my pictures of Elly's English and American homes. It was not a very skillful Perpendicular Gothic. But the New England neo-classical, luckily, is just down Main Street, so my memory can be daily refreshed. Elly's does not need it.

11 ⋅ Professionals
as Human Beings

I HAVE JUMPED ahead of my story. Let me erase the glimpse just given, to return to four-year-old Elly, just arrived in England. That Elly was not the child I have just described enjoying my renditions of comparative church architecture. That Elly had shown a capacity for seeing pictures only for the past six months. She was not yet able to ask even the crudest question or respond to the crudest answer. She had just recovered from the severest illness of her life and it had left her narrowed and subdued. It was this child that, as soon as we were settled, we made arrangements to take to the Hampstead Clinic.

We had planned to do this even before we left. Dr. Blank had written Miss Freud the day after we spoke with him. That had been a major reason for my anxiety when I found the Institute had not made out its report; I knew we would need it in England, and soon. My letter of appeal to the Institute's director reflected the desperation and pressure of the last days before departure. I remained shrewd enough, however, to make it clear that we wanted the record, not for Dr. Blank or for our small-town clinic, but for Anna Freud.

An answer arrived by return mail; the silent psychiatrist himself wrote it. He quite understood my anxiety; he had delayed the report because he wanted to write it himself; he would make sure it went out promptly. I was past charity. I reflected that there was hierarchy in this profession as in others. The great provincial archdiocese need not exert itself for the little country parish—but now we were going to Rome. After six months I could still recall the reverential tone in which the Institute psychiatrist had spoken of the Hampstead Clinic.

And Rome it was. No footsore pilgrim was ever welcomed in the holy city with warmer hospitality or more healing kindness than we experienced at Hampstead. Dr. Blank had said that whatever our language was, Anna Freud would speak it. As things turned out, we did not see Anna Freud. We did not have to. What happened was something more remarkable still; her spirit so permeated her clinic that *everybody* spoke our language. The building was little different from what we knew already; clinics for disturbed children seem to run to shabby, aging houses with many rooms. The examining team was the same—social worker, psychiatrist, and testing psychologist. As far as I know, their theoretical presuppositions were not markedly different. I even recognized the puzzles that Elly worked for the intelligence test—the same old-fashioned browns and pinks, the same nineteen-twentyish dress. Yet all was different. The chill, noncommittal professionalism that we had found in America was missing here.

We could have guessed from the ease with which we made our appointments. The Clinic seemed to find no particular difficulty in answering letters. That was professionalism, in its proper place. For the rest, from the time we walked in the door of Number 21 Maresfield Gardens, we were treated, not like sick children, but like adults, human beings, and friends. Perhaps, as truly practiced, this is professionalism too.

What should one say further about anything so natural? Why should it be worthy of mention that the psychiatrist and social worker talked to us together as well as separately, that they asked questions and answered them, that they discussed with us matters of theory and nomenclature? We conversed with sensitive and intelligent people on a matter of mutual interest. They picked up cues from our voices and manner and allowed us to do the same from theirs. We smiled and joked, although all concerned were aware that our errand was not funny. With everyone there we experienced that delicate progress of mutual adjustment which we call communication and which is one of the great pleasures. In our own land we had been treated by strangers as strangers, and strangers we had remained. We were not strangers here.

The psychologist laughed with me as we watched Elly solve the now familiar puzzles. We went rapidly through the rest; they had the Institute's report and they had obviously read it, and the medical history as well. The social worker asked if I had any photographs of Elly. I had not; remembering the Institute, I had left them in America. Encouraged, I mentioned my notebooks. Certainly, of course they would want to read them. I sent for the photographs and turned the notebooks over. When we came again a week later they knew what was in them.

I had determined that I would not repeat my mistake of eight months ago; whatever it cost me, I would make sure they saw me play with Elly. It cost me nothing; playfulness was easy here. The social worker was interested in our play; she had read my records. Knowing that, I could elaborate on episodes I had only sketched. I described for her, much as I have described them in Chapter 4, the slow stages in teaching Elly to turn on a tap. This is the sort of thing, I suggested, that you can help me with. I will not forget her reply. "I think," she said, "that we will be able to learn from *you*."

I could scarcely believe I had heard it. But it must have been so, for after more conversation about particulars came something for which I was even less prepared. "I suppose you've often been told," she said, "that this is a very interesting case." Often? Interesting? No one had told us anything, least of all that. I felt better at once; if one's troubles are heavy it helps that someone

finds them interesting. But I had not heard it all. What was unusual about the case—the words dropped into my mind like
balm—was the persistence and energy shown by the parents.
Regressions had been kept temporary. "A massive regression
now appears unlikely."

I did not, I think, begin to shake. Kanner's control stood me in
good stead, though my skin seemed a frail integument just able
to impart its usual definition to the trembling chaos of animal
gratitude within. One is less vulnerable to pain than to understanding and kindness. One develops defenses against slights or
insensitivity; against kindness, none. When one has been long in
such straits, one has a terrible greed for kindness. Before one
feels real pain one may think—I thought—that one would want
people not to notice, to aid one in the attempt to carry on—
business here as usual. It is not so. Business may seem as usual
but it is not. What one wants is that people should know that.
What one wants is sympathy, understanding, not tacit but openly
given. What one wants is love.

Too much to ask? It is surprising how freely it is given in some
quarters while in others it is not given at all. I remember, I think,
from those years everyone—everyone—who was kind to me. I
should, for I lived on kindness, I consumed it like fuel. I remember the friend, herself a trained social worker, who tele-
phoned me after a visit to her house where Elly, only two, had
misbehaved and been disciplined and then loved, merely to tell
me "how beautifully you handled that child." I remember from
the chill months in England the loud-voiced checker in the local
Co-op who called me "ducks" and understood when Elly
screamed because she couldn't touch the candy, who asked
after her when I left her home, and who went out of her way to
say how much she had improved. I remember the man who,
when I apologized for some embarrassing caper of Elly's with a
muffled "not a normal child," smiled and replied, "Well, I'm not
normal myself." My honor roll is long—too long for inclusion

here. The list of those who have helped us contains the names of amateurs and professionals. What they have given us may have seemed to differ on its surface; at bottom, it has not differed at all. The measure of my gratitude is greater to those whose kindness, because institutionalized, has been more prolonged. But it does not differ in kind.

Perhaps this would not be true if the professionals had access to a sure body of knowledge about psychotic or defective children, which they could have imparted to us. But they did not, nor did they pretend to. What they had was a body of observations, some of it crystallized into theory, on the behavior of a large number of children and what appeared to affect it. These children were different from Elly and from each other; conclusions drawn from their problems or solutions were of doubtful applicability to this particular child. In the absence of sure knowledge in this case, these professionals did not substitute theory. They gave us instead the gift that amateurs and professionals alike can give—their sympathy, understanding, and support.

Not that they withdrew from the attempt to apply what they did know, to place Elly within the categories they found meaningful. In this, as in other things, they were candid. The severity of her condition, which we had uncertainly divined from the gnomic generalities of the Institute, these people made quite plain. Up to this time we had had, as a guide to prognosis, only a small number of case histories that Kanner had got together some years before.* Its utility was doubtful, since very few of his cases had had time to grow to maturity, but such as it was it could be used to predict any kind of future for Elly. The cases showed a complete range of functioning, from quasi-vegetative existence in a state hospital to (in one case only) apparent normality. But Hampstead, like the Institute, did not seem to find infantile

---

* Kanner and Eisenberg, *op. cit.*

autism a valuable category, and they did not encourage us in any vague hopes based on observation of it. The social worker emphasized that Elly had missed out on the most formative years of childhood, and that those lost years could never be made good. The psychiatrist discussed the difficulty children can experience in realizing the boundaries between themselves and others; his final report speculated that "the defect may lie in the integrative processes of the ego." He brought forward the terms "childhood psychosis" and "schizophrenia," only to stress their extreme generality. The term childhood schizophrenia, he suggested, would in time be seen to cover a variety of conditions we could not as yet distinguish.

Elly, as he spoke, was absorbed in play. Compulsively she turned on the taps in the playroom washbasin, filled it, and emptied it again. She was tense with excitement. This was a new fixation; in any building now she sought out sinks and tubs, screaming if she was prevented. The unexpected presence of a washbasin here made any contact impossible. Back in her citadel, she was incommunicado. The Institute psychiatrist, eight months before, had fared better than this.

The whirr of running water made a background for the doctor's words: "The prognosis is not good." When he said that she could not be expected to become an integrated personality, I knew that he was not thinking merely of a withdrawn woman who collects stamps and never marries.

Yet it was the painless evasions of the Institute that hurt us, not this hard candor. We were grateful for much, but most of all for the fact that these people respected us enough to trust us with what they thought. It was, after all, that for which we had come.

And if we could no longer strengthen our efforts with inchoate hopes of full recovery, we had been given another source of support. "A massive regression now appears unlikely." The wise and gentle professionals of the most famous children's clinic in the world had given me the reassurance I could not give myself. They did not think that in my lonely and presumptuous work I had injured my child. They thought I had helped her. Their present recommendation was not that Elly begin analytic therapy, but that I continue to work with her as before, with one difference. I would now have professional guidance. One of their analysts was transferring her practice to the city where we were living. I could see her there.

I saw her three times a week at first—a lot, it seemed to me, not enough, to her. The sessions, to my initial surprise, centered not on Elly but on me. It was not until much later that my husband told me the one thing that the Clinic had withheld; that they had thought that it was less with Elly's emotions I would need help than with my own. We talked about me for several weeks, stirring up a good deal of mud and taking a good deal of time I didn't have—the analyst the while cheering me on to find more time to myself, to read, to write, to meet the English, and generally encouraging me to feel talented, heroic, and unappreciated. It was a rather enjoyable process. The things she said were flattering and sympathetic; as no one else, she seemed to realize how hard my job was. But I grew uneasy. I was grateful for the support, but as time went on I feared the pleasure was self-defeating. The process seemed to breed self-absorption and self-pity, and at this juncture there was no use I could make of either.

What happened then was a tribute to a good analyst's perceptiveness and flexibility. We seemed to reach our conclusions almost simultaneously. Abruptly she shifted her approach. She came to see Elly at home. We talked, not about me, but about her problems. I came less often. The analyst became, and remained, a trained adviser, wise in the ways of children, giving me the benefit of her knowledge. But she was an adviser who now knew me well.

I knew her too. She too became a friend. She tried not to, for it is contra-indicated in the training. She told me that; I had not known it. But we had too much in common. We could not inhibit our friendship, and it was as a friend that she helped me.

That help took various forms. There were, for example, words I used which revealed certain presuppositions. Several times I had spoken of a "breakthrough." Gently the analyst asked me what I meant by that word. "What are you expecting?" I saw then how much had been involved in it—how many romantic notions, fostered by how many accounts of cures that seemed like miracles but presumably were not to those who understood the dark mysteries of the unconscious. I had been told—though not by Hampstead—that Elly had no mental deficiency. Yet in all but a few areas of actual behavior she was grossly defective. What could be the explanation, then, but some emotional blockage, some log jam of fears and repressions, which could be opened up and removed? We had already begun to remove them; with Jill, with the children, with her father, with me, was she not now often laughing and affectionate, more open than ever before? If she was healthy in body and had no mental deficiency, then her trouble must be all emotional. And was that not tantamount to saying that there was a normal child hiding inside her, and that if we could find the right things to do we could call it out?

All that, I now saw, was inherent in my use of the word "breakthrough." Though I had not been told so, I had unconsciously assumed that underlying the practice of psychiatry was this kind of optimism. I saw now that the wiser practitioners had too much experience to make such naïve claims for their method. There were miracle recoveries, to be sure, and well-publicized ones — a recent book* tells the story of a child who could have been a stand-in for Elly, restored by good therapy to intelligence and affection. No doubt it happened. Miracles do. But I was in the presence of someone too wise to claim she could chart the

* Barry Kaufman, *Son-Rise*, Harper and Row, 1976.

164

processes to bring them about, or to allow herself or me the illusion that one was in preparation here.

Sometimes we talked of words, more often of things. We began
and ended with specifics. At the time our sessions began, I was
in dire need of specific advice; Elly, whose toileting had never
given any problems greater than those posed by minor cleanups,
abruptly began to withhold her bowel movement for days at a
time. Controlled as she was, withholding was easy for her; what
was hard was letting go. For months she had been urinating only
two or three times a day, but that had bothered neither her nor
us. She had defecated regularly every day or two, in pants by
day, or diaper by night. (It had been years since we had put her
on the pot.) But this changed suddenly when David and I, luxuri-
ating in the freedom provided by the loving and intelligent girl
who was now living with us, went to Paris for an unprecedented
eleven-day trip. All went beautifully in our absence. Elly was
cheerful all day, and some slight nighttime disturbances soon
righted themselves. Everything was as usual, except that though
she gorged herself on canned pineapple and imported American
apple juice, she had no movement all the time we were away.
Even when we returned she could not let go. She suffered extraordinarily little discomfort, but clearly the situation could not
continue indefinitely. It was no simple matter to find a cathartic
that Elly would take; Elly as a rule allowed no unfamiliar substance to pass her lips. When she rejected Ex-Lax, however, I
wondered if she were clairvoyant; never before had she refused
chocolate. Finally she accepted syrup of figs, only to become
frantic at the realization that her movement, now artificially
liquefied, was out of her control. She would soil the diapers we
now had to put her in and cry inconsolably, as never before.

The analyst at this time was an invaluable support. She suggested that Elly's withholding was a silent protest against our
absence; she checked with pediatricians at her London hospital

and found a less frightening cathartic, which prevented Elly from withholding her movement for more than four or five days at a time. Consulting the doctors, she was able to assure us that this could not harm her—an assurance we have had constant need of, for this was another of the sudden changes in Elly's behavior patterns that became permanent. We were lucky that this problem did not arise before we had help. It would have been hard indeed to ride it out alone. Modern parents have become so sensitive about toilet behavior that it would have been nearly impossible for us to proceed with steadiness without the feeling of a professional behind us.

Not that professional support gave us any remarkable solution, here or elsewhere; it merely helped us to adjust to a modus vivendi in which we avoided absences and trouble. The profit I got from my sessions with the analyst lay less in the recommendations she made for affecting Elly's behavior, or the occasional interpretations she made of it, than in the general atmosphere of her approach.

She told me at the beginning that I should expect her to make mistakes. For that I respected her most of all. She gave much good advice. Mixed with it was much that turned out to be inapplicable or irrelevant, and some that was wrong. How should it be otherwise? If there is to be trial, one must expect error. In our common groping for a forward way, what reassured me was exactly this: to find pragmatic flexibility where I had anticipated dogmatism, allegiance to fact where I had expected applications of theory. I had thought I would be led among the verbal mazes of Freudian analysis, but "ego," "id," "complex," and "libido," are words that occur more often in the course of a New York cocktail party than they did in my months with the analyst. It is true that there was a bit of "oral" and "anal," but considering our particular problem that was not surprising. I soon found that it translated down to "let Elly play with stoves and refrigerators and let the bathtub and potty toys go." That seemed good enough. Elly in fact paid lukewarm attention to cooking toys, none to potties, and there was no possibility of cooling her interest in tubs. I never did find out to what extent "oral" and "anal" applied. But my friend the analyst's interest was clearly not in matters of theory. She brought forward few interpretations of her own and she was less than enthusiastic when we ourselves came up with ingenious hypotheses to explain the increasing complexity of Elly's behavior.

One of these concerned Elly's new ability to count. Naturally, this delighted us. Yet it had queer liabilities. Instead of expanding, as a normal child's will, so that the child learns to count higher and higher, it hardened into a fixation. She had to have four washcloths in the bathroom, four cookies on the floor. She had to have them; they were so important to her that we called them her status symbols. We knew that intuitively she could subtract, because if one or two were missing she would reject any but the right amount required to make up the number. This was a gratifying display of intelligence, but awkward if the Co-op ran out of the proper biscuits so that lost or broken ones could not be replaced; it was then almost impossible to comfort her.

Focusing on this behavior, as perforce we all had to, we noticed that the week after Jill came to us Elly added one cookie—and one washcloth. A short time later, she added two more—chocolate biscuits this time, somewhat larger than the others. Then, on our Paris trip when Jill and the children were left alone, the two chocolate cookies disappeared and four Ritz crackers took their place. A total of nine, grouped as five and four, was now indispensable.

Psychology is a game any number can play. Our Cockney cleaning woman, who was extraordinarily good with Elly, had suggested already that the four biscuits represented the four children, raised to five at Jill's arrival. From then on the interpretation burgeoned. Jill put her fine young mind to work; the exigencies of replacing cookies which got lost or stepped on kept the problem in the forefront of everyone's attention. Might not the two chocolate cookies represent the two parents? When they left the family circle, the five were retained, but the original four were now added to represent the confusion in Jill's status, since it was no longer clear whether she was functioning as a child or a surrogate parent.

This hypothesis afforded us all a certain intellectual satisfaction. Myself a gingerly theorist, I had had no part in it, but I thought it a handsome attempt and reported it in one of my sessions. It had the air of some of the things I had read in the psychology books, and I thought it was the sort of thing the analyst would like.

She didn't care for it, however. She cautioned me "not to make constructs." I was surprised; I had thought applied psychology to be more than the method of trial and error I had been pursuing, cautious, hesitant, guided more by action and reaction than by overarching explanations. I was startled and pleased to find professional sanction for playing it by ear, especially since it was the only way I knew how to play. Her caution against constructs helped me, not to reject constructs altogether, but to feel free to judge them by their correspondence with the facts and not by the glories of their internal consistency. There were few constructs indeed, however probable, that made much difference to what I actually *did* with Elly. I could refrain from flushing out dirty diapers in her presence, as the analyst had told me to do, because the bowel movement is "the child's first gift to its mother." But since she continued to pay the process no attention, whether the change in routine reassured her or hastened toilet training I could not see that I would ever know. "Constructs," whether our own or the work of professionals, were certainly interesting. In other cases, their applicability might be verified by the child's positive response to changes in routine which they suggested. In this case, if there were such constructs we did not light on them. The only construct working here was one so obvious and so deeply shared that we did not need to talk about it: that all children, sick and well, feed on love, and that the job of the lover is to love, not in ways satisfying to herself, but in ways the child can accept and use to grow.

So we were back to specifics again: what to do with Elly, how to fill her empty days, how to encourage such spontaneous play as she originated, how to supply new and usable experiences where she originated none. As before, I learned best by watching. Twice the analyst came to our house—further evidence of her flexibility, for many children are treated by people who never see them at home. She was thus able to check out some ideas of her own in a direct way that would otherwise have been impossible. She could satisfy herself that Elly's fastidiousness did not reflect compulsive orderliness at home (one look at the living room took care of that!), and that her low performance was not a reaction to the inappropriately high standards of a middle-class family. And while she observed, I was able to watch her play with Elly. It was an impressive sight, for she was one of those people who could involve her in action without making demands on her. Most people tried to talk to Elly. This therapist, though highly articulate, was an expert in nonverbal communication. She played the piano for Elly. She got out the cups and saucers she had brought and got her to play tea-party. She sat down on the floor beside her to paint. Elly, used to my drawing sessions, tried to get her to do the drawing herself. She did not refuse, but kept her markings as crude as Elly's own, so they could set no unattainable standard. A year before, when I had begun drawing with Elly, I had deliberately made my drawings as realistic as I could to aid her uncertain recognition. The technique had had considerable effectiveness, but I could now see its drawbacks. Elly was more likely to draw for someone else than for me.

The analyst had brought a flower pot. She tried to interest Elly in filling it with earth. She had little success beyond satisfying herself that Elly could take dirt or leave it, but I saw something that might be usable later. As I watched the therapist I had the impression of an enormous reservoir of skills, most of them as yet inapplicable to this very simple system, yet still something I could learn from for the future. I wished I could watch her with other children. That was impossible, but she was willing to tell me about some of them. The children she described seemed much less severely afflicted than Elly; even those who didn't talk had shown that they *could*. I tried to imagine Elly playing, like the little girl I was hearing about, with the contents of my pocketbook, and in the process revealing tensions and hostilities invisible on the surface. I couldn't. If I gave her my pocketbook what would she do but ignore it, or at best lay the objects out in rows? I put the idea away for the future. One day, I hoped, she would reach that degree of complexity.

She was growing all the time. We led a quiet life in England; inside the walls and fences of our neat suburb children played, but there was no way I knew to get Elly near them. Even at home, on the open lawns full of children, she had done no more than run beside them. Here except for her own siblings there were no children to run with. Yet I sensed a frail new readiness. I often took her to the village green, where she would swing unseeingly among strong wiry boys and girls who paid her no more attention than she paid them. But one day, as a squad of children marched out of the adjoining school yard, she did an unexpected thing—she suddenly shifted direction and ran directly among them. I reported this to the analyst, and other incidents that tended in the same direction. It was then that she made the move that has benefited Elly more than any other single thing that has been done for her. It was she who made the contacts that made it possible for Elly to go to nursery school with normal children. That Elly, from that time to this, has been able to go to school is largely due to the intelligence and devotion of the teachers at the extraordinary school the analyst found for her.

They too were professionals. The school was no plushy private foundation, but run with tight public funds as a demonstration school for the local teacher's college. The analyst did not think a place would be found there for Elly—our best hope was that the principal would see her and recommend some tiny, mother-run class where Elly could at least see other children. We were foreigners. We did not even live within this school district. There was every administrative reason to send us on our way and none to welcome us. Yet the principal took us in—both of us, for the way she found to reconcile regulations with need was to invite me to come in with Elly, so that her status could be that of a guest, not a pupil. And as a further dividend, I could watch the work of teachers who were such subtle masters of their calling that no one could say, in this school, where teaching ended and therapy began.

For we were not the only waifs welcomed here. Elly was not even the most severely handicapped child in the school; she functioned far more ably than the overgrown, affectionate Mongoloid who moved clumsily about among the toys. I learned later that parents who wanted a place for their normal children in this fine school enrolled them at birth. Not that it was a school for misfits; normal children formed the great majority. But for children whose need was severe enough this principal would somehow find room. Whether their trouble was physical or emotional in origin, caused by deprivation or by family upheaval, they became contributing members of the school, even if like the little Mongoloid all they could contribute was their helplessness. More fortunate children, imaginatively treated, could learn much from that. Here imagination and competence bound waifs and healthy children into one thriving community, where by a miracle daily renewed fifty small people ranging in age from near babyhood (the youngest two and a half) to almost five were not only taught and fostered, but given their main meal of the day. The staff consisted of the principal and two teachers, helped by a student trainee and a pleasant woman who ran the kitchen. The school kept a seven-hour day, although Elly, as a guest, came only for an hour and a quarter twice weekly. American administrators, I suspect, would think this impossible. I wish they could, as I did, see it done.

My hours there were lessons in resourcefulness. Nothing seemed to escape these people. They observed Elly as closely as if they had nothing else to do. The analyst and I had been occupied for some time with Elly's tub and basin obsession, which had lasted now for some months. The principal had needed no more than the bare mention that Elly liked to play with water; the first time Elly came to play, tub, cups, kettles, and waterproof apron were set out for her. No better introduction could have been chosen. Elly was delighted; she made loud, cheerful birdlike noises, she sang. Soon, however, a little boy came up. He wanted to play too. Elly, of course, had never in her life played except by terms she herself had set, and never with a child her own age. Rarely, indeed, had she appeared even to see another small child, although she now often focused on her siblings and on adults. She saw this child well enough, however. She warned him off with edged, anxious noises. Other children gathered. She did not mind them; they were not using the water. The little boy took the kettle and poured. Elly squealed, shrieked, jumped up and down, made the rhythmic intonation that I knew mimicked our "that's enough!" Calmly the principal kept on with the game. While another teacher suggested new activities for the watching children, Miss J. found a new washing activity that Elly and the little boy could share. Elly calmed down a bit and the little boy drifted away. Everything was fine then, naturally, but when another child came and she began to shriek,

Miss J. gently explained that Elly had not learned to share yet, and let her have the tub alone. The rest of the session was dominated by water. Elly tired of the tub and, leaving the playroom, found a faucet she remembered from her first interview at the school, with a large bucket beneath it. It was no toy—children did not ordinarily play in this room, which combined the functions of clean-up room and toilet, equipped with large washtubs, four tiny toilets separated from the room by half-open curtains, and four tiny basins. Here Elly was allowed to play apart from the other children, who came and went on their own errands. Elly filled the bucket and emptied the heavy, awkward burden (weak Elly!) into one of the little toilets. She filled it too full and spilled some on the floor and on her tights. She wept furiously—a sound quite different from her former anxious shrieks—but when the water was mopped up she returned to the bucket. The next time, and all subsequent ones, the water level was exquisitely adjusted to avoid further spills. Except for an excursion into the playroom to get a doll to perch on the bucket and another to watch the assistant run water into the washtub she played in hermetic isolation until her time was up. She left with reluctance; her last act was to return to the bucket and empty it in the toilet. Miss J. said, "Bye-bye, Elly." No response. She leans down, puts her face close in front of Elly's. Elly doesn't see her. She kisses her. Elly's face is expressionless. We go.

An unpromising beginning, but two days later we are back. Elly is reluctant to enter the school gate. I carry her to it, set her down, and wait. She goes in under her own power. This time the watchful overseers have provided two basins, and dolls to go with them; Elly is able to play uneventfully with her basin beside another child. But difficulties arise that Miss J. could not have anticipated; she does not know that Elly's doll must sit in its bath and must have jointed legs in consequence. By chance, the other child's doll is jointed, but Elly of course cannot be al-

lowed to grab it. I look for another but can't find one. Elly
shrieks. Calmly, the tubs and water are taken away, while Elly
is introduced to less sensitive playthings.

Next time Elly was able to transfer her water fixation to the
small hand-basins. This was a less isolated activity; she watched
the children wash their hands in fascination, especially since the
pipes led into an open drain into which water whished visibly
every time a child removed a plug. As one child finished
washing, Elly, who had been watching from a distance, went
up to her and touched her arm. I interpreted: Elly was asking her
to go through the process again. The little girl was reluctant, but
did so when I explained that Elly might feel braver if she could
see her do it. The second child that Elly asked refused. I offered
to fill the basin myself, but Elly did not want that. She returned
to touch the child, at which point a third little girl, who had
been watching, did it unasked. And then Elly did in fact feel
brave enough to put in the plug and turn on the water herself,
retreating eight feet away to watch the water gush into the drain
when the plug was removed.

The staff did not take part in this compulsive activity, but
they were aware of it. Elly began each session at the basins. At
first they let her play there go on as long as she liked, but after
a few sessions they decided that she was ready to have it cur-
tailed in favor of freer activity. The school was simply but well
equipped with toys—books, puzzles, play-dough (made by the
busy staff), wagons, slides, paints. Halfheartedly, Elly began to
explore these, encouraged by the teachers. There was a high
rocking-horse, splendidly painted and accoutered by a grateful
father; there Elly, and other children in need of a temporary
retreat, could retire and in rhythmic motion survey the life of the
school without taking part in it. After a time a teacher would
come over, to reinvolve the child who had been alone too long,
to facilitate taking turns, to sing the pretty rocking-horse song
that became Elly's leitmotif for school. When her turn was over,

Elly would come down and be led into play. She was no longer interested in puzzles, though she did them without difficulty. She gravitated straight to the doll-house bathtub, but with skill it was possible to divert her to a toy telephone or even a wagon. She tried out the paints, filling a sheet of paper with neat parallels. We had paints at home, but for months, whatever my strategies, she had only mixed and poured colors from vessel to vessel. Here, seeing other children use the easels, she made a picture almost daily—abstract figures in pure colors, never puddled or mixed. Once she made a little girl; Miss J. gave it to her to take home, a departure from the rule, since to save paper all sheets were normally used on both sides.

She began to respond to the teachers as people; after two weeks had passed, in her fourth session, with a brilliant smile she showed one of them a toy horse. Although she paid less attention to the children, by the sixth session she was actually sharing water in the tub. By the eighth she no longer required the full attention of a teacher. After four weeks Miss J. asked me to retire into the office; I could watch through the window, but Elly was able to function on her own.

Elly liked school. She might not herself be able to vary the monotony of her activities, but she welcomed variation when it came from outside. The analyst had told me to watch for signs of tension at home and to be ready with extra indulgence. None, however, appeared. Yet I could see the ambivalence in Elly's attitude toward this demanding new experience. At first she had tensed with pleased excitement as we approached the building, but on the sixth day—the third week—as we passed in the car a turnoff which though ten minutes away she recognized as leading to the school, she sang a bar of the rocking-horse song and began to cry bitterly. She kept on crying until we arrived. I parked the car across the street as usual and wondered what to do. She had seemed to like school—and besides, tolerant as the teachers were, I hesitated to introduce a crying child into the peaceful building. It would be better if she could go of her own free will. So we sat still in the car. I made no move to open the door, but waited. Crying, she put her own hand on the door handle. I opened it. Crying, she moved forward to be lifted down from the high Microbus. I put her on the pavement. Crying, she made the move to cross the street, to open the gate, to run up the path, to enter the school. She stopped crying as soon as she was inside and she did not cry again. The next time she merely whimpered. Then the approaches to school were no longer marked by tension. She was learning to take it for granted.

Elly was able to go to that school for five months. Then we had to leave. We would have had to leave anyway, for in a month she would have been five and too old for the school. It's idle to speculate about what progress she could have made there. Miss J. had shown me a boy Elly's age, playing, talking, kissing the teacher, apparently normal except for an odd mincing walk. Two years before, she told me, he had been admitted, silent, withdrawn, diagnosed as deaf-mute. The staff noticed first that he winced when objects were dropped; gradually—I had seen a little of how—they had drawn him into activity and speech. Miss J. said that Elly was very like what James had been then, and James was going to an ordinary school in the autumn. But Elly was five and James had been two and a half. And none of us were diagnosticians—James's problem may have been quite different. In any case we could not remain here. Yet our experience was ours to take away—invaluable training for me and for Elly, who on her return home was able to enter a small local private school in the nursery class. She has been in school ever since. That this has been possible we owe to the kindness, flexibility, and intelligence of the professionals of England.

We found these qualities in every professional contact we made there. I had noticed it in the busy school administrators who solved the transfer problems of my normal children; I noticed it again in the university official who found me a graduate to take home to replace Jill, who would be leaving us for college. We experienced in our scheduled appointments in the offices of English professionals all the openness and warmth—I might almost say affection—that Americans expend so lavishly in their private relations. Private relations in England are neither warm nor open—at least until the participants have known each other many more months than were at our disposal. An American can only wonder at the reversal of what he is used to. It is as if all the Englishman's dammed-up potentiality for warmth overflowed into the practice of his profession. Perhaps one cannot have it both ways, though I cannot see why not. At any rate, nowhere in England did we come across that chill routinization of human contact which too often passes in this country for professionalism.

Too often, but not always. On our return, on the analyst's suggestion, we sought out an extremely well-qualified psychiatrist who had newly moved to a nearby town. We went to him with our usual shyness, but he received us with the flexibility and welcome we knew from England. We thought that now Elly was settled in one place he would begin direct work with her. We were not entirely easy about it, from the point of view either of utility or of expense. But he did not. After three or four sessions, all dealing with Elly, he put me on my own once more. He even suggested—I lived on it for months—that I work with children professionally. He even said that Elly could have done no better in the best residential school for disturbed children than she had done at home with us.

I return with Elly once or twice a year, and he tells me how much Elly has improved since he last saw her. We could not do without him. He acts as a buffer between us and the world. He provides documents, classifications, terminology, and these reassure the bewildered administrators and teachers who have to work with Elly. What school would accept her if she had only her parents to speak for her? But she has her credentials; she has

a psychiatrist. We luxuriate in his encouragement and support.
It is he who suggested that I write this book.

One day he may feel that Elly can benefit from analytic
therapy, but four years have passed and he has not suggested it
yet. In the meantime, he is willing to accept that parents can
be partners, even senior partners, in the treatment of their child.
He does not consider that he presides over a privileged arcanum
into which we are not qualified to set foot. What he knows that
can help us, he imparts. What he can do, he does. It is both little
and much.

When, smarting from our first encounter with professionalism,
we took our disappointment to Dr. Blank, he told us we had
expected too much. Psychiatry, he said, was a gift, not a science.
We agreed with him; it was not scientific knowledge we had been
looking for. We had indeed expected too much, but it was something else that we had expected. What we had asked, and with
incredible naïveté thought to get, was nothing less than the
counsel of someone loving, wise, and good. We had been hurt
and disappointed when we had not received it. Yet we had no
right to surprise. Few people are wise and good. It is remarkable
evidence of the American faith in the power of cash that a profession should arise that puts wisdom, goodness, and love on sale.
Socrates did not. We had no right to be shocked that at our
first attempt our money failed to buy us these commodities.
Should we not rather be astonished and grateful that it is ever
possible for money down to provide access to the rarest human
virtues, that some psychiatrists are wise and good, true coun-
selors, whose love and wisdom, if not their science, can help heal?

12 ⹀ The Amateurs

It is obvious enough why psychiatrists seldom welcome parents as co-workers. Even if they do not try to convert them into patients on the hypothesis that it is their pathology that has caused their child's, professionals can find other reasons, some of them very good ones, for doubting the capacity of parents to work with their own offspring. Not only professionals, but any outsider may well wonder how father and mother can function as therapists under the handicaps inherent in their position.

Although detachment is necessary for wise action, parents are inextricably involved with their child, their natural emotional commitment intensified by constant physical proximity. Though they must be content to work from day to day, they cannot avoid the long perspective; they must think as heads of households, and the fruitless question "What is going to happen to him and to us?" is one they learn with difficulty to suppress. Because much is at stake, they may be drawn to exert pressure on the child, and if they are, the opportunities afforded by family life are endless. If their involvement and concern does not produce a nervous and harmful overactivity, an opposite possibility presents more subtle dangers: loving their child, they may not be sufficiently armed against the slights and rebuffs that those who deal with troubled children must expect—against the rejection that seems deliberate even after one knows it is not. So many overtures repulsed, so many words unheard, smiles unseen, touches unresponded to—the danger is that they will be too bruised to mount another assault, for rejection does not cease to hurt when one has grown accustomed to it.

Even if they escape these inward pitfalls, a more straightforward one remains: how can untrained people know anything like enough to do what is there to be done?

No parent is likely to deny these handicaps, knowing them better than anyone else. But since we parents, in clinical literature, have found few eulogists, it is up to us to put our handicaps into perspective. Since we are conscious of them, we can go a long way toward overcoming even the severest. And we, and others, should realize that they may be counterbalanced by special advantages that even the most gifted psychiatrist cannot match.

The first of these advantages is a considerable one: total familiarity with the case since birth. Every child psychiatrist who concerns himself with his small patient's past is dependent on what its parents tell him, however he may decide to discount it. Even if he manages to call out of the child's consciousness some fugitive memory which he can use to enhance his understanding, he must go to the details of the child's history to make sense of what he has found, and his source for these will almost certainly be the child's parents. The younger the child, the truer this must be, especially if its dysfunction affects speech and the therapist must work at mind-reading. The parents of a psychotic child are quarries of information which no psychiatrist has time to work to the full. If the child is obsessed with an object or a place, who but they know where he has been or what he has clung to? Who else knows their baby's characteristic approach to food, to sleep, to play? Who else can say what threatened him and what delighted? Yet how much of what they know, which might prove relevant if the psychiatrist knew it, finds its way from their minds to his? Psychiatrists and parents both explore an unknown country, but parents at least hold a map that shows the major landmarks. They may not know all they need to, but they know more than anybody else. As long as the child develops rightly and they have no need of all they know, they may not even realize that they know it. If the time comes, however, it is there to be used.

The second advantage is another version of the first: as well as a fuller knowledge of the child's past than any doctor can have, parents have a fuller knowledge of its present. They can observe the child in the complete variety of situations to which it is exposed, not merely in the artificial situation of the therapy hour. Children's conflicts and anxieties become evident to skilled therapists through their displacements onto things; sibling rivalry becomes visible through the doll family with which every therapy room is equipped, training problems through the miniature toilet in the doll-house. The parent can learn to use toys too, but he needs them more for stimulation than diagnosis since he can observe these things directly. He knows how his child responds to each of its brothers and sisters, to grandparents, teachers, passing visitors. He (or, more probably, she) knows what the child is like at breakfast and in the bath, how it reacts to strain, how it behaves at a party, in a supermarket, at the circus. It is she who quicker than the best psychiatrist will notice the deviation from customary behavior that may suggest a new explanation or initiate a new stage. She will not, of course, do this because she is cleverer than he, but merely because she is there when he is not. I have written in the previous chapter of the time when Elly suddenly ran toward a crowd of school children, and of what we made of it, mother and analyst together. That moment could not have come at all in the analyst's office, in the daily hour.

Parents are *there*. Because they are there they can act when the child is ready. In the first years of life, more often than not, one parent or another is on hand, in actual or potential contact with the child, twenty-four hours a day fifty-two weeks a year. Books on child therapy state that the experiences of bedding, feeding, and awaking are especially significant to a child: this is one of the reasons that many psychiatrists recommend residential treatment. Those out of reach of such treatment may reflect, however, that experienced parents do not need to be told when their child is most receptive. Their knowledge, transmitted through the generations, has been absorbed into the rhythm of family life, institutionalized in the family meal and the bedtime story. Even Elly smiled straight into my face when I got her up in the morning.

When you are in twenty-four-hour contact, every experience can be considered for potential usefulness. The fertile course of daily life offers you far more material than you could think of for yourself—a trip to the dairy (it was on one of these that Elly first climbed into the car under her own power), to the bakery where a lady's kind hand provides a cookie and eventually Elly will begin to chirp "thank you," a visit from a little girl who eats peanut butter so that Elly begins to eat it too. There are lessons in dustpans, sinks, pebbles, and bowls of cereal. And when you have known a child since birth you have as good a basis as anyone can for judging which of these experiences a child is ready to make use of and which he is not. Its withdrawal, or the edge in its voice, teaches you the difference between stimulation and pressure.

Growing out of this intimate knowledge is a curious advantage I have become conscious of only slowly. The parent knows his child, and he also knows his mate and his family. Individuals in a family differ markedly, and the parent is of course aware of that. But he is also aware of what is less obvious—of the ways in which they are alike, the patterns of behavior that might seem strange to an outsider but are not so to parents, who see them in their normal children as well as in the deviate, and who also recognize them in themselves. My husband could recall that, like Elly, he had rocked his crib until it had to be nailed down. Elly's relative passivity was not unfamiliar to us. We all shared her physical caution, though in us it stopped short of pathology. Looking at Elly, I could remember Sara, who even as a baby never put a foreign body in her mouth, and Becky, who cried when I pressed her to turn the faucet. Matt, apparently strong and well co-ordinated, was four before he learned to push the pedals of his tricycle hard enough to propel it forward. None of my children opened medicine bottles or explored unauthorized cupboards or jars, any more than I myself had as a child. All when excited waved their arms in a tense way unseen in other families. All were reluctant to apply pressure; long before Elly was born I had raged inwardly at three healthy children who cried "Mommy" at a resisting door that my neighbor's children would open with one energetic shove. We do not rush at life. The six of us have lived a total of a hundred and forty years (albeit mostly concurrently, of course). The only bone that has been broken among us is one big toe, and there is no antiseptic in our medicine chest.

So that in a curious way Elly belonged in our family. She would have driven my energetic neighbor beside herself, just as the activity of my neighbor's children would have been too much for me. Therapy begins in acceptance. We could accept Elly more easily, all of us, because we knew her in ourselves.

This deep knowledge of the child in context finds its climax in what is perhaps the most important of all the parents' advantages: that they know the child's language. The extreme difficulty of work with very young children, or those whose speech is defective or absent, is to a great degree one of language. Yet their difficulty in communication is a measure of how much they need help.

The parents—and their allies, their other children and their household helpers, who in some degree share in all these advantages—know this language. They have learned it the natural way, over months and years, gesture by gesture, sound by sound, word (at last) by word. Their understanding of it has deepened to intuition; their grasp of it is quicker and surer than any outsider's can be. They hear the anxiety in the high squeal the outsider cannot distinguish from laughter; they understand that assent is conveyed by running across the room or jumping up and down. They will understand the new word in its fluctuating indistinctness because they first encounter it in the situation that brings it into being—and if it carries emotional or symbolic overtones they will know it if anyone does. It was not until her fifth year that Elly began to acquire words in any quantity, and what they gained in number they lost in distinctness. Who could expect a stranger to understand a child who says "buh" for six different words from "baby" to "fish"? That summer in Austria Elly would say "huh" and cry with frustration if we could not guess from context whether she meant us to draw a house, hand, hen, hat, or horse. (If *we* said "huh" in imitation she was never satisfied; she heard the little differences she did not reproduce.) Might her frustration have led, in the skilled hands of someone who could *not* rely on basic understanding of her language, to attempts to speak so she could be understood? We tried that then, saying gently that we couldn't understand and waiting for her frustration to produce a more refined pronunciation. But she wasn't ready; communication didn't interest her enough to provide a motivation. Now, four years later, it is beginning—only beginning—to.

Had Elly gone into professional therapy at five (and even that would have been years after the onset of the condition) it would have taken months for a psychiatrist to learn her language, and even then it would have been as a tourist, not a native in her world. Even if he had by some miraculous philological instinct realized that "Ih-ih huh" meant "England house," he would hardly have recognized it for a request to draw a remembered building and he would have had no clue to the frustration that would have occurred when he failed to respond. How many interpretations go astray from lack of the knowledge that any parent has? The English analyst, when she learned that Elly had once said "pee-pee," assumed that it must be a toilet word. I deserved no particular credit for knowing that Elly had said it only when she saw our neighbor's child Peter, or that "pee-pee" was a word she had never heard and so could not have used. It was merely that I knew her language.

Skilled therapists do wonders without talk, working with objects and with direct play. But they must come to words at last; if the child is to move into a speaking world, they must acquire his language with him until he can speak the common tongue. When I took Elly, at five, to her present psychiatrist, he recognized how far he was from understanding her and how long it would take him to begin to do it. This was, in fact, an important reason why he left me on my own. In so severe a case the process was long, he said, and the advantage doubtful. And—as neither of us had to remind the other—psychiatry is a well-paid profession. Which brings me to another advantage of using parents as therapists. They work for nothing.

It would be more graceful, perhaps, not to press this point, particularly since we were fortunate enough so that for us it need not be decisive. But for many parents it is—for us it would have been if Elly had been born when we were younger. To overlook it would be unrealistic and unfair. Children with severe afflictions—call them psychoses, defects, or what you will—need intensive therapy if they need any—if not in a residential school, then daily. But the price of intensive contact continued over years is beyond the resources of all but the well-to-do, and even they cannot absorb it without strain. The family that cannot afford therapy, or enough of it, has one recourse. The parents are going to be on hand anyway. Every family can afford the services of its mother.

The last advantage possessed by parents, and by other amateurs with them, may well be a certain humility. This humility will grow out of their very consciousness that they are *not* professionals, and still more out of their sense, daily and hourly reinforced, of the mysteries and ambiguities of the condition which confronts them. Again and again they will have reached some explanation which has seemed plausible until the fact comes along which contradicts it. Living their lives among questions, not answers, they are natural empiricists in a field that—they may be pardoned for suspecting—is not yet ready to press beyond empiricism. They have learned to feel their way; they have learned it not only from their experience of abnormal children, but from normal children too. Years before Elly was born, in the course of one of those mother-to-mother chats by which parental expertise is spread, a friend told me a story. It contained a lesson, and since it has become as sure a part of my education as anything I have read in a book, I must tell it here.

My friend and her husband, traveling with their children, had arrived in Germany. They had come to visit an elderly relative, the husband's great-aunt, never seen before and barely known through infrequent correspondence. His parents had left Germany sixty years before; these young Americans were nervous about the visit, aware that the free-wheeling spontaneity of modern academic children might not pass muster among German ladies of an earlier generation. So when they arrived they were relieved at the old aunt's suggestion that they sit inside while the children played in the garden. After a few minutes the mother went out to check and found to her consternation her four-year-old son standing beside a broken sundial. A mother both permissive and understanding, she gently explained that everybody knew that accidents happened and that little boys made mistakes and that it was very much better to own up to a thing than to pretend you hadn't done it. Hand in hand they went inside and the little boy told his aunt how sorry he was he had broken her sundial. The old lady looked at her young relatives with amused puzzlement and told them that the sundial had been broken for years.

Elly's comprehension is still too primitive to tempt me to offer her any interpretation of her behavior; the "why" and "because" of human motivation are words and realities she does not yet understand. But even if she did, I would think carefully and long before I told her why she did a thing, remembering this story and knowing how easy it is for an admired adult to convince a child of his own interpretation. Not all therapists are as cautious as the English analyst who warned me against "constructs." In the case histories I have read I have come across interpretations both brilliant and ingenious, and the more ingenious they are the more they frighten me. An interpretation must be pretty obvious if it is to be safely offered. I have read of a little girl, no older than Elly and talking no better, whose psychiatrist guessed from obscure words and actions that she feared she had injured her mother. And so she may have. No one ever found out, for she did not get well. But it is well to be humble in the face of facts; for a therapist to verbalize that a child, for example, feels guilt may liberate it from an oppression it cannot face, but it may also suggest a responsibility that was never felt and create guilt where none existed. A parent, seeing so much more of a child than does a professional therapist, will be chary of interpretations, both because he has not been trained to make them and because he feels his immersion in a complex reality which at any time may prove them simplistic, or harmful, or wrong. One can know too much as well as too little.

Yet I am far from denying that parents know too little. I do not mean to make ignorance a virtue; it is one only under the rather special circumstances that obtain when specialists know—as Mark Twain remarked of the human race in general—"so many things that ain't so." Yet although many of them may know—about castration-anxieties, masturbation, rejecting parents, and the like—many things which in particular cases are not so, they also know an immense amount that is, and that a parent will have to learn. One of the most famous of child psychiatrists, whose therapy for disturbed children depends on a complete separation from their parents, has written that Love Is Not Enough, and he is right. One must know *how* to love as well. Far from denigrating the knowledge of psychotherapists, I only ask that they let parents share it.

I learned what I had to from Elly, slowly and painfully, she and I together. But I would have learned faster, and with fewer gaps, if I had been in contact from the beginning with skilled and sympathetic professionals (the plural is deliberate). People whose profession is working with children—I do not limit my statement to psychiatrists—possess a great arsenal of the techniques of siege-warfare. Lacking access to it, I had to develop my own, with difficulty and duplication. I had nothing to guide me but common sense and a till then unverbalized knowledge of three normal childhoods, to which I could add the imperative that an eminent mathematician has given as a two-word definition of the scientific method: "Try everything." When I came to read case histories, it comforted me to find that was what the professionals were doing. They might indeed have theories to guide them, but they led to no agreed-on therapeutic regimen. Qualified, trained people dealing with children like Elly were trying everything, drugs and shock treatment, massage, all kinds of play therapy—even love.* But they were in contact with each other and with professional literature, while we were alone. No one person, trained or untrained, will think of everything, or even everything in the limited range of possibilities relevant to one particular case. It was for this reason that I profited from those

---

* For a suggestion of the range of therapeutic techniques (and nomenclature!), see Caplan, *Emotional Problems of Early Childhood* and *Some Approaches to Teaching Autistic Children*, ed. P. T. B. Weston, Pergamon Press, 1965.

case histories, lacerating as I found them, and that I was glad of the chance to observe the Institute people and the English analyst operate with Elly. Four hours at the Institute, four with the analyst—that was my training until Elly was four and a half. Then fifteen hours or so at the Blankshire Nursery School—if only they had come earlier! Later, Elly's present psychiatrist suggested I visit Dr. Carl Fenichel's League School for Seriously Disturbed Children, where I was welcomed and acquired in a day suggestions for months of work. These experiences were the most valuable help I could have had, but only the last was planned and recommended. The others occurred almost by accident and there were not nearly enough of them. Professionals conscious of the problem could have helped me to have many more. Far from underrating professional knowledge, all I wanted was for the professionals to let me watch them work. But this desire was so unorthodox that it took years for me to reach a point where I could articulate it. I was, at the time I needed to, quite unable to make it known, and I am afraid I can guess what would have happened to such a request at the place where I was told that case histories were bad for me. Yet with all the expertise about, it is strange that in mid-twentieth century a mother should be left to her own devices and such assistance as she can get from *Saturday Evening Post* articles * and biographies of Annie Sullivan.

Parents need help, but not in the current American understanding of the phrase. They may need it from the same people, but they need a different kind. I appeal for a breakdown of the separation between parents and the psychiatric profession. At present it is common practice for a child to receive psychotherapy for months, sometimes years, without its mother or father having any direct conversation with the child's psychia-

---

* Rosalind Oppenheim, "They Said Our Child Was Hopeless," *Saturday Evening Post*, June 17, 1961. Parents who consult this article will find help and comfort, as we did.

trist. Especially is this true in large clinics, where the social worker exists as a kind of mediator (or buffer) between psychiatrist and parent. It is thought best that the parent, even of a small child, know nothing of what goes on in those privileged sessions, and the only way she may hear what the expert actually thinks of her child's case is if he is kind enough to speak to her if she passes him in the hall. Yet there is so much that she must learn that he could teach her.

How can parents learn? They can read, and they can watch and listen. Yet they find out fast that psychiatrists do not like them to read; display of the slightest knowledge of their child's problem suggests exactly that cold intellectuality which many professionals expect to find. Even after I met psychiatrists who trusted me enough not to veto professional literature, they did not encourage reading, or suggest what it would help me to look at in this vast field with which I was almost completely unfamiliar. Even from my random reading I learned something—here was a child astonishingly like Elly, there a technique that seemed worth trying. How much more might I have learned from an intelligently selected bibliography, especially if I had been able to discuss what I read with a professional?

And if I learned from reading, how much more might I have learned from watching? Let parents into the therapy rooms and the special schools. The difficulties are obvious, but they can be overcome. An observer's presence may disrupt the therapy, and children—especially other people's children—cannot be made into guinea pigs. Fair enough. Use microphones then, and one-way glass. An untrained observer will not understand what she sees. Convert, then, the session with social worker or therapist into a question-and-answer training period. If the mother's reactions need analysis, they will be better understood, by both her trainer and herself, in the mutually experienced context of the therapy room than when shakily reconstructed from memories and dreams. But the parent's personality may be totally unsuited to this kind of work. Of course—in many cases it is bound to be so. But the radically unsuitable are less likely to wish for such training. If they should, they can be excluded after they have proved themselves so.

Severe mental illness in children is far too widespread for it to be possible to provide intensive professional treatment for every case. The answer must be to train nonprofessionals *—unless there is to be no answer at all. Above all, it must be to train parents to do with skill and effectiveness what they have got to do anyway. Mothers (and fathers who have time) will make ready pupils, as people do when they are learning what they have immediate need of. And it may happen that their training will pay social dividends beyond their own particular cases; such parents, if the time comes when their own child's need is no longer paramount, may make use of what they have learned in helping others. The professionals may find that they have unwittingly created a corps of valuable assistants who will amply repay the time and effort that have gone into their training.

I have spoken so far of the special advantages of parents of abnormal children—those they possess by the very nature of their position, and how they might be enhanced by sympathetic training. I must not overlook, however, another advantage—not a special one, this one, but so commonplace that it is easy to forget it entirely or to doubt its relevance. This is the homely expertise already possessed by parents of normal children. I have often thought of the Institute psychiatrist's musing words—"It's hard—it's very hard—even to bring up normal children." It is hard, perhaps, but it is something that millions of people have done. When viewed from the vantage point of the expert, con-

---

* For an impressive account of the achievement of untrained "teacher-moms" working with severely disturbed children in an ordinary public-school situation, see Sol Nictern and George Donahue, *Teaching the Troubled Child* (Free Press, 1965). Donahue, however, does not believe that parents of disturbed children belong in his program.

scious of the vast field of parental error, it may indeed seem miraculous that children ever grow up undamaged. Yet most of them do. Parents must not sell themselves short. Let them be conscious not only of how little they know, but how much.*

Without guidance, through Elly's worst years, I brought up Elly as I had brought up my normal children, with no more knowledge of psychology than Dr. Spock affords an unpracticed mother. Perhaps I should not imply that that knowledge is a little thing, for Dr. Spock is the premier example of a psychiatrist who is loving, wise, and good. His book was written for ordinary parents of normal children—it is not a handbook for the nurture of psychotics. Yet it is astonishing how much that one has learned from living with normal children is applicable also to the disturbed and defective.

I have come to see mental health and illness, soundness and defect, not as the separate entities the words seem to describe, but as a continuum. The needs of the defective and the sick are more imperious than those of the well, but they are not different in kind. Sick children need to be accepted, supported, comforted, corrected—like well ones. Above all, like all children—like all people—they need to be respected. Good parents have no magic key to dealing with children beyond this almost foolishly simple one: to try to imagine each situation from the child's point of view. Some people do it by instinct, but it is a technique that one can learn—to turn in upon oneself at need and ask, "What would I feel like *if?*"

But the child is ill, its thought processes are incomplete, distorted? So are we ill, by turns and chances, and we are no strangers to distortion and incompleteness. Indeed since our

* A trained psychologist, writing in a highly specialized professional journal, solemnly records his anger when his new jacket was soiled by a small autistic patient, and explains that he chose an old one for the next session. Any mother of young children could have instructed him in this elementary principle.

children tend to be like us, we may have a special insight, based on our own self-knowledge. Our memories of our own childhood will guide us as we try to understand our children's.

I remember a little girl, seven years old, shy to the point of incapacity and so tense that every social situation was liable to flood her in helpless nausea. I remember a father less known in daily familiarity than in arbitrary incursions and descents bringing with them fear and distrust the child could not acknowledge, since children learn early that it is customary to love one's father. I remember a weekend of crisis so acute that the doctor had been called—the little girl had been able to keep nothing down for two days and the doctor and her mother had agreed that she should not be forced to eat, in hopes that the tension would abate of itself. I do not forget the unwonted apparition of the father in the kitchen, tall, handsome, intense. *He* would get the child to eat, these people knew nothing, it was all a matter of the right approach. He would make it with his own hands—a simple, tasty meal served in attractive circumstances. They would see that she would eat for *him*.

And she did eat, while he stood over her; she ate everything down to the last bit of applesauce, fighting back nausea with every mouthful. She thought that this would be the way to satisfy him, to give him what he wanted so that he would leave her alone and she would never have to eat again unless she was able. She could not guess that he would take her gift as proof that what she had done then she could do always, and that a genuine and terrifying disability (which has followed her all her life) was merely a spoiled child's malingering. That memory is also part of my education. It taught me, when my own children came, not to confuse gallantry with strength. Respect must grow out of knowledge—knowledge of what a child can do, and what is at present and perhaps forever beyond its power. When Elly came I at last formulated what I had learned so long before— that a result that has been achieved once because of some unusual motivation may have taken every ounce of strength a child possesses, and that it must never be construed to commit the child to that level of performance.

Every parent has been a child—more likely than not a child in some way like this child of his. Every parent has incidents he can remember and learn from, from which he can assess his children's vulnerability or strength. The bringing up of children is an exercise in self-knowledge and in the respect for others that grows out of it. The millions of families that function in comparative happiness are evidence that ordinary parents have intuitive knowledge of this principle of respect. They are expert in many things, but penetrating and modifying everything they do is their expertness in the application of that golden rule which governs all personal relationships. Family life is the first school in which we learn the techniques of love, and if it is not perfect, still I know no better.

I have not dared to set down in my list of advantages a parent's love for his child. Love is not only not enough—we have almost been persuaded to admit that it is a disadvantage. Yet I cannot think that we are disqualified for working with our child because we love her. Detachment and objectivity are techniques too and can be learned. Psychiatrists themselves work by love—in their strange language it is called transference. It is usually understood as the love the patient feels for the person who is helping him, but psychiatrists have learned from their master Freud that it works both ways and that they love whom they help. It is in fact to prevent their being consumed by the power of reverse transference that they have learned to set limits to the therapeutic relationship—and this knowledge is part of what they can give to parents. They have learned, too, the dangers of a love that uses the creature that it loves to satisfy its own needs. It is quite true that parents can exploit children to build up their own egos. Teachers can exploit students, ministers parishioners, psychiatrists patients. "Love seeketh only self to please,/To bind another to its delight"—the love that builds a hell in heaven's despite is one we must all recognize. Most of us learn to recognize it in the school of family life, from the childhood of others if we have been lucky, from our own if we have not. We learn it from reading, watching, listening—in as many ways as we are able, for it is the single indispensable lesson. Never to make Elly feel guilty for having taken so much of our time—never to voice the words "the best years of our life"—always to remember that though she may have needed what we gave her, she never asked us for it, that we gave of our free choice what must remain a gift and not a claim—luckily these are not recondite principles. We must remind ourselves of them continually; no expert can do it for us. Though others may help us to it, such analysis as we make must be our own.

So it is that we must be aware of the ways to go wrong in loving, ways that help not the person we love but ourselves. But our consciousness of these should not be too acute, lest it immobilize us for the work to be done. We need to learn the lesson, but not to be made afraid by it. Insight, overdone, becomes cliché; if there is a cliché more widespread than that of the rejecting parent it is that of the possessive mother.

Physicians of the soul do the ·thousands of afflicted children no service if they undermine the confidence of their parents in what they can accomplish by intelligent love. Intelligence and love are not natural enemies. Nothing sharpens one's wits for the hints and shadows of another's thinking as love does—as anyone who has been in love can testify. Blake's poem describes as well another kind of love—the love that "seeketh not itself to please,/ Nor for itself hath any care,/But for another gives its ease,/And builds a Heaven in Hell's despair." There are millions of parents —as well as teachers, and social workers, and doctors, and ministers, and psychiatrists, and ordinary men and women—who practice this love daily, knowing that love is a technique as well as an emotion.

Ordinary men and women. The point needs emphasis; the special advantages of parents are not unusual but widespread. It is some time since I myself have felt shut out by professionals. Those with whom I have lately come in contact treat me almost as if I were on the inside. But their amiability has a corollary; they seem to think, as some readers may think, that I have done something extraordinary, something that few parents would have been able to do. I do not believe that. I learned from my Cockney cleaning woman that an uneducated mother of six can have a delicacy of touch in dealing with a psychotic child that few can match who are trained to the business. Of all the types of success, the most widespread is successful parenthood; the species survives because this is so. It is also the most inconspicuous; it is precisely those millions of parents who successfully pilot their children through illness and crisis who never come to a psychiatrist's attention. No one, professional or amateur, should underestimate the immense fund of goodness, knowledge, and resourcefulness possessed by ordinary parents. Let it be understood that I am no miracle worker. I am not "good with children" or particularly fond of them. I knew none before my own, and even now I would never voluntarily seek a small child's company. Such qualified success as I have had must not be thought of as unique.

Once, in an access of mingled self-congratulation and self-pity, I was describing all I had done with Elly to a friend, herself a mother of three. When my torrent of words had ceased she replied with healing matter-of-factness, "Well, you couldn't have done anything else, could you?" Of course not. She did not have to tell me that she would have done the same.

Psychotic children are a congregation of mysteries. So little is as yet understood about them that the distinction between amateur and professional has hardly begun to acquire a meaning. There are many parents who, like us, have had no choice but to make themselves experts in their child's abnormality. I have met some of them. They should not have to work alone.

13 · Towards Speech:
A long, slow chapter

I HAVE described Elly's first four years in almost complete detail. To describe her second four as minutely would be impossible, even in a much longer book. Not only has her behavior become more complex, but as her withdrawal has lessened and helpers and teachers have been able to contribute more and more to her development, I have not, as in her first years, been aware of everything she said and did. I have been aware of most of it, though, and it is a measure of her progress that at length I have more data than I can record. Elly has gradually begun to live a richer life than can be got between the covers of my notebooks.

On our return to America, Elly was five years and two months old. The devoted intelligence of the English teachers had socialized her to the point where she was able to enter a small private school in the community. Here she adapted to the school routine and enjoyed the minimal stimulations of the nursery class—clay, paint, music, and dance. She remained two years in the nursery and then went into the kindergarten. She was older than the other children, but it did not matter much. Socially she was far less mature than the youngest of them, and though she coexisted in the same classroom, she interacted with them hardly at all. The children tried to talk to her at first, but receiving no answer gave up the attempt. Only the most aggressive of them could make a contact—I remember a small boy taking hold of her sash and pulling her around the room while she laughed in pleasure. But such things did not happen often. Most little children are too shy and too self-absorbed to function as therapists. Elly responded to the kind and gentle teachers, not to the children who should have been her companions. It helped her to be in the same room with them, doing the things they did—that we took on faith. Quiet still, and docile, she did not disturb the group though she contributed nothing to it. She was at least kept constructively occupied while she learned to respond to simple spoken communications of adults outside her own family circle.

For as she grew, the problem of her speech took precedence over all the others. It was through speech that she must join the human race. Kanner had found no better indicator of future development than speech. Five was his year of decision. By her fifth birthday, Elly had in fact begun to develop communicative speech.

The reader will recall that, according to the count made the month she turned four, Elly had in her life spoken thirty-one different words, fewer than half of which were then in current use. In the course of a week she would speak no more than five or six. She responded to a number of routine commands. That was all.

This situation began to improve that year, the year we spent abroad. There was no sudden change; it happened gradually. Four months after her fourth birthday the word count had reached thirty-eight. More important, when I counted the different words she had spoken in a single week, I found twenty-one. Two months later, although only three new words had been added and she was still using about twenty words a week, they were by and large the same ones. Instead of the frustrating come-and-go of her earlier vocabulary, she was acquiring a core of speech on which we could depend.

Along with this came a new interest in getting us to name things—the letters in her alphabet set, the fruits and vegetables on the pretty curtain I had found for her to darken her bedroom and give us a little more sleep. She would try herself to say "strawberry" or "celery"—the barrier against imitation was at last breaking down. But she mouthed them so clumsily that they were nearly unintelligible even at the time, and totally unrecognizable out of context; they did not get included in the word-count.

All Elly's speech was indistinct; only those who knew her well understood anything she said. She never pronounced a final consonant, and often the initial consonants were ambiguous or wrong. Words of more than one syllable were rare, and tended to turn into Polynesian, so that Becky's name would come out Beh-Beh, recognizable only because Elly would perhaps be looking at her sister's picture. In this indistinctness, as in so much else, there seemed a queer deliberateness. The first time I ever heard her say "all gone" she said it distinctly; I could even hear the terminal "n." I remembered the clear "scissors" she spoke before she was two; I remembered her limpid "El-ly." I smiled; she smiled back mischievously and said the words again, less distinctly. "Ah-gah." It was "ah-gah" for years after that. Her pronunciation did not improve as she began to acquire words more easily; it grew worse. It was as if (*as if*) now she was beginning to talk she had still to maintain her reputation for unintelligibility, to obscure—to herself? to us?—the significance of her entry into the world. At this same time began a new phenomenon which, though unconnected with speech, seemed comparable to her verbal indistinctness. Often, now, she would squint up her eyes, sometimes to the point of actually walking around blind. This would last a few seconds—at most a minute. Her face would have a little smile on it. The action seemed to express a kind of separateness, now she was becoming one of us, and yet it was a game of withdrawal rather than withdrawal itself. She kept it up, with decreasing frequency, over the years —a teasing game which denies withdrawal while affirming it, since it is done with our reaction in mind. We suspect—we cannot know—that the indistinctness of her speech has been similarly functional.

When Elly was two months short of her fifth birthday, the number of words on her vocabulary list was up to fifty-one, more than half in current use. That list was the last I made. That summer she began to learn words rapidly, and by Christmas of that year—the year of our return home—it was clear that there was in effect no limit on the number of common nouns she could acquire. That barrier was down. Anything she could see, actual or pictured, we could name and she could remember and identify. Anything—from aardvark to zebra. Familiarity made no difference. If I had shown her, at bedtime, a unicorn or a hippogriff, she would have known the words next morning. The problem now was no longer to add words to her vocabulary, but to extend the kinds of words she used and to combine them into larger units of meaning.

As she added word to word, her progress seemed astonishing. It hardly seemed that this could be the same Elly who for five years, of all the words we spoke to her, had retained so few. Yet it was. If we had expected that, now Elly had become open to words, everything would be different, our expectations were disappointed. Elly learned new words with the ease of the normal two-year-old she had never been. But she did not learn to talk like a normal two-year-old.

I have just said that there were no limitations on the number of nouns she could acquire. But even among nouns, the easiest words to learn, there were severe limitations on kind. She could learn immediately a word like "igloo" and remember it, although its relevance to her own experience was nonexistent. She could learn and accurately apply the words "oak," "elm," and "maple." Yet words which were, one would think, much closer to her experience she could not understand or learn. Such terms as "home," "sister," "grandmother," "teacher," "friend," or "stranger" were beyond her at five; "friend" and "stranger" are beyond her today. Proper names she acquired with a slowness that seemed clearly related to the weakness of affect. A name, after all, defines the importance of a person, his individual significance. Except for "mama," in occasional use, and "da-da," which made a few rare appearances, Elly got through her first five years without naming a single member of the family. Crude approximations began to appear that fruitful summer of her fifth birthday; in a few months, "Sara," "Becky," "Matt," and "Jill" (the much loved mother's-helper) were semi-intelligible and in frequent use. We could refer to each other by name and Elly would comprehend—"Go to Sara." We could add some of her new nouns: "Take the doll to Jill." People were beginning to be worth naming, although the familiar resistance was still there. At school she hardly looked at the children; she gave no sign that she distinguished them at all. One day, however—she was about five and a half and had been in the class three months—the teacher tried an experiment. Arranging the children in a circle, she asked, "Elly, where's Mark?" Elly, head down, eyes on the floor, jabbed a finger, not at Mark, but in his direction. "Where's Andrea?" Another jab. "Where's Sue?" Another. There were thirteen children. Elly, it turned out, knew them all by name.

It has been speculated that what is impaired in children like Elly is the capacity for abstraction, and it is true that Elly was, and for the most part still is, incapable of giving meaning to words like "love," "hate," "fear," whether used as nouns in their full abstraction or more directly as verbs. But my experience suggests a different formulation—not in terms of abstract and concrete, but in terms of relative and absolute. It is true that an abstract word such as "fun" was beyond her capacity. But she was equally slow to grasp that least abstract of entities, the particularity of a specific individual as manifest to sight and touch and expressed in a name. Moreover, she grasped with especial ease a whole class of word-concepts that are generally considered the product of abstraction, in that the mind in order to arrive at them must proceed from a number of individual experiences, abstract their significant common characteristics, and fix these in a word. Even at two and a half Elly had applied the general term "ball" to objects as different as a flattened rubber oval and a sphere of perforated plastic. This was not very impressive, perhaps—until you reflect that at this time when she had only five or six words, one of them was a product of abstraction. (Balls that *looked* like balls did not elicit the word; Elly was responding to the concept, not the appearance.) At three and a half the idea of a circle was so clear in her mind that she had commandeered music to do duty for the word she did not know. At five and a half, when she was at last ready to learn words in quantity, she learned "triangle," "square," and "rectangle" as easily as at three she had distinguished one block from another. The simple ideas behind the words "Where did Becky go?" or "Do you like candy?"—questions to which an average three-year-old can respond—were beyond her comprehension. But her teachers could say "Draw a red triangle, Elly," and she would do so. When she learned the other words for shape they came so easily it could hardly be called learning. Her sisters showed her them one summer morning, to amuse her: pentagon, hexagon, heptagon, octagon. . . . There was no hesitation, no need for practice or repetition. They spoke the words once; thereafter she simply knew them. Six months later she asked me for "heptagon." I thought she'd said "hexagon"; those we sometimes drew and talked about. Not so. Making a heroic effort at clarity, she said "hept*agon*—seven sides!" It was as if she had had the concepts for years and had been waiting for the words to describe them. And of course she had; when people had still been invisible to her she had responded to shape and color. Rectangle, a diamond, a square—these words are nothing if not abstract. When ideas

were significant to her, Elly had no difficulty with abstraction. We had not been able to teach her any color words until that fruitful summer of her fifth birthday, although of course we had named colors before, as we had named shapes. As soon as she did learn them, however, she used them to record the niceties of a color sense more acute than even we had suspected.*
"*Pink*-orange! Green-blue!" This at five—by seven, peacock green and peacock-blue cars were carefully and enthusiastically distinguished. Color was so important to her that I could use it to call attention to things she would not ordinarily notice. I would say "*purple* mountains," "*brown* horse," and Elly, who had little interest in animals and none in landscape, would see horse or mountain, which had now acquired significance from its color, and learn the word for it. It was not, however, the particular thing which interested her, but the generalized notion of color, which could be applied to any object.

There were many such abstract words she could have learned, but I was concentrating on the human, the ordinary and familiar. Like the Victorian governess whose charge described the shape of the earth as an oblate spheroid, I thought that it was much *nicer* for a little girl to say that it was shaped like an orange. It was more than a year later that it occurred to me to teach her "curved" and "straight." Only one drawing was necessary. Again it had been the word, not the idea, that was lacking. Elly demon-

---

* The most striking confirmation of her color-intelligence occurred when she was six. I had bought several boxes of powder paint for her, and mixed small quantities on demand, so she could paint at home as well as at school. The colors, of course, came out pure—plain red, blue, black—and Elly seemed quite satisfied with them. When we returned to the store for more she asked for white, and we brought a box home and put it on the shelf with the others. A week later she asked for paint, and when I asked what color replied "pink," "light blue"—colors she had never before requested. It was obvious to her that we could now make these colors, that white was the ingredient needed to produce pastels—something many normal six-year-olds have to be taught.

strated that on one of our walks. As we approached a house we had not visited for a year or more, Elly suddenly spoke, loudly and intensely. "*Curved* stairs!" I rang the bell in some excitement. I myself had never noticed the staircase, though I had been here more often than Elly. I might have known I could rely on her. As we entered the hall I saw that it swept up and around in a splendid curve. Certainly her capacity for making this kind of abstraction was not impaired. It was in fact so great that it had been able to sustain itself in her mind over months without the support of any words, to surface when they were supplied.

As we observed Elly's developing speech, it seemed divided into words she could learn instantly once they were pointed out to her, and words she could not learn at all. For a long time there seemed to be no middle ground. What she was able to grasp were absolute terms, whether concrete or abstract—those that reflected concepts that could be defined and understood in themselves. "Box," "cat," "giraffe." "Rectangle," "number," "letter." What she could not understand were relational terms—those that must absorb their full meaning from the situations in which they occur—situations in which the human element plays a part. Elly acquired the word "man" a year before she learned the name of any specific man—"man" is an absolute concept. Once you know the word for a being with short hair and trousers, you need understand no more; from then on, men as such will be recognizable. "Man" is absolute and abstract, but particular men are people, to whom one relates—if one does. "Teacher" is a word which, like "man," is the product of abstraction, but it is first learned in a relational situation: "my teacher." Similarly for "sister," "friend," or "home." It is characteristic of the average child that he learns concepts best in situations in which he can find a personal relation. With Elly, the personal relation seemed at best irrelevant, at worst a hindrance. We wanted to give her words that would enable her to function in the familiar world of a small child. But it was we who defined what a child should find familiar; Elly did not see it our way. Which was more familiar to her, a rectangle or a friend? Her sense of what was important, or unimportant, was simply different from our own.

I recall her, some months past five, looking at a Dick, Jane, and Sally pre-reader with the familiar pictures in series. Dick is painting a chair, in four stages. He has a brush and a can of red paint. I am trying to encourage Elly's new ability to learn names. Pointing to the picture, I say "boy," and meet with comprehension; I then say "Dick." Elly reacts instantly with unusual pleasure; she smiles, she bounces up and down, she repeats the word, she applies it to the succeeding pictures. I am pleased too. For her to learn a personal name so fast is unheard of. But suddenly she gets up and goes to the wall. It is painted blue. "Dick," she says, with emphasis and satisfaction. She moves into another room, goes to another wall, a pink one this time. "Dick." I realize what I should have known; what she has abstracted is not the boy's name, but the concept of "paint," which is also inherent in the picture series, and which to her is both more interesting and more available than the "simple," "direct" idea of a person with a name.

Elly's weakness in understanding human situations was especially marked in her difficulties with personal pronouns. She was six before she used any pronouns at all. This was not as surprising as it might have been; instinctively, in search of sure comprehension, we had spoken of ourselves and her by name, as one does to a two-year-old. But when we did begin, deliberately, to substitute "Would *you*" for "Would Elly like a cookie?" we realized the severity of the problem. The answer, at six, would be, not "yes" (that came much later, not spontaneously, but as a result of careful teaching), or even "I like a cookie," but a simpler echoing: "You like a cookie?" This echolalia, complete to the rising intonation of the question, was, we knew, part of the autistic syndrome; autistic children who, unlike Elly, do speak at a normal age, still speak not flexibly, for communication, but like parrots. Elly had not shown that symptom earlier because she couldn't talk that well. Now she could, and here it was. "Daddy gave you a present," I would say. And as time went on she did more than echo after us; she herself would volunteer the words, with full enjoyment of the fact of the gift. "Daddy give you a present." And now we recognized another specific characteristic of the speech of autistic children. In any statement, "you" is the equivalent of "I" or "me."

There was no confusion or ambiguity in this usage. My experience does not support the conjecture of some psychiatrists that this phenomenon is a sign of the weakness of the ego and the vagueness of its borders. Elly knew who she was. She was "you." The usage was exact, denotative, certain. The whole family understood it. It simply reversed the usual meaning.

It is perfectly logical, when one considers it. Elly thinks her name is "you" because everyone calls her that. No one ever calls her "I." People call themselves "I," and as a further refinement Elly began to call them "I" herself. The reversal of meaning seems nearly impervious to teaching; now, at eight, when Elly says "I like that" it means not that she herself likes it but that her interlocutor does. What can I do? I can tell her to say "kiss me" and reinforce it by kissing her; I can refuse to give her a shove in the swing until she says "push me." But these rare ways of dramatizing the correct usage cannot hold their own against the hundreds of incorrect reinforcements that every day provides. "You made a mistake," I say, and Elly replies, "You made a *mistake!*" "No, I didn't make a mistake, *you* made a mistake." "You made a mistake!" Everything one says makes it worse. Twice—on occasions a year apart—Elly has used "me" correctly, to refer to herself. "Becky gave me a book," she said recently, the book in her hands. Hurrying to encourage her, I caught myself saying, "Yes, she did give you a book," thus destroying the effect I had meant to reinforce. I have come to wonder how it is that ordinary two-year-olds can grasp anything so subtle. Yet they do. As mothers know, many of them have this same difficulty as they begin talking, but it rights itself spontaneously in a few weeks. How? As a psychiatrist—not one of ours—remarked to me at a party, the correct use of the first- and second-person pronouns * cannot be grasped by logic. The social sense must take over and straighten things out—the sense, or complex of senses, that assesses the relations of people in a given situation, how they think of themselves, and consequently what words they use to identify themselves. Elly's usage is rigidly consistent, severely logical. What it lacks is that social instinct which guides even the dullest of normal children in the labyrinth of personal relations.

This lack affected Elly's acquisition of all the parts of speech. She learned nouns more easily than verbs simply because there are more nouns whose meaning does not depend on surrounding situations. On the veldt, in the zoo, or in an ABC book, a giraffe is a giraffe. "Go" or "come," however, is something else again. It is harder to draw a picture of a verb, as you will find if you try it. Since action requires an actor, and often an object acted upon as well, there is more than one meaning to be abstracted from the simplest verb-picture. Unlike a noun, a verb implies a situation. From it, Elly must draw out the right thing— right not in her terms but in ours. The Dick-paint episode illustrates the ambiguities inherent in pictures—themselves so much simpler than real situations. We soon discovered that the drawing by which we tried to teach "play" might teach "swing" or "girl" instead.

But in spite of this difficulty, verbs slowly followed nouns

* For the record, I should say that Elly did not become conscious of third-person pronouns until she was nearly eight, when she spontaneously picked out "they" from a pile of word-cards as the one she wanted to learn next. The same week added "he" and "she." But though she can recognize them, she has said them only once or twice, and is only beginning to comprehend them securely. Ultimately, it seems plain she will acquire them, but there is nothing natural about the process.

into Elly's speech. "Walk," indeed, had been one of her first words, used, though not comprehended, before she was two. Four years later it was joined by "look," "jump," and "run," and later, in her seventh year, by such words as "give," "move," "push," "open," "shut," "cut," "hurt"—words easily illustrated in pictures or in action. The children, my good co-therapists, taught her "cough," "laugh," "cry," "scream," and "burp"; she and they took a mischievous delight in testing, usually at the dinner table, her ability to perform these actions on command. "Die," they would say, and Elly, gagging and choking, would collapse onto the floor. Other verbs were more immediately useful. By the time she was eight she responded to "say"—"Say 'butter,' not 'buh-buh,' "—and within a few months she used the verb herself. I found no way of illustrating "see"; Elly was seven before she acquired it, as a kind of tributary of "look," which by that time she could both understand and recognize in print. "Hear" is even worse; I'm not sure she comprehends it even today, and she does not use it. "Know" and "understand" are as yet beyond her grasp, although for three years I have responded to an unintelligible pronunciation with "I don't know" or "I can't understand that." Such nearly indefinable words as "have," "put," "take," and "get" are only now coming into use, and their boundaries overlap in distorted ways. She may suggest, if Daddy is sick, that "Daddy ha' broken arm," using "have" correctly— only to follow it up with "Daddy gi' temperature hundred." And by another strange reversal of normal learning order, these simple words, which children absorb from the environment long before they can manage the symbolic representation of them, Elly has learned only when she was shown them in writing. The visual experience of recognizing letter-combinations has focused her attention on words of which, although she heard them constantly, she seemed unconscious. She had never spoken the word *is* until she was seven, when her kindergarten teacher asked her to write it. Her statements were (and for the most part still are) of the form "Becky *girl*," "cup *broken*." Once she saw the word written, however, she began to hear it, and now will use it if she is asked to. The word "equals," however, which functions as a restricted form of "is," she learned with ease and uses freely, volunteering such relatively recondite statements as "seven plus five equals twelve." She has much more difficulty with "seven and five *are* twelve," although "equals" and "plus" come from a set of words proper to age six while "is," like "and," should appear much earlier. The meaning of "equals" is absolute and clear, however, not dependent on the multitudinous shifts of situations.

It is not surprising, then, that Elly made do for years without the verbs that cluster around the ideas of affection, desire, and need. The words "I wanna" characterize the small child, but this child who at two wanted nothing was six before she spoke the word "want"—of course without the "I." In those long intervening years, her desires, never numerous, were conveyed, first by gesture, then—in the expansion of speech at age five—by naming what she wanted. That she should be able to ask for something in words seemed great progress; we hoped—I think we expected —that the realization that language was power would bring with it further appreciation of the joys of communication. And it is true that now, nearing nine, she has a new flexibility in requests; at a single recent mealtime she used four different patterns, not only the primitive "Peanut butter?" but also "Eh' (Elly) ha' vanilla yogurt?"—"Nee[d] egg?"—and "Wan' pie?" If words fail to communicate, as with her indistinctness they often do, she will occasionally, if asked, pronounce them better; more likely, she will do as she did at two and a half—lead you to the wanted object, or make your hand approach it. Certainly there is progress here—but the reader who reflects how many ways there are to ask for something, and how often children make use of them, will realize how far there is to go.

And if "want" and "need" came so slowly, what of the verbs whose function it is directly to express emotion? "Love" and "like" lagged behind "want"; although we of course made a point of telling Elly we liked, loved her, she was nearly seven before she herself used the words. Remembering Annie Sullivan, imagining how she made love real to Helen in her prison, we had accompanied word with act, and Elly "understood" it. My journal entry records: " 'Love' now freely used. Means 'hug,' 'caress.' Will she extend to its full meaning?" Two years later I am still not sure of the answer.

If Elly picked up few words for the positive emotions, for negative ones she acquired fewer still. I remember Becky at eighteen months frightening us with the intensity of her "Go away!" Elly has never said anything like that. To deal with the things she doesn't like she has developed nothing beyond "no" and the anxious, edged voice of her wordless years. I did not think of teaching her "hate," for reasons that, if not wise, are at least obvious. She does use "don't like," but in a way that well illustrates the complex of difficulties confronting us. Beginning with "no like," which though primitive was clear and useful, she progressed to the more conventional expression. But "don't like" is a complex form of words, combining with a contracted negative the irregularities of the verb "do"; its shifts through "doesn't," "don't you," etc., can be reproduced only by a child whose brain has already recorded their patterns. Elly's lazy mouth converts the phrase into "like," preceded by a virtually inaudible "n," thus shearing it of the negative which is its primary indicator of meaning.* The words are rendered useless; even to me they are intelligible only in certain contexts and with great good luck. But Elly does not seem to feel the loss; it is a phrase she can do without. Simple avoidance is enough.

The same relational problems affected her acquisition of ad-

* We have other indications that she lacks the sense of what sounds carry the burden of communication. Soon after she learned "without" she dropped the "with"; nothing will induce her to put it back. Her indistinct pronunciation drops essential indicators of meaning; she forms no plurals and inflects no verbs because she will not pronounce a final "s" or "d."

jectives—if anything, more severely than nouns and verbs. Her first adjectives have already been described—the color and shape words she learned so readily. "Big" and "little," being relative terms, came less easily. "Long" and "short," "near" and "far," were harder still. She is exploring comparatives now, with a kind of fascination; at bedtime, as I turn off the light, she says "dark, darker, darkest." But she is nearing nine years old. The most striking lack, however, was of course in adjectives that express affect, that should convey her reactions to the world around her. Imagine how important the word "bad" is in the ordinary three-year-old's vocabulary, and then imagine a child with a vocabulary of hundreds of different words who has never needed the idea enough to pull a sound for it out of the environment into her own use. Elly's first use of "bad" (and its companion "good") did not occur until she was six years and four months old; the month before she had learned not only "real" and "pretend" but "left" and "right," concepts which mothers and first-grade teachers know are not easy. The sequence seemed symbolic. I was tempted to elevate it into a definition: an autistic child is one who finds the concepts "left" and "right" more easily available than "good" and "bad." The autistic child is one who, having minimized its interaction with the world, feels no need for words to express opinions about it. When small, it does not request. As it grows, it does not evaluate. "No" is enough.

Elly, at any rate, for years existed in apparent comfort without any value words at all, and though at length she found some uses for "good" and "bad," she has not made much of them. Language for her remains a mode of identification, a means of labeling phenomena; she is as yet not able to use it to express emotion. Small children say "bad" with every gradation of fear and fury; Elly now says "bad" too. But she says it with serene pleasure, to set a phenomenon in its proper category: "Bad can," she says as she collects beer cans from the beach. "Bad dog," she remarks, surveying an overturned garbage can. Elly does not care for dogs. If one comes too close she clings to me; if it jumps up she whimpers. But it would never occur to her to verbalize her emotion. She would not say "bad dog" then.

For all her color sense, she does not say "pretty," "lovely," or "beautiful," all words which she hears often. Nor does she say "ugly." She gets much more mileage out of "dodecagon" and "carnation-pink." She has acquired "right" and "wrong," but only in the unambiguous, objective sense of "correct" and "incorrect" ("Wrong foot," she says, deliberately putting left shoe on right foot). She enjoys using them; she has always been amused by mistakes. The summer she turned seven she acquired "sad" and "happy"; she sang the "don't be sad" song the children made for her, and when I drew a sad face and a happy one, Elly herself volunteered "mouth down" and "mouth up." She knew what sad and happy looked like. Perhaps she had known for a long time, as she had known curved and straight; perhaps not. At any rate, the words had made the ideas usable, and now and then she used them. We and the children would reinforce them by simple dramatics. We'd say "Sara is sad," and Sara would cry crocodile tears, to Elly's amusement. Elly would say "Be happy," and Sara would brighten up. The comprehension of these crude approximations of emotion was light-years beyond her old imperviousness. Yet they bore the same relation to the subtleties of actual emotions as a road map bears to the colors and forms of a living landscape.

"Young/old" and the adverbs "fast/slow" came as she neared eight. "Funny" she got from a word-card; though she laughs a lot, it applies as yet only to clowns. I taught her "tired" and "resting"; she picked up "sick," and "feel better." A skimpy list, and I may have overlooked a word or two that should be on it. But it is virtually complete. If she had said—or shown signs of comprehending—anything like "worried," "friendly," "danger-ous," "angry," "mad," "afraid," "scared," or "nice," be sure I would have remembered it.

Prepositions are by definition words that show relationships.

As late as six and a half Elly comprehended no prepositions, and of course used none. By this time she was well able to respond to such simple commands as "Bring me the pencil"—but in spite of her uncanny sense of orientation, she was still unable to understand the simple descriptions that answer the question "Where is it?"—a question that she never asked. Where is the pencil? *Under* the bed, *in* the drawer, *behind* the bookcase. Useful words, these; in her seventh year I decided they were too useful to wait for. I couldn't find a set of pictured preposition word-cards,* so I made my own. With these, Elly learned the printed words overnight, the spoken ones in a day or two. I taught only four or five of the most useful and easiest to illustrate; she understood them in commands, and gradually began to introduce a few into her own language. Such short words as "in" and "on" are easily slurred, however, and hard for the hearer to recognize. Though Elly's primitive "spoon [is on the] *table*" gave way to "spoon-uh-table," her effective communication had not advanced very far. Later—after seven—when she understood "say," I could ask her to "say it better," but that was in the future. And even then there was a great gulf between speaking intelligibly on request and speaking intelligibly habitually.

But the problems presented by these words were easy compared to the problem of conveying the untidy miscellany of adverbs, articles, and conjunctions, the unsung heroes that give our conversation its preciser meanings. These words are relational in their very nature. But. If. Whether. Maybe. Because. Soon. When. Yet. Like. Except. The words seem unimportant until you try to imagine doing without them, and simple until you try to find ways to teach them. Teach them? No one teaches such words—the small child seems to draw them out of the air. But Elly did not even pick up "and," the simplest connective of

---

* Later I ran across some by chance. But this is the sort of thing a good counseling service would make available to parents.

them all. She was seven before I thought of a way to convey it, and characteristically it was in terms of color. Our neighbors had a gray house with a blue trim; Elly called it "blue-gray house." Though Elly might verbally confuse blue-gray with blue-and-gray, I knew she was incapable of confusing them in actuality. So I drew two houses, colored them, labeled them, and pronounced the words. From then on she could understand "and," and read it on occasion. When pressed, she could even produce a sound to represent it. But who can draw "if" or "when"? Who can draw "but" itself?

It is words like these that convert vocabulary into language. A collection of words—even a large collection—is not equivalent to speech. They must be combined.

The average child begins, like Elly, with isolated words, and sometime between a year and a half and two starts to put these words together. Elly was nearing six before we heard her speak two words in combination. "Laura *girl*," she said of the small child next door, and this kind of statement, three years later, remains characteristic of her speech. As with a normal child, but much more slowly, two-word combinations gave way to larger aggregates—three, six . . . as the years passed she might sometimes say eight words together, with obvious logical connection. But these were not normal sentences—the almost total absence of articles, conjunctions, prepositions, verb-inflections for tense * or person, and the verb "to be" ensures that though her language grows in complexity she is still speaking pidgin.

---

* Her first use of the past tense came the summer she was eight. There have been few since. The two instances in which she has conveyed an idea of futurity are instructive: told I'd come in a minute, she said "Gi' minute Mama come"; in autumn, as we speak of storm-windows, she says "Be winter, ha' 'tor' window." Her comprehension of tenses is limited; asked "Did you have your lunch?" she will reply "Yes" when she hasn't, because she thinks I've asked "Do you want your lunch?" Tense understanding requires situational understanding. "Sara little. Sara grow bigger" can lead to "was" and "grew."

And it is a distorted pidgin at that, for Elly's grasp of word order, in English the most powerful indicator of meaning, is very weak. When a normal child says "Give Becky a green lollipop," we know who is to get the candy; it has been signaled by the word order. When Elly says it, however (dropping, of course, the article), it may mean what it appears to, but may also mean that Becky is doing the giving. "Dr. Mama doll gi' medicine" is meant to mean that Dr. Mama is dosing the doll. The order of the words is scrambled, and the listener must interpret from the context. Elly will say today, "No four find daddy peanut"; it means "I can't find four big peanuts." Responding to a picture of a hat on a table she may get it right—or she may say "table on a hat." She says she will "grow be ten"—I tell her, as I can these days, "Don't forget the 'to'—'grow *to* be eleven.' " Good-naturedly she does as she is told: "Elly grow *be to* eleven," she says. Her word order is correct more often than not, certainly—but that is not very much to say of the extremely simple speech of an eight-year-old child.

Elly has been a stranger in her world, and the course of her acquisition of speech has not been so very different from that of a tourist learning a foreign tongue. He learns the nouns first and easily: the things that can be pointed out. Verbs and adjectives come more slowly—they would come more slowly still if he were not helped, as Elly could not be, by the possibility of referring them to equivalents in his own language. Word order and syntax he acquires more slowly still; simple correctness may be the work of months. Years later he is still discovering new delicacies of situational appropriateness and unsuspected shades of meaning. Those who realize how difficult is the process of learning to feel at home in another language will be able to imagine a little girl experiencing the same difficulties in settling into her own, and marvel at the linguistic achievement of ordinary children between the ages of one and four.

One learns a language more quickly and better, of course, if one has reason to do so, if there are things one wants to find out and people with whom one wants to communicate. People learn a language because they want and need to use it, and if they do not want or need to very much they do not learn it very well. It is impossible to discuss Elly's slow acquisition of language without considering the part played by motivation. The old familiar weakness, inertia, and isolation had not lost their relevance.

Elly was still—is still—not very good at wanting things. The patterns of her childhood persisted; a word was more often than not used, not to ask for an object, or even to call attention to it, but simply to name it. "Milk," she would say. There is milk. Milk exists. No more. In the general expansion of language in her fifth year, she began, as I have said, to use words as requests. "Milk?" Thrilled, delighted, we fulfilled her requests the instant she made them; we would show her that language worked, that speaking sounds made good things happen. It helped. She requested more things, more often. She requests things now. But not very many things, really, and not very often. The discovery that words could alter circumstances did not effect a miraculous opening of the possibilities of communication, like Helen Keller's first understanding of "water." It was an episode, like another, in her slow progress. She learned names, as I have said. But what are names for? They are to identify, indeed, but also to call, and a child will use them as much for the second purpose as for the first. "Mom? Mom? *Ma*ma!" The sounds ring in my ears. In sixteen years I have become attuned to the frequency of each child. I can hear the voices in my imagination, I can hear them through walls, but Elly's voice is not among them. She has not yet called me. She has not called her father, her sisters, her brother, except—the exception is as instructive as the generalization—recently, when we have been able to *tell* her to call one of them for dinner. Then, imitating the very intervals of our voices, she will do as she is told. "Sa-ra! Beck-y!" But she is not calling for any purpose of her own. Recently, too, she has developed a new game for herself. After eight years, she has found out my name. "Cla-ra!" she sings—the characteristic descent, fifth to third, of a loud call into the distance. I am right there in the room, but that makes no difference. She isn't calling me really, as becomes clear in a moment: she puts forward her doll Deedee (imagine it, she is naming her dolls now!). "Deedee 'Cla-ra!' " It's Deedee who is calling me, not Elly. People do call other people. After eight years you notice it, imitate it, dramatize it. But you yourself don't do it. When Elly is actually looking for me she doesn't call "Clara," or "Mama" either—she wanders from room to room saying "hello?" Marvelous progress, we think, since for all these years, though she moved with me almost always when I was in the house, she didn't look for me when she mislaid me, or say hello, either. It looks as if—when she is nine perhaps—she will one day be ready to call my name.

Speech is used not only for requests but for responses to the requests of others, for the answering of questions, the conveying of information. Although in her sixth year Elly could respond to a wide variety of commands (though nothing like as wide as a normal child), she could answer no questions of any kind. By six and a half she could say "no!" if you asked her did she want more meat; this is a form of common self-defense, and perhaps it is the natural first response. As months passed the ability broadened: "Is Matt a girl?" "Is Becky's dress blue?" "No!"—with gay laughter, as always, over the ludicrous mistake. It was not until she was seven that we taught her to answer "yes." * She can now answer correctly any question that expects a yes-or-no

* The absence of this word has been called a specific symptom of infantile autism. Elly took three months to learn to use it. We would confront her with a situation to which she could be expected to respond positively and ask her to say "no" or "yes." "Elly, do you want ice cream? No or yes?" She could echo the "yes"; at length she could use it spontaneously. Contrast her instant acquisition of "difficult" words like "heptagon."

answer, if she comprehends the terms. She can also answer a variety of other questions that expect an answer of a prescribed form. Some of these are apparently quite sophisticated: "What's today?" "What's four times three?" "How many —— are there?" The ability to answer each of these questions was not acquired spontaneously, but taught. I do not mean, of course, that I had to teach Elly what day it was or how to keep track of a number of objects. For things like that she did not need teaching. It had been apparent from the time of her cookie fixation, at four, that she could count, and by the time she was six she would look at a collection of objects in one of her number books and say "seven" or "three." Unasked, that is. She could not answer when I said "How many?" It was the question itself she did not comprehend. When I realized the problem, which was not for a long time, I set myself to teach her the word-patterns of question and answer. I myself said "How many?" and answered my own question, and asked her again. After I had done this for several days (every evening at the same time, with the same book), Elly could answer the question alone. Other question forms came more quickly, as Elly began to understand the routine, but there is still a very limited number of them (limited by my powers of invention, as well as Elly's comprehension). Elly has picked up none on her own. Most significant of all, she can answer no question that requires an open-ended answer—one that asks her to reach into the great variety of her surroundings and come up with something that fits. We can ask "How old is Granddad?" and get a precise answer, for Elly is fascinated by ages and never forgets one. We can ask "Is Granddad upstairs?" and get a correct yes or no. If we ask "Where's Granddad?" however, we will get no answer. Pointing at a person close by we can ask "Who's that?" But we cannot ask "Who's your teacher?" or "Who's that in the kitchen with Sara?" We are even farther from being able to ask her "What did you do at school today?" or even "What did you have for lunch?"

She herself never asks a question—for the "Hot dog?" or "You like a cookie?" or "Gi' candy?" are not true questions, since their expected response does not consist in information but action. Though I taught her to answer "What's that?" a year ago, she never asks it. She never asks "When are we going downtown?" though she will say "Downtown?" as a request. The powerful word "Why?"—which introduces a far more complex kind of question—Elly cannot comprehend. Most crippling of all, for we need the words daily, we cannot ask her "What do you want?" or "What's the matter?" If she cries, if she shows anxiety or tension, in spite of her hundreds—it may be thousands—of words, we must still guess why, as when she was two years old.

This, then, has been the situation in Elly's second four years—speech rudimentary and distorted, but constantly expanding in scope and usefulness, and increasingly open to modification from without. It is clear already that Elly's speech has not been the free product of spontaneous development, that we have interfered constantly in the process as we have tried to teach what in a normal child needs no teaching. We are amateurs in speech therapy, as in all other therapy; we can guess how much we do not know. But we do know something about teaching speech, not in lessons, but in a total environment, and we know what approaches have worked for us. Most of these have already been suggested. It may, however, help someone if I review here, explicitly and in detail, the principles by which we worked and the methods we found workable.

I will begin with the most obvious, the method everyone suggests. "You should try not giving it to her until she asks for it." And of course we tried that, and tried again. So did other people; the teacher at the English nursery school tried witholding a sweet until Elly said "please." Elly was four and a half then. It didn't work for the teacher, as it hadn't worked earlier for us. All anyone got then was indifference, or, if the object was really desired, bewilderment and frustration. But children grow, and a year later it *did* work. Not as well as one would hope; rather than make the effort Elly would still too often cry or do without. But that it worked at all seemed wonderful to us. Remembering Pavlov, we rewarded her requests instantly; I leapt to my feet in joy when, instead of pulling at my arm, she said "Get up, please." When she said "candy," she got some. The effects on discipline and teeth were not wholly salutary; in trying to show her that speech worked we came uncomfortably close to demonstrating that you had only to speak to get what you asked for. We had to compromise. Yet we could not backtrack so far that she would conclude that words were not useful.

Above all, she must not conclude that speech was an untrustworthy instrument. If she must find her own speech to be effective, she must also be sure that ours gave a true account of reality. By this I do not mean merely that we could not lie to her. That goes without saying. But beyond that, it became second nature for us to examine our statements to make sure they would not be disproved by events. If we said, "Grandma is coming at five," it must be true; if there were the slightest uncertainty, we should say nothing. If I promised a trip to the store I must make it whatever the inconvenience, and since I knew that, I weighted my predictions and promises carefully. In those first years of Elly's speech I had still no words in which to explain change in circumstances, and the meaning of "perhaps" and "maybe" was out of reach. We are only now beginning to focus on the modes of speech that deal with uncertainty; we could not afford to perplex her with them then.

The second approach to speech was also an outgrowth of something old and obvious, the practice of naming things, which had finally, in Elly's sixth year, begun to get results. Naming of course remains a primary method, but its uses are plain and need no rehearsal. Less obvious are the possibilities of reinforcing spoken identification with the written word. It would not have occurred to me to do this had not Elly spontaneously been interested in letters. She had made her first mysterious "E" at three and a half, and had chuckled when, a few months later, I had written "Elly" on her hand; the day after we returned home from abroad, she had found her old letter set and spontaneously spelled E L L Y, ingeniously inverting the number seven in order to provide the second L, which the set lacked. Clearly she liked letters, and since I did so much drawing with her it was natural that I should begin to put written labels on the things I drew. I printed slowly and clearly; her eye followed the word as it took shape. I wrote the label before I drew the picture, hoping anticipation would tempt her into recognition. And by her choice, not mine, I made the same word and picture over and over. It was thus not surprising that at five and a half she could recognize "house" and write "window." In the next year, by a series of games incorporating successive steps forward,* she learned to recognize sixty words on cards, initially with pictures, then without.

I cannot explain the strange reversal of the natural order of events in which a child learns speech through the written word. But this is not the only instance in which I have understood traits in Elly by looking into myself. There are people, and I am one of them, whose comprehension is better oriented to the written than to the spoken word, who can hear something and not retain it, but who when they see it written will learn and remember. The configuration of letters itself seems to crystallize the word for them, makes them able to hear its pronunciation, and renders its

---

* I was encouraged to continue with simple reading by watching the work of the teachers at Dr. Carl Fenichel's League School for Seriously Disturbed Children. The welcome I received there was a model to show what help skilled professionals can give to parents. I watched for a full day a classroom of children as remote as Elly, and came away with new strength and ideas for months of work. Without this experience, and without the encouragement of Elly's psychiatrist, I do not think I would have presumed to teach Elly reading.

spelling an inseparable part of its identity. I could imagine that in some such way it worked for Elly. Perhaps one natural proof-reader begets another.

Yet though the printed word came easy, I had no startling success with reading as such. When it became clear that there was no upper limit on the number of word-cards I could teach Elly to recognize I stopped adding new ones. Elly could not yet understand the story of the Three Bears when I read it to her; how could she read herself? I did not want to see her "reading" degenerate into rote recognition; it was important that her words not outrun her comprehension, since reading, at this time, was valuable not in itself but because it intensified the experience of speech. So instead of increasing her recognition vocabulary, I started putting the words she already knew together in short sequences, picture above word to make sure the symbols kept their meaning. "Elly [of course I had made a card for *that*] hurt finger red blood cry." I could pull her through the sequence, but slowly, slowly; the words she could memorize overnight and recognize instantly were much less available when meaningfully connected. She liked them less, too; she no longer seemed to enjoy our bedtime word sessions, and she would not recognize her familiar words when pointed out in a book—indeed it was hard to get her to look at them. I found another bedtime game and put the cards aside. Meaningful reading still lay far in the future. The cards, the words I printed, could only point toward that. Their present use was valuable enough: to focus her attention on sound and meaning. Like our drawings, like our drama-tizations, they intensified her experience of speech. Without the cards, without my ready pencil, Elly's understanding of verbs would have been much delayed. We would have had to wait—who knows how long?—for "and," "the," "a," "is." I do not think she would have understood "in the box" to this day.

Through letters, too, we could approach speech by a third way. The look of a word could be used to help correct the indistinctness of her pronunciation, more noticeable than ever now she talked more and there were more words to confuse. Letters could direct her attention to a fuzzy initial consonant or a nonexistent final one. They could, that is, if she could understand how letters function. I had failed to teach her less difficult lessons than this one, which required not only comprehension of symbols but the precise discrimination of sounds to which she seemed so oblivious. It was fortunate, then, that the function of letters lay in the category of things that Elly learned without teaching. I had said "E for Elly," "B for Becky," without expectations, hardly thinking what I was doing. I had not expected that Elly would soon be volunteering "c for cup" and "b for bed." Simply, she liked letters, as she liked shapes and colors. She liked them very much—enough, even, to think about them. Intuitively, in spite of her own mispronunciations, she guessed their simple significations. Sometimes she would give unasked the initial letters of words she neither knew by sight nor could pronounce; her "S" was a muffled distortion between T and D, but we knew its sound well enough to recognize it and be astonished when she said "S for Stephen."

Using letters and pictures together, her father developed a pronunciation game. Recalling the technique of immediate reinforcement that underlies all teaching machines, he would draw a picture or print a word, then give Elly a tiny marshmallow if (and only if) she could clarify her pronunciation of it. Under this stimulus, he confirmed what we had always suspected: that Elly could pronounce a great deal more clearly than she did. Elly's pronunciation at two was, we think, potentially normal, but four years of semi-mutism had taken a toll; there were now real difficulties in sound formation. David, whose linguistic gift is oral as well as visual, was able to analyze his own pronunciation processes well enough to assist Elly in forming the problem sounds. If he had not been, we should have had to look for a book to give us clues. As it was, there must be, of course, many tricks that speech therapists know that he did not hit upon. We presumed in this, as we presumed in most other things where we did not seek professional help. But Elly could have been reached, at this time, only by a most unusual speech therapist; she was already good friends with her father. She could sit by him at bedtime, bathed, warm, and snug, and accept his fingers in her mouth. Eventually—perhaps even this year—Elly will be able to benefit from professionally administered speech therapy. In the meantime, her father and she make good progress.

Not remarkably good; in this, as in other things, what Elly learns in one context is only slowly extended into another. Her new clarity seemed less for use than for display. In the framework of the game, marshmallows were a worthwhile compensation for the effort required. But that effort was more than she cared to expend for the doubtful rewards of communication. Yet as months passed the effects of the marshmallow game did begin to rub off onto ordinary speech; at her seventh-birthday visit the psychiatrist remarked he could understand ninety percent of what she said. (At five, when he first saw her, she said little and he had been able to understand nothing.) We can count on simple initial consonants now, and many final ones. Sometimes we even get one in the middle. One day, I think, pronunciation will no longer be a major bar to her intelligibility.

Yet pronunciation, however important it might be to Elly's contact with others, was a matter of detail. It affected single sounds, or sounds in combination. But in our work with Elly, behind every approach to a specific problem lay a decision which would affect not isolated words and word groups but everything we said. How should we speak to Elly if we wanted her to believe in the possibility of mutual communication? If some of what Elly said was still unintelligible to us, we could not forget that most of what we said was unintelligible to her. We must consider our own speech as well as hers.

We could tell when Elly understood us and when she did not. If she did, she acted appropriately or jumped up and down in enthusiasm. Incomprehension brought indifference or a clearly inappropriate response. Of course we had in the back of our minds the stories everyone knows, of children who had seemed to hear nothing and yet were found to have recorded everything; the social worker at the Institute had suggested that Elly might understand far more than she let on. Even then this had seemed improbable, much as we would have liked to believe it. In the years since, we have watched for evidence of hidden comprehension and found none. It has been only in the past year that we have seen her pick up anything out of conversation not pointed directly at her, even its general subject. As she sits with us at dinner, as she moves among the children on the playground, she is still surrounded by a foreign tongue. Like a tourist in his first weeks abroad, she can understand what she expects to hear, if it is unambiguous, is clearly addressed to her, and falls largely within her own vocabulary. We all know the difference between our hotel French and the French the waiters speak to each other. I have heard Elly as she imitates me on the telephone. Giggling, she says "Tah. Te tah. Pah pee pee pee pah." The syllables suggest how meaningless to her is the sound of most speech.

Of course we did not want our speech to be meaningless to our daughter; that she should regard speech as at least potentially intelligible was our overriding concern. It was this that led us to a decision that many people will find questionable. We decided that if we wanted Elly to believe that speech had meaning, we must speak to her in her own language.

Of course this was in fact no great decision, only a verbalization of what we had been doing for years, what most parents do intuitively as they talk to their babies and toddlers. Using short, familiar sentence patterns, they speak to them in words they can understand. They do not think about the subtle process by which words build into speech; they do not have to. Automatically, with no one's conscious attention, the vocabulary and sentence patterns of the child's speech come to approach the range and complexity of the parents'. Gradually the parents drop their unconscious simplifications, and somewhere between three and five it turns out that everybody is now talking English. But when Elly was five we were at the beginning of this process, not the end of it. Elly was not talking English, she was mouthing words. We had the choice of confronting her with sentence patterns of normal complexity and length and hoping she would come to understand them, or confining ourselves to those she was reasonably likely to find intelligible. We chose the latter course.

We talked pidgin, but we talked it with a difference. Though we wanted Elly to understand, we did not want to imprison her within a primitive language, but to help her move toward more refined and complex structures of meaning. This meant that our pidgin must be one step ahead of hers. But not much more than one; nothing we had seen of Elly had led us to believe in her capacity for any great leaps forward.

To give details of how we spoke to Elly is impossible here, but the general approach can be conveyed. It has been rather as if one applied the familiar method of the Dick-Jane-Sally readers to speech. The influential creators of Dick and Jane do not introduce new words in clusters, but one at a time. The new word is introduced in several contexts, it is repeated ad nauseam. No step in comprehension is omitted, even if it seems obvious, and to a verbally gifted child *is* obvious. Stages the average adult would skip over have been identified and incorporated into a program that gradually leads the child to feel at home with a large number of printed words. The inventors of Dick and Jane know that many children will learn "go" without being able to extrapolate to "goes" and "going," that "can't" and "cannot" will seem to them totally different words. As it was in their reading, so it was in Elly's speech.

I learned much from Dick and Jane. When talking to Elly I tried not to burden a sentence with more than one word I knew to be unfamiliar. I was prepared to repeat the sentence again and again; autistic children do not find repetition nauseating and their parents cannot afford to. I tried to remember to use the word or phrase soon after, in another simple context, and to use it the next day and the day after that.

I spoke to her in her own vocabulary and I used her syntax as well. I tried to use it in a more civilized form—but only slightly more civilized. The gap between "Elly go store?" and "Elly, I'm going to the store now to get the eggs, do you want to come with me?" is fifteen words and several constructions wide. I could not, I thought, bridge it all at once, so what I actually said was a compromise, and a compromise nearer to her terms than mine.*

We had at first expected that once she began to talk, Elly would begin to pick up language like a normal child. And she did pick up words—especially nouns—that we had not taught her. She was much slower to pick up constructions—so slow that at length we began to take a more active part in the process. In addition to speaking ourselves so she could understand us, we began to find ways to nudge her own expression ahead—not merely to speak simply to her, but deliberately to feed her new patterns of communication that she would find usable if she knew them. We did not begin this until her seventh year. We were for a long time primarily word-conscious, and it was not for some time that we thought of conveying whole statements by repetition, as one would teach a word. A few of these were superficially sophisticated, like the arithmetical sentences with "plus" and "equals" mentioned earlier in this chapter. Most, however, express simple ways of coping with the world—less simple, though, to Elly than the relations of arithmetic. "Don't forget the ——." "Don't be sad, be happy." "Come back another day."

---

* As I typed these words, I received a call from the mother of an autistic child in a city half a continent away. She described the limits on her boy's comprehension, how he could not reply if she said "Tell me," but could respond if she said "Say the words." The counselor at the clinic she attended had overheard such an exchange and asked how she could expect the child to learn to talk if she herself talked such strange English to him. It is a natural response—to one who has not lived with the problem.

"Oh, we made a mistake." "Never mind." Ideally we would have imagined what patterns she needed to deal with her experience and provided them. If I were writing a handbook for parents of autistic children that is what I would counsel them to do. But in fact we were seldom so conscious or so clever. Only recently have we addressed ourselves consciously to the problem of giving her the words to handle recurrent situations in her experience. It has worked well enough so that we wish we had had the wit to think of it earlier. Better than anything else, it has enabled us to cope with the situations of frustration and anxiety that occur when everything doesn't go according to plan. Uncertainty exists, and we cannot protect her from it always. It is progress indeed when words can be not only a tool but a shield. This summer I developed the pattern "Sometimes buy candy, sometimes *don't* buy candy," and it has proved possible to extend it. "Sometimes go to school, sometimes don't go to school." "Sometimes we go home this way . . ." The words themselves are the first real help in dealing with autism's severest emotional difficulty: the commitment to routine and repetition. Life must be orderly, its forms must repeat, yet they cannot always do so. We can't always take the same route home, nor should we; we vary it deliberately. We have come far enough now, Elly and I together, so that the resulting anxiety can be mediated by words. "Sometimes . . ." The familiar frame becomes the fixed point in the changing world and Elly will insist on its application. She motions to my mouth with the familiar gesture of a conductor cuing in the violins. If from contrariness or inattention I miss my entrance, she will supply the whole pattern herself, even if she is crying from disappointment because "sometimes *don't* have candy." The patterns are clumsy, but Elly is beginning to alter them herself to fit new situations. On Matthew's birthday I remarked that "Matty is twelve." "Sometimes Matty eleven, sometimes . . ." and then, sensing that that couldn't work, she substituted another stock pattern. "Matty eleven last *night*."

Elly's speech is much improved. The psychiatrist says so, and so does everybody else. We can never be sure, however, that she would not have progressed further had we made the other choice—to let Elly find her own patterns, to speak English to Elly and wait for her to understand and imitate it. The teacher at Dr. Fenichel's school told me, "I always speak normally to them —they get it eventually." Perhaps Elly would have got it eventually, and got it better. With time at our backs, however, we chose for her a meaningful world sooner, even if worse.

We were more comfortable in our choice because Elly was of course in contact with other people who spoke naturally. She heard daily all degrees of speech between pidgin and English. Each person in the family spoke differently; we did not want an imposed uniformity. Since they wanted to be understood the children also spoke pidgin to her, but less carefully than I. Her father too was less in contact with the day-to-day expansions of her language; he spoke simply but with a wider vocabulary and in more conventional patterns. So did the mother's-helpers. The teachers at the nursery school talked to her in the same language they would use to any three-year-old. My hope was that what she learned from my simple conversation would aid her to make sense of the wonderful variety of sound around her; others could build on my foundations.

The foundations have risen. Elly at eight comprehends much of what anyone would say to a four-year-old. But though she speaks better pidgin than she did, she speaks pidgin still. I cannot know whether I have accelerated her progress toward speech or retarded it. I am sure, however, that I accelerated her comprehension. And it was through comprehension, even more than speech itself, that she must move into the world.

"I endowed thy purposes with words that made them known," said Prospero to Caliban. How little have we wished to play Prospero to our small daughter! How far from our ideal of education is this supplying of conventional patterns into which thought, which above all in a child should be spontaneous and free, is to be poured. But we have seemed to see a choice between a moderate and increasing range of conventional, suggested patterns, and a much slower rate of increase. We have chosen not to wait for a spontaneity which may never come.

The process has not snowballed, as one might expect of a child who, people still tell me, has "normal" intelligence. But it has at last begun to acquire its own momentum. Our hope has been that what Elly learned to understand and say with our guidance would make it easier to absorb the language of the world at large. And it has done so. Though she picks up much less, much more slowly, than a normal three-year-old, she does pick things up untaught, and every month she picks up more. We can now, perhaps, look forward to the day when we can retire from her learning process.

Meanwhile, she moves forward. Recently I sat and listened to her chatter, cheerfully and comfortably, for two minutes without a pause. It would have seemed a miracle, I suppose, if I had not experienced every step that went into its making. I set her words down here as I transcribed them—only a bit of the pronunciation has been rendered more intelligible. The reader will assess it for himself.

"Go Roger' house. Ha' little Christmas party. Come back go bed wake up ha' Christmas open stocking. Jill come *back*. Jill come back Christmastime. Elly go-uh-dolly house see-uh-dolly Christmas tree."

Suiting the action to the word, we move to the doll-house. Now Elly astonishes me; she speaks the very words that not two months ago, when I began this chapter, I wrote that she had never said. "Nice, pretty room. *Pretty* day. There Christmas tree. Yes. Look. *Two* candy cane. Eat up, dolly. [*Singing:*] Oh Christmas tree. Dolly ha' two TV. Color TV, black-uh-white TV. [Not fantasy, but a statement of fact; her dolls are well equipped.] Doll ha' Christmas tree. *Yes!*"

14 ˏ Ideas of Order

As WE assemble for dinner, Elly surveys the table. "Only five for suppertime! Six minus one equal five! Sara? Sara?" Anxiety is sharp in her voice. "Sara went to baby-sit," we say, and Elly repeats "Sara go baby-sit." The words help her come to terms with the situation, but she is not really satisfied; she asks again, and once more after that. Then she goes and gets a doll to set in the empty chair, and peace is restored.

Another day her uncle, aunt, two cousins come—the house is full. Elly is delighted: "Ten for suppertime," she informs us—restive, however, until we all sit down and make her prediction true.

My mind shifts back two years. People are in the living room, sitting, standing, moving in and out; there are a lot of us. Elly is uneasy. We must sit down, all of us, side by side, in rows around the room before she is satisfied. A few minutes of that and we are free again. It was one of her more inconvenient obsessions. Like all her obsessions, it had held sway for a time, and passed. I had forgotten it. Yet here it is again, refined, verbalized, numeralized, so to speak—another instance of that passion for arbitrary order which we had lived with so long that we had to remember to realize how strange it was.

At two and three it had been blocks in parallel rows or a deck of cards made to stand vertical in the cracks between the floor-boards, each card a neat half-inch from the next. At four it had been configurations of washcloths and cookies, unerringly kept track of by a baby who had no words for number but who knew at once if any were missing, and how many. Elly could grasp an ordering principle with astonishing rapidity. She needed only to be presented with the opportunity to arrange objects by shape, color, and size, and later, by kind and function, and she would do so. The classification exercises given in kindergarten pre-readers were obvious to her. She had no need to listen to the teacher's instructions; she may not even have heard them. As-sociate the cats, eliminate the dog: the pictures themselves told her that. Elly could grasp without words what was wanted be-cause that was what she wanted—an affirmation of formal order in a changing world.

It was not that Elly's life was especially neat. We ourselves do not keep a particularly orderly household. Regarding Elly's fas-tidiousness as pathology, we had not reinforced it, and we had tried to keep her routines from becoming sacrosanct. Elly's room should not be visualized as an untouchable arrangement of toys on shelves, and Elly had no interest whatever in conventional tidiness. Her play consisted, as often as not, of dumping and scattering objects, or of mixing them and running them through her fingers. Her arrangements were little islands in the general disorder—configurations that seemed to come out of nowhere, give intense satisfaction, and then become binding for a time, so that the delight of their completion would be matched by the anxiety that arose if completion became impossible. But anxiety was in no sense primary or frequent; she made the arrangements because she liked to, and since they were in general easy enough to fulfill, they usually brought satisfaction. Once fulfilled, Elly learned to accept their disruption, since a new one could always be made. The real pleasure lay in the making. Obsessive, perseverative, it seemed yet a genuine delight, as if the mere keeping track of things were an activity in itself worth while.

In an ordered world, one keeps track of things in space, and events in time. In Elly's sixth year, one of my helpers devised a simple calendar of different-colored cards for the separate days of the week. Elly learned them easily, and we began to notice that without having been told she knew what things happened on what days. "Wednesday Mama go college!" "Saturday no school!" In one of the typical autistic reversals, relational time-words like "tomorrow" and "soon" were much more difficult because they had no exact denotation; Elly still does not really understand them. If she is disappointed because we cannot go shopping today, a promise of "tomorrow" will not cheer her as "Friday" will, even if Friday is days away. "Three o'clock" works well, where "soon" does not, and Elly will be on hand to remind us when Friday and three o'clock come.

As she grew, Elly could appreciate larger orders of time. At seven and a half, she produced a series of four nearly identical paintings: a little girl and her mother outside a house, the only variation in the pictures the color of the simple landscape which surrounded them. Pale green, green, orange, white. "Spring, Summer, Autumn, Winter!" she told me—just like the seasonal pictures we had looked at together in her educational children's books. As she neared eight she became interested in ages, her own and other people's, in past and future as well as present. Number could order time and was a significant aspect of people as well. "You [read, of course, 'I'] eight." "Becky fifteen." "Mama forty-two." With satisfaction she anticipated birthdays, making the necessary adjustment: "Ha' birthday Mama forty-three!" Events were located in a future ordered by number: "You fourteen see Rosemary!" (For Rosemary, the last of our mother's-helpers, had returned to England as Elly turned seven and none of us could contemplate not seeing her again. Elly had invented "fourteen"; we shall try to make her prediction come true.) Elly's numbers ordered a future in which, to our delight, she grew steadily bigger and more adequate.* Leveling her hand two inches above her head to show her future height: "You nine like that see mirror better!" "You ten like that!" "You nine, 'sixty-seven," she said one day in 1966—when, of course, she was eight. "You twenty, glug down big pill!" The past, too, took on numerical reality. As we looked at the family photographs we had enjoyed for years, "See Sara baby?" was replaced by "See Sara one?" But her keenest interest was of course in herself. She still asks me to re-create her past, but now it is exhaustively catalogued by number: "Draw Elly zero?" "Draw Elly one?" "Draw Elly two?" . . . and number by number, picture by picture, the tiny baby crawls, walks, grows, and reaches the present.

Space, of course, she had organized far earlier than time. I cannot know by what methods the two-year-old Elly had recorded her indelible map of houses and streets, but she had done so. Nevertheless it was five years before it occurred to us to show her a real map, and even when it did we tried it almost as a joke, it seemed such a quixotic thing to do. But continuing the old methods of dealing visually with experience we could not talk about, when we bought a summer house in Rhode Island and moved there, leaving once more home behind, we thought we might reinforce Elly's sense of security by showing her the road map of our trip south. It was an instant success. Our town, the turnpike, the pancake house where we stopped for lunch, the ferry, and our island resting place were located with delight,

---

* She was helped in this by her pleasure in two books that I name because other parents may be able to use them: Phyllis Krasilovsky's *The Very Little Girl* and *The Very Little Boy* (Doubleday, 1960, 1962). In these, a story so simple that even Elly can follow it traces by pictures the growth of a tiny child towards strength and adequacy. I would also urge all parents of defective children, especially those who do not draw, to photograph often the houses and people that constitute their child's past.

over and over again. In a few weeks we shifted to the big atlas and retraced the European trip now three years in the past, as my hand turned airplane and flew to England. Vroom-vroom: we drove to Southend, flew the Channel, entrained (chug-chug) for Munich, reached St. Gilgen, returned via Le Havre. Each new understanding, however formal, can be used to render experience more manageable. Now absences could be talked about: I could say that Rosemary was in England, that Jill was in Pennsylvania (space) and would come back to see us at Christmas (time). The elaborate projection-map of our college town produced tense, excited delight. I had had to guide her across oceans, but she herself could trace her familiar walks and reach the beautifully rendered library, the church, Daddy's lab. She became fascinated with road signs; I remember a long night drive with everyone torpid but Elly, who was crowing "Two! Seven! *Curved* arrow! Arrow *straight!*" When she returned to her town map she was ready to discover "Route 2 *west!*"

Six months later we were back in our summer house. Elly was not quite eight. We had arrived the day before and everyone was busy settling in while Elly played unnoticed with last year's happily rediscovered crayons. I did not look at the sheets she had produced until next day. The marks on them were quite different from any she had ever made before—superficially less orderly than her usual pictures, they consisted of long, sinuous triple parallels interspersed with occasional squares and rectangles. Snakes? The word brought no response.

Suddenly I saw. Two borders, a line down the middle. Roads! "Did you make a road, Elly?" "Yes!" And now I understood: here was a square for our house, a road leading out, with no line down the middle, however, but filled in with rough penciling. "*Dirt* road!" said Elly. I followed it as it made the left turn and joined the main road where the white line began. I followed her map all the way to town. "Hardware store!" "Market!" "Ferry!" The important buildings were there, the major turns

235

correct. It wasn't perfect; Elly had put the hardware store on the wrong side of the street. But there are normal children older than she who do not grasp the concept of a map at all.

A map is one of the most demanding of the possible orders of space. Controlled by the reality to which it corresponds, it fails to the degree it is spontaneous or free. If Elly drew a map (and she has drawn only two), or drew the seasons (she has drawn them only once) she was not composing freely; she was reproducing an order in the external world. But her painting and drawing was no less orderly when it was not bound by fidelity to an external original—rather it was more so.

It happens that all of Elly's drawings I have mentioned so far have been representational. They have been easy to call to mind, for the very reason that they were so untypical of her usual work. There were six or eight of them, perhaps, over a period that produced hundreds of nonrepresentational pictures. Only in the past year and a half, in fact, have renditions of external reality —people and things—become at all common. Before that it was almost all "nonobjective painting." From the time she first began to draw and paint without reluctance *—roughly age five—her work exhibited the same characteristics of order and control that we observed elsewhere.

Its most obvious characteristic was its neatness. Though she had never before painted on an easel, she rapidly mastered the problem of paint that drips or runs. She showed no particular anxiety; painting did not seem to engage her emotions. She simply learned to take on her brush the right amount to produce a clear, pure, easily controlled line. Colors were neatly placed contiguous to each other, never superimposed. Most nursery schools have learned to make their work easier by limiting the number of colors to three, changed daily; Elly was more than content to

* She began to paint in the English nursery school, at four and three-quarters, and painted daily in her American one. She also painted intermittently at home.

use only those that were set out. Though she knew how two colors combine to produce a third, she herself never mixed colors on the paper. She never splashed or scrubbed the paper, never added red to green to blue to produce a glorious mud. Her brushes were the cleanest in the class. Not that she was painfully neat; she worked too quickly and casually for that. Rapidly but judiciously she made lines and figures which organized the full space at her disposal. Balance came easy to her.* Usually she painted in lines against the white background of the paper, not filling in the total space with color, but when at length, encouraged by her teachers, she made areas of color to cover the whole paper, her colors exhibited the same purity, the same clarity of edge. I have sheafs of her paintings. Covering a three-year period, they show no technical progress; I do not think anyone could date them unassisted. All but a very few are nonrepresentational. There are lines, parallel, wavy, or straight; zigzags, stripes, circles, squares, rectangles, triangles, in different sizes and assorted combinations. She would introduce a motif, repeat it daily with small variations for a week or two, then abandon it entirely—in sharp contrast to her representational drawings, which were always one-shot affairs, coming seemingly out of nowhere at intervals months apart.

Once she made a car with a tall aerial upon it. Cars were not particularly important to her, and our own car didn't have an aerial. She had had a week-long flurry of interest in aerials, however, and had learned the word. The car appeared on her easel one morning, and was never seen again. Similarly with an occasional house, stair, or bed. The only occasion on which we were able to surmise from her drawing a personal or emotional meaning occurred when she was something over five. It took on a special

---

* When her paintings were unbalanced, they were unbalanced in an orderly way—for example, three shapes at the bottom of her paper, every day for a week.

significance by its very rarity, and is worth describing here not because it was typical but because it was not.

She drew a figure standing in the door of a room. The door, with its knob, was clearly recognizable, and a bed was visible beyond it. Though the figure was crude, with no hair, arms, or clothes (she added these to figures in the next year), the drawing was spatially sophisticated enough so that it was evident what was behind what.

At that time we were fresh home from our year abroad. As we had anticipated and hoped, Elly had been thrilled to return; there was a real surge of interest and alertness in rediscovered things, even people. But by ill luck, the college revarnished our floors before we had been home two weeks. Chaos came again as furniture was piled in hallways. The home that had been lost and found was lost again. Elly, who had settled in so joyously, did not complain. She solved the problem her own way. She went into her room and shut the door, and for weeks she would remain only in a room whose door was closed.

Although she accepted companions on her side of the door, she still shut out in this way a great deal of the life we wanted her to share. So I talked about this to the psychiatrist, and he was glad to see the picture of the open door; he thought of what it might mean when I had not. And in fact she did begin to allow the door to stand open. But she produced no more drawings that could tell us things, and I think her paintings might have baffled more skilled and ingenious interpreters than we. At five and six, she might go for four months making a picture every day, and never a representation among them. If she did draw something recognizable, as once or twice she drew a house, it seemed a mere object, no more expressive than the ones I drew for her at her request. Once—it was six months after the figure at the door—I broke in on her pattern series and asked her to draw a girl. (Always it is in one's mind that she has forgotten how.) Efficiently, carelessly, wholly without interest, she sketched a figure—head, body, arms, legs. "Put a hat on," I said, and in a single stroke she did so. Nothing could have been plainer. She seemed to say, "You wanted a girl and you've got one. Now let me paint my way."

Her way was nonrepresentational. Yet did we really know that? How could we be sure her pictures represented nothing? Might not the patterns she repeated so often have significances beyond themselves, significances we could not see? Parallel zig-zags, a circle, a square—pure and abstract as they might seem, there are such things as symbols. Why should we assume we would recognize such representations as Elly drew?

We could not, and to this day we cannot be sure. We could only wonder, and try to fit things into the totality of Elly's experience, and our experience of it. And we could check: before some bright, balanced pattern, "What's that, Elly?" I would ask, pointing to the picture. "Green," Elly would answer, or "pink" or "brown," depending on what area my finger had inadvertently been directed toward. And green it was.

Should I have been taken in? Perhaps this non-representational, matter-of-fact objectivity was merely a cover for her true pre-occupations.* That might be true. It might also be false. We could only watch and guess. "A primrose by a river's brim/A yellow primrose was to him,/And it was nothing more." There are

---

* At seven and three-quarters she made, all on one day, a most interesting series of drawings that showed she well understood the process of visual abstraction from a human situation. She began with a picture of a birthday party, represented as a rectangle surrounded by recognizable heads—not the full figures she had drawn occasionally before. These she identified verbally as "girl, lady, boy, girl, lady, boy" around the table in strict order. A second picture showed the same rectangle, but the heads had turned to simple spots of color, still identified by the same words. Later pictures in the series show members of her family, identified by name, as mere blocks of color. But this series remains unique. It is no longer uncommon for her to draw members of the family, and she even labels them herself in writing. But only this once have human beings ever been hidden by abstractions—or, rather, not hidden, but represented, since the whole process was conscious and deliberate. It was also accompanied by considerable gaiety.

people like that. I remembered one of Kanner's differentiae between schizophrenic and autistic children: that schizoid children lived among fantasies and even hallucinations, whereas autistic children did not seem to hallucinate at all. As Elly never seemed to; I had never seen any sign that she related, negatively or positively, to anything that was not objectively there. It fitted with all I knew of Elly that to her a red circle should be a red circle—only that. On the rare (though increasingly frequent) occasions when she departed from pattern-making, the departure was evident. It was unnecessary to ask "What's that?" We could see what it was. But if we did ask, after the idiotic manner of grownups, Elly did not answer "red" or "peacock blue"; she said matter-of-factly, "stairs," "bed," or "girl." She could draw, if she pleased, people and objects, or she could draw patterns. The two realms were not confused, nor, apparently, did they overlap. Real things were not patterns, and were not treated as such. Her representational drawings were markedly less ordered than the great body of her work; figures, objects, did not repeat, and they might be clustered at the bottom of the page or to one side. It was as if she knew that the world of reality and the world of pure form were distinct—and knowing this, preferred the world of form.

I write surrounded by scraps of paper on which I have jotted down Elly's ideas of order. The problem of selection here is severer than anywhere else. Elly has the kind of mind that given the series 2, 4, 6 . . . will spontaneously supply 8 and carry the series to 100. She will do the same thing with a progression by 5's, 10's, 11's, 100's. She will do it with 3's and 4's, but with more difficulty; though she can add 9 plus 3, she may make a mistake on 49 plus 3. What is illustrated is not her ease in performing arithmetical processes, but her grasp of an ordering principle. The grasp is more remarkable because we do not *ask* her to supply the next number, any more than the psychologist who tested her at three and a half had to ask her to pile five cubes in order of decreasing size. It is simply apparent to her that that is what is there to be done—that the system itself demands it.

When she was first learning to count verbally, at five and six, she still had difficulty with new words. Two words for the same thing confused her and I avoided them where possible. Consequently I anticipated difficulty with ordinal numbers (for "first" and "second" are very different words from "one" and "two"), and also with the verbal shifts as she must move, for example, from ". . . twenty-eight, twenty-nine," so orderly and easy, to "thirty." But she grasped ordinals at once, even making the effort necessary to put a slight noise on "fifteen" to adumbrate "fifteenth." And though she did initially say "twenty-ten," she knew without being told that twenty, thirty, etc., were different from other numbers and like each other, and in a day or so was spontaneously correcting her seventy- or eighty-tens to "eighty" and "ninety." Not only were numbers readily available to her, but words as well, if only they reflected an ascertainable order.

Elly's natural grasp of ordering principles seems to tell her what defines a system and consequently what is needed to make it complete. I had deferred teaching her zero; I knew it was a sophisticated mathematical concept, and what the Greeks had lacked, Elly, I thought, could do without. But Elly picked it up somewhere, at kindergarten perhaps, and brought it into common use. I had not forced numbers on Elly; she was seven and a half before I suggested that $1 + 1 = 2$, $2 + 1 = 3$. She had intuitively added larger sums for years, and I made sure to associate the abstract symbols with blocks or objects. She was now in kindergarten and it did not seem too much to teach. I was, however, unprepared for her critical reaction: "No zero!" She wanted $0 + 1 = 1$ and I supplied it. Then, "Oh, we forgot! Zero plus zero equal zero!"

Similarly, she could grasp the principles behind the verbal representation of numerical order. A few months after she was eight, at a time when she had been able to count correctly for years, we found her making numbers on a sheet. "One-ty nine, one-ty eight, one-ty seven . . . one-ty one, one-ty zero, zero-ty nine" . . . all the way down to zero-ty zero. What could be a clearer verbalization of the way our notational system works? If 29 is represented as "twenty-nine," the word "two" buried in the "twenty" (as of course we had never even thought of teaching her), then "one-ty nine" will be the equivalent of "nineteen," and "zero-ty nine" of "nine," and when one gets at last to zero-ty zero there's reason to shout out what had become Elly's new cry of triumph, "Yo ho! yo ho! yo ho!" *

Yo ho indeed. For a year zero has been Elly's favorite number.† She uses it interchangeably with "no" in common speech ("zero car in garage"), and she has even developed a purely verbal system in which "nobody" and "somebody" (an especially difficult concept for her because indefinite and inexact) become "zero-body" and "one-body," occasionally joined by "two-body" and "three-body," depending on the number of people in question. (Alternatively, the opposite of "nobody" may be "yes-body.") Elly, in fact, focuses on hard-to-get ideas through

---

* The reader will by now have noted how many of my transcriptions of what Elly says carry exclamation points, and wonder why. To appreciate the tone of Elly's speech, it is important to realize that (requests aside) it consists largely of assertions, made with varying degrees of emphasis ranging from simple underlining through enthusiasm to transported delight. A musing or inconclusive tone is rare. Anxiety almost always leads to a questioning rise in intonation, and question marks or exclamation points could really be put after almost everything she says. A "no," for example, that she is sure will be honored is "No!" One that she suspects I may not accept but which is still important to her will be an edged "No?"

† I can imagine one famous theoretician-therapist explaining to me how an autistic child takes hold of a symbolic representation to express its inner emptiness and despair, saying as clearly as it can that the only way it has found to defend itself against its destructive environment has been to make itself a cipher. I supply this interpretation to show that I can do it as well as another. But it was an analyst who warned me against constructs.

systems as she once focused on them through color. The shifts in such relative notions as dark and light are hard for her, and she has been slow to acquire comparatives and superlatives, but one of her favorite games now is to darken a room, and as she shuts its door the diminishing light from the hall illustrates "dark, darker, darkest!"

She is delighted when words exhibit ordering principles. The actual principles behind English word order, being so deeply situational in nature, she grasps (as I have noted in the preceding chapter) less well than a normal three-year-old, but it is quite otherwise with a principle that is not rooted in situations and usage, but arbitrary and devoid of content. We watched, incredulous, as Elly, just turned eight, extrapolated from what she had at long last learned: that the plural of "man" is "men." I had been able to convey it by a picture: the two words first, and below them, one man and several. The next day, Elly, totally absorbed, produced five pictures of her own. One was a reproduction of my man-men original. Next came MAMA-MEME, illustrated, of course, by one mama and several, followed by DADDY-DEDDY, SARA-SERE, and MATT-METT, each illustrated with a single figure and a group. (The single member of the family whose name did not contain the letter A was of course not pluralized.) The utter divorce from common usage (Elly still does not form conventional plurals, though she knows how to, since S is for her the most difficult of the final consonants), the total disregard of human and situational plausibility are obvious; so too is the spontaneous abstraction and application of an ordering principle. One is no more extraordinary than the other.

Again and again we had felt it; something more than a simple lack of interest in things human—a positive commitment to, a genuine pleasure in that which is abstract, arbitrary, devoid of content. The passive two-year-old Elly saw the parquet formboard out of the corner of her eye and actually made the effort to go upstairs so she could play with it. Elly four years later could go into an ecstasy that tensed every muscle in her body as she communicated the simple observation that some sleeves are short while others are long. Today she says to me, "Do 'rithmetic?" and as I sit on her bed and transcribe the sums and answers she dictates, the springs shake as she jigs and bounces, smiles, chuckles, squeals, laughs aloud in the intensity of her pleasure. If an experience is empty of content, of a sort that the average child would find particularly uninteresting, Elly is almost sure to enjoy it. She has just discovered our zip code number—01267. Of course she loves it.

Of all things in the varied world—cars and houses, animals, flowers, and people—why should Elly be interested in the conventions of notation? At five and a half, as I sat and drew for her, she asked for "pea." Pea? I thought. Peach? Pear? We often drew the forms from her fruit-and-vegetable curtain, and she was so indistinct I could never be sure. I tried out all three. They weren't right. Elly's frustration mounted to the point where she made a supreme effort to communicate. "Lelluh?" Lettuce? I wondered, and drew one without calming her in the least. And then I caught on: *Letter!*" She laughed, bounced, that was it, she wanted the letter P. From then on I felt less need to defend myself against possible charges that I was pushing my child into activities that would satisfy my own intellectual pride. If I wanted to be proud of a child who—like the rest of her family—liked letters, I had one. Elly had had a set of plastic letters for years—twenty-six capitals and ten numerals. It was with that that, at five, she had spelled her name. When she was seven, in kindergarten and already able to recognize many words, I got her a rather elaborate set of wooden letters—a real compositor's chest, full of e's and a's, enough to spell words in plenty. You could choose between capital letters and small, and I had bought the small, since she had the others. As Elly played with the letters I heard her say some curious syllables. "Uh-puh-cay? Uh-puh-cay?" "Apple-cake?" I said uncertainly. Though Elly had no special interest in apple-cake, it seemed a possibility; it was the sort of thing a child might say. Perhaps she had apple-cake at school. It was strange, at any rate, how she kept repeating these sounds. "Uh-puh-cay?" Some urgency came into the voice. I looked again at the letters and suddenly I knew. "Upper-case?" No uncertainty now: "*Up-uh-cay!* I got the old set of capitals and began to make words, but Elly was not interested in them. Instead she occupied herself happily in producing the set of 26 upper- and lower-case pairs.

Now I was primed for them, the syllables for "low-uh-cay" became recognizable. Where could she have got them? I did not use them. I was sure they did not use them at school. Then I remembered. We had taken her to try the "talking typewriter" at the hospital in Cooperstown, where Dr. Mary Goodwin was using it with children with autistic symptoms and getting some strange and interesting results. Elly had enjoyed her half hour with it, and although she had produced nothing strange or interesting in this single visit, Dr. Goodwin's understanding and encouragement had been well worth the trip. We did not repeat it; the five and a half hours in the car was too long, we thought, for Elly and for us. But I remembered the typewriter now. Developed by Dr. O. K. Moore for the rapid teaching of reading to pre-kindergarten children, it combined sound with visual stimuli —when a child pressed a letter or a symbol, a recorded voice identified it. Elly had spent a half hour with the typewriter, six months before. She must have learned "upper-case" then. Without any reinforcement, she had preserved it over the months between. Intrinsically without significance, it was significant to her.

The more meaningless a convention, the more purely formal, the better Elly liked it. She liked punctuation. She liked her letter set, but she liked it far less when I used it to spell the words she knew from cards. She never used it this way herself; she preferred to make arbitrary arrangements, or to mix the letters up together and sift them through her fingers. She was fascinated by a book of different type fonts; predictably, she learned the word "serif" at once, and had I wished I would have had no difficulty teaching her "black letter" and "Gothic." Spontaneously, long before handwriting was introduced in school, she tried to turn her capitals into cursive by supplying florid connections, saying "handwriting" as she worked. She noted that the top of the printed numeral four is closed, whereas most people write it open; from then on she insisted on a "different four?" She took to Roman numerals at once; recently she spent a happy hour typing out the numbers from I to L. Her sisters, having learned the deaf-and-dumb alphabet from their high-school production of *The Miracle Worker*, taught it to Elly without difficulty. When Sara learned the Greek letters I asked her particularly not to teach them to Elly; I was afraid she'd learn them.

It was difficult enough to put meaning into the symbols Elly knew already. The phenomenon I noted in the preceding chapter is again relevant here: she could learn the look of a new word overnight; the job was not to retain the word itself, but its meaning. None of her words began as rote acquisitions—with pictures and action, I saw to that. But as soon as I abandoned orderly word-card drill (cards set out in rows on a drawing board, print-side up, reversed to show the pictures as she identified each one, correct identification of them all rewarded by a new word-card) and tried to make of words an avenue to meaning, Elly resisted. I would point them out in familiar picture books or assemble them in statements meaningful in her experience, and she'd look away, or shut her eyes, or slow her activity to a crawl. Correctly identifying sixty word-cards according to a settled routine—that was a pleasure. Reading for meaning was not—so definitely that she no longer likes to look at books with me, lest I should ask her to recognize a word.

If I follow her lead now, even the pictures that I draw are reduced to number. "Draw Elly cry?" "Draw Elly 2 tears? . . . 4 tears? . . . 6 tears? . . . 8 tears?"—all accompanied by the cheeriest good humor, unless, of course, I should refuse to complete the series. When her baby doll lost both its legs I thought she might mind, remembering the horror of deformity I felt as a child. Not at all; she was delighted. "Draw baby zero leg?" "Draw baby one leg? . . . two leg? . . . three leg?" . . . "Draw baby eight leg?" To me it looks nastier with each addition. Dead-pan, I suggest it is a spider-baby and meet with enthusiastic assent.

I recall an incident so characteristic of Elly that it can stand as an archetype of what she seems to be. Elly was six and a half. I had been gone all day, and returning, coming into the bedroom, I found Elly at the typewriter. Leaving it, she ran to me at the door and for the first time in all her life said "Hello, Mama!" Then, back at the machine, she chirped "Comma! Exclamation point!" In my happiness I had still to reflect, "It is the 'hello, mama,' that surprises you. The 'exclamation point' does not."

What kind of child was this, who could take six years to learn to greet her mother (a greeting she has seldom repeated) but whose mind unerringly recorded meaningless terms mentioned once without emphasis weeks or months before?

It was, apparently, an autistic child. Dr. Blank had first thought of autism, long ago, at Elly's first visit, when he heard of her interest in arrangements. Autistic children were often good with numbers; some showed extraordinary abilities, far beyond Elly's. Elly's exact shape discrimination and her acute perception of the missing members of a set were not isolated phenomena, but typical of the condition. So was her ear for music, most abstract of the arts. Even the concern with the preservation of sameness, which Kanner considered a primary symptom, can be thought of as part of the autistic commitment to order; the patterns established, whether in space with cookies or washcloths, or in time with rituals and routines, must be preserved and completed. Elly could accept my outright refusal to draw for her, say, the numbered series of triangles with which she ended every day. We have had some success in moderating her compulsiveness, and I could, especially as she grew older, say that it was too late for the usual twenty-six, but that we had time for twelve. But if I once began the series and was interrupted before the twelfth one came, Elly would be beside herself with distress.

Series must be completed, order reaffirmed, limits observed. This was still the same child who at three had sought out fences and enclosures. At first it was I who colored the pre-bedtime triangles, for though Elly wanted them done, she did not want to do them herself. As I colored, of course, I used the full spectrum that Elly's crayons provided; it never occurred to me to do otherwise. Gradually I was able to draw her into the coloring routine; I colored one triangle, she the next, until all were done. At first I chose my colors while Elly chose hers; later (and there are some hundreds of these sheets of triangles, one for each bedtime; much of Elly's arithmetic has been learned from them) she chose my colors and handed them to me. "Only two colors?"

Her voice grew urgent as I reached for a third crayon. "Just green and yellow-green, yes!" Inspecting the triangle sheets after weeks, I realized what had escaped me as we colored night by night. Not only was Elly using a strictly limited palette, she was providing the same color combinations every night in almost the same order. The first five would be successive combinations, two at a time, of orange, red, peach, and pink. The next four would combine green, yellow-green, and pale green. The next would be orange and blue. Only after that would she choose with any flexibility, and even then she would allow no third color.

Some such limiting principle seemed to lie also behind her tendency to stereotype her environment and activities. When Elly was three I could see no trace of Kanner's prime symptom, the commitment to the preservation of sameness. Elly had no routines then. But the symptom lay in waiting (it should be noted that Kanner did not always see his patients as early as three). It developed later, with the capacity for self-assertion—the pathological symptom accompanying what we take as a sign of health. When Elly was three and four, more withdrawn and less assertive, she would walk with me anywhere. At five she began to want to turn right or left at a certain corner, if we had done so before. At seven and eight—today—she will, if not opposed, reduce any walk to sameness. There is one path to take downtown, one for our return. If we pass a landmark where I have previously invented a game Elly has liked, Elly will repeat the actions even if I have forgotten them. If I have spoken words there, Elly will repeat them for me and cue my mouth to make me speak my lines. She is not unyielding about it; by introducing minor, tolerable variations I and, still better, others are able to maintain some flexibility. She will now readily accept a deviation introduced for a reason—lateness, or a changed destination. But if I merely suggest that we walk home a new way, her anxious "no?" vetoes it unless I decide to make it an issue—and if I do, the new option will probably be incorporated in the next walk. The commitment to an environment that can be kept track of remains.

Recently Elly spent more than an hour making a series of pictures—twenty-one sheets of carefully crayoned paper, each displaying a large numeral, starting, of course, with zero. Upon the zero, inside it, a small figure sits. She is standing against the one. The numbers continue to twenty. In each of them the same figure stands or climbs or sits or hangs. Sometimes the figure is "Elly," sometimes "girl." Elly enjoys talking about them; she explains with delight, "Girl hang-uh seven!" (The hanging figure's hair, obeying gravity, hangs straight down.)

A new series carries the process one step further. The body has disappeared and the girl has merged completely into the numeral. Only her schematic head remains.

Girl into number. Elly, I fear, is a natural Platonist. Though she no longer lives in it, she prefers a world stripped bare of the adventitious accretions that to ordinary minds make it interesting and precious—a world reduced to its essentials of pattern, shape, and number. That preference can of course be seen, for her as for Plato, as a retreat, an abandonment of the real, disorderly world which causes anxiety and pain. Yet sometimes I think that to interpret it so is to miss the point. That golden baby circling its spot laughed aloud with pleasure. Elly's delight is spontaneous and free. If it seems unnatural, that is because it is uncommon in young children. Joy cannot in itself be unnatural or unhealthy. Few of us share the joy Pythagoras must have felt in his theorem, but we can all recognize it. Order in the world is something to take joy in—on this theologians and mathematicians agree. Elly's joy is of extreme simplicity compared to theirs, yet I think it is of the same kind. I cannot be sorry it exists, only that it comes so much easier than the other, more human kinds of pleasure.

Elly herself can end this chapter better than I can. We shall watch her as she plays with her new map, the one she insisted on getting as soon as she saw it in the college office. I saw no reason to bring it home, as she already had one posted, but we did, and with uncharacteristic effort she has found some tape and has put it up near the other. "42a," she says. "42a this map. This? This?" I do not understand, but her insistence makes me examine the map and I perceive what evidently she has known all along. The maps look identical but they are not. Five or six buildings, perhaps, out of a hundred have been altered or replaced, necessitating a revised legend; 42a is a new addition.

Elly continues: "Zero heating plant?" I contradict; understanding her to mean "no heating plant," I reassure her. "One heating plant, there's the heating plant." But she goes on saying it. I do not understand why until she takes my pencil and herself writes in a zero by the picture of the building. Then I see that all the other buildings are numbered. Only the heating plant is not. "They forgot," I say, falling into one of our familiar frames.

"They forgot!" crows Elly, over and over again, eight, ten times in succession. I hear her, but my eyes are elsewhere, and I do not notice what she is doing. When I look up I see that she is laboriously printing, as the first item in the legend, 0 HEATING PLANT. She miscopies, but she does not lose her cool. "They forgot!" She erases, corrects. "Forgot!" And we go down to breakfast, after one half hour of happy activity.

After breakfast she returns to the map. Fascinated, she enjoys it, singing a little song. Now and then she tenses, shivers in a paroxysm of pleased excitement, but mostly she is relaxed, absorbed in the delights of notation, enjoying the relation between abstraction and reality. "Walk downtown?" And in her mind she does. "Don't cross-uh street! Buy six M-uh-M? Buy four Necco? Buy seven shoestring candy? Buy five gumdrop! Little gumdrop. Get out-uh candy store. Go bakery. Buy-uh two cookie. Get-uh one big cake. Get-uh lot-uh cupcake. Go drugstore. Get a tempacan [temperature = thermometer]. Elly too sick [she is laughing]. Buy three new bottle. No. Zero bottle. Buy eight candy box. Buy nine new gumdrop. Buy ten new candy box. Buy eleven star candy. Buy fourteen new Necco. Lot-uh new M-uh-M?"

The hairs of her head are numbered.

15 ' Now and Later

ELLY has been under siege now for six and a half years. What is she like today?

Someone who saw her now for the first time and had no knowledge of her history would probably not think her autistic at all. Speech penetrates to the ears that for so long seemed not to hear; the eyes that saw not can now register the full variety of the world. The autistic isolation itself is much attenuated. Seeing her laughing and squealing with her sisters or enjoying the marshmallow game with her father, an observer might remark the immaturity of her affection but he would not think of her as a child particularly withdrawn. It might even be possible for him to hear her sense of community break through into words, as when, taking a hand mirror, she snuggles close, contemplates our two images in the mirror, and says "Mama *love* you!"

If he came when I was out he could see how she relates to someone who is not a member of the family—to the warm, understanding woman whose help makes it possible for me to get away at all. Mrs. Gerry's best qualifications are her own six children and eighteen grandchildren. She brings Elly surprises, lets her watch while she mixes and bakes, persuades her to pull her boots on, gives her firm and loving discipline when she gets out of line. Elly goes to stores with her, visits her at home. "Mrs.

Gerry ha' color TV!" Like the live-in mother's-helpers I can now do without, Mrs. Gerry is another focus of Elly's increasing capacity for affection.

One no longer has to be a miracle worker to reach her; any friendly person who is at home with two-year-olds can do it. If you were to come to our house and wanted to get to know Elly, it could easily be done. She would indeed pay no attention to you at first, as she has come to expect that adults begin by talking in ways she cannot understand. So I would put her hand on yours to bring you into contact,* tell her your name, and from then on it would be up to you. If you roughhoused with her, or drew pictures or provided candy or took her for a ride, she would "relate" to you as satisfactorily as you please, smiling, laughing, taking part in your games, even talking about them. If, however, you asked her hard questions, like what her name is, or talked in language above a three-year-old's comprehension, she would lose interest. She would ignore you again—not look through you or beyond you, as long ago, but ignore you as any child ignores an uncomprehending adult.

If you were then to turn your attention to me and we were to talk at any length she would become restive, then demanding. "Mama talk!" she would complain, but her annoyance would go no farther into speech than that. It would express itself in undifferentiated squeals and creaky-door noises, in a crescendo of anxious, edgy (but still ludicrously accurate) evocations of rock-and-roll, in tense and jerky dancing up and down, in awkward imitations of falling down—perhaps if it all went on too long, in crying. I would either terminate the conversation then or take a firm stand: "Sometimes I talk to you, sometimes I talk to other people." Elly would then retire, probably to her bed, and bawl,

---

* I remember the question of a psychologist-friend who came to visit: "Did the psychiatrist say you could do that?" I said I hadn't asked him, but that when he saw Elly he seemed very pleased with her progress. "It certainly is an unusual arrangement," she said.

and after a while she would stop and I would hope everything was all right and that this experience would be, not a trauma, but in fact what I wished it—one more infinitesimal step towards the realization that she cannot totally possess even those whom she loves best.

I am going to interrupt the narrative at this point. Where Elly is today can best be communicated, not by summary and inter-pretation, but by presenting a few glimpses of her as she has appeared in action at different times in recent months. The reader will be able to make his own interpretations—among them, no doubt, some I have not thought of—and judge for himself how far Elly has come and how far there is still to go.

Elly is in her room playing with her doll house. Having picked up some of the scattered toys and books, I am sitting near her on the floor occupying myself with an interlocking gear toy. I am bored and quiescent. Elly is playing well, with little reference to me, but if I read she will find a way to bring my attention back and if I go away she will stop and follow me. I have learned that it works best to saturate her desire for community, to let her possess me completely for an hour or two; then when she has had all she can use she will be ready to do without me—for a little while.

Now she is perching all the little dolls in a row on the doll-house roof. She has a lot of them—the conventional family and many extras. She moves the hinged roof and they all fall down. She laughs with pleasure; clearly, that's why she put them up there. I suggest, without emotion, that they are crying, are hurt. She laughs some more, says "Can't ha' supper on *roof!*" I agree. She begins to imitate, in a high falsetto, the sound of dolls crying, with excited amusement. Noticing my gear arrangement, she has an idea: "Doll go merry-go-round, feel better." She puts them all on the merry-go-round, one per gear, and they stop crying. "Wan' be happy, yes!" says Elly. One doll begins to cry again. Elly puts her back on the roof, again to fall. "Poor girl," she says, laughing.

"Ride-uh-boat?" She neatly sits them all in her pull-toy ark, a game I suggested some two weeks before. I had, in fact, suggested that the boat take them to the A&P, since Elly had remarked that they had no car and could not go. But I've forgotten this, and so I ask if they are going to the island in the ferry. But of course they are going to the A&P. They will continue going there, and the dolls will continue falling off the roof; new ways to play do not come easy. Yet they come, bringing with them two questions which are perhaps only one: why do they come at all, or why do they not come more often?

A month later, Elly has another doll-house game. "*Walk* to A&P, get a bo'll wine, drink all up!" She picks up a tiny bottle from the doll kitchen and, making as if to uncork it, produces with her curved tongue a perfect pop. We both laugh, I with surprise, she with pride. She has been praised for popping with her tongue, but this is the first time the trick has had meaning. She begins to offer wine to the dolls. In a cheery chirp she anticipates their reaction. "Baby 'no thank you'! Grandma drink all up! Teacher drink all up! Boy 'no thank you!' " I ask, "Elly, do you want some wine?" "Elly 'no thank you!' "

Elly's dolls go to the hospital, they sit on the pot, they have parties. They do these things repetitively and in patterns, but still it is a pleasure to watch them. There are other ways of playing, equally cheerful for Elly but less so for the observer.

It is Saturday. "Nice day," says Elly. "Vacation day." With a gaiety that seems particularly relaxed and spontaneous she begins to play: she is arranging objects on a tray—a doll, a puppet, some National Wildlife stamps, a plastic Indian, a hairbrush, a catalogue, two books, six assorted doll-garments. Happily she lays them side by side, patting each. "And shoe—and cloth"—she covers them with a red handkerchief. "Pretty!"

The arrangement is without meaning. The objects have no relationship in actuality. Fantasy would be hard put to it to provide one, and there is no sign of fantasy here. These are a set, in the mathematical sense, and Elly is pleased with it—the set of objects on this tray. At other times a rudimentary fantasy will give an arrangement an eerie social meaning, as when Elly sets out the letters on the scrabble board and informs us they are having a dinner party. Other games are even more discouraging. These we do not share. Daily Elly empties her toy-basket, pulls her books onto the floor, systematically dumps out every jigsaw puzzle in the house to sift the pieces through her fingers, as she sifts marbles, peanuts, even dolls. If I could always be playing with her, feeding her imagination and sustaining her attention, perhaps she would not play like that. But I cannot. Her play covers the whole range from utter sterility to the amusing surprises of the two incidents I described first. But such incidents, though increasingly frequent, are not typical. They exhibit the extreme of inventiveness and flexibility that Elly can as yet reach.

Play has its surprises, and (so far have we come) conversation has them too.

Elly says, "Elly three hundred!"

I say, "Three hundred is too old, Elly will die." (This is a concept that will bear some work, since it is so far based exclusively on squashed mosquitoes.)

Elly says cheerfully, "Too old, die," and mimes it. "Great big dead, too old! Carry me? Elly too tired? Elly three hundred, yes!"

Elly has been talking a good deal about dirt recently—dog dirt, doll dirt, our dirt. It means feces. We have accepted this, particularly since her fuzzy pronunciation does much to denaturize the word in company. But her speech is improving and she is, after all, in school. I want her to learn, even if she cannot understand, that dirt is not an all-purpose conversational gambit. So I say, "I don't want to talk about dirt." Yesterday at dinner I had said the same thing. Elly remembers—not only what I said but where and when. She makes a supreme effort to imagine what not wanting to talk about dirt might entail. We are not at dinner now, but for her the words are still embedded in their first context and it is in that context that she must envisage what I might regard as suitable conversation. She says trimphantly, "I [equals, of course, 'you, mother'] want to talk about corn muffin!"

So slowly understanding grows, and even concern for others. "Becky eye *pink*. Need ointment." I recognize my own voice in the conventionalized tones of her concern. "Becky eye all better, Becky ha' pink eye, yes! Don't touch-uh-eye, make-uh-*itch*! Leave eye alone, Becky. Feel better, yes. Becky eye all better, yes. She *hurt*. Ow! Ointment in it. See? All better. Sore eye. Becky get sad. See, Becky eye itch. Look. Becky cry? No! Becky be happy! Becky sad? No! Becky put-uh-ointment in it."

And gradually the forms of social interaction are refined. Coming in from my day at the college I greet her.

"Hi, bird."

"Hi, bird," she echoes.

"Say 'hi, *Mama*.'" (On second thought) "Am I your bird?"

"Yes."

"That's all right, then you can say 'bird' too."

"Hi, bird too."

This is Elly in her own home, occasionally frustrated and anxious (if she has decided that the number of those dolls is significant, there will be hell to pay if she loses one), but in the main gay, active, full of cheerful noises and cheerful words. But if you were to watch her outside it you would see something very different. Outside, children play, familiar children who have lived long in the neighborhood. No such conversations take place with them. They play in ways Elly does not share. They pull wagons, ride tricycles, run in and out of houses for toys and

257

equipment, organize tea-parties, snow fights, and hide-and-seek. Elly swings and swings, or eats snow, or plays with sand as of old, dribbling it from a spoon. I can get her to make cakes, but why should another child make the effort, or accommodate itself to her rigidities? "You want to put icing on it, Elly?" Anxiously Elly replies "No?"

The children have learned not to talk to Elly unless I am there to act as interpreter—an interpreter not even of speech, but of behavior. It is simply too hard for them. Sometimes there is a brief contact, as in taking turns on a swing. But where, either because of inability or shyness, neither party will take the initiative, there can be no real interaction. I am trying to encourage Elly to answer when a child says "Hi, Elly." So far, I am encouraged—but the child is bewildered—if she echoes "Hi, Elly," back.

But here too there are mysteries. Elly can be contrary, and she knows how to tease. She will rarely greet someone she knows well, but on occasion she will rush up to some college boy she has never seen before and embrace him on the street. He, of course, is as embarrassed as I am, and Elly looks at us with mischief in her eyes. Or she makes—not often—a clumsy overture to another child, an overture that would have been reciprocated had she made it when she was two, to another two-year-old, but that normal children now find bizarre and frightening. It is hard to build sociality on these fitful and easily discouraged advances.

Elly is now in the class for the educable retarded at our local public school. After three years with normal children, the private school considered it impossible to move her into even their extremely small first grade. Ironically, it was because she had made so much progress that they could not keep her. She was no more strange than she had always been, but as she has improved her strangeness has acquired a much higher visibility. Now that she can "act out," she is no longer the silent child who took directions and caused no trouble, but a spring-tight, hyperactive little girl who uses her voice and her whole body to express the emotions, positive and negative, that are at length available to her. Newly at large in the world of feeling, she must learn to control it, and that without converting control into repression.

It is not easy. Her first weeks in the public school required manifold adjustments and imposed severe tensions on teacher, pupils, and administration—tensions that were absorbed with a flexibility, imagination, and good will that quite literally pass belief. That I do not describe them here at length only illustrates that there is never space for all the important things. Elly's new teacher knows that Elly's very difficulties show that she is now ready to profit from what no home care and no one-to-one relationship, however devoted, can give her; the opportunity to be led, step by step, with imagination and understanding, into minimal interaction, not with a sympathetic adult, but with her peers.

Elly is learning a great deal in the new school. Slowly and reluctantly she moves through the primer. With eager enthusiasm she fills out the exercises in visual perception that the other children find so hard. Stage by stage she advances in arithmetic. But all this is secondary; the teacher does not need me to tell her so. For Elly, for whom each interaction must be learned separately and again and again, the important subject is Deportment. To speak in greeting, face up, voice audible, while standing neither so close as to embarrass nor so far that the greeting goes unnoticed—to share attention—to respond to an overture—to take part in a game—to listen with patience and ultimately with comprehension to a storybook or to a schoolmate's simple account of the rabbit he keeps in his backyard—these are Elly's lessons. She may be solving quadratic equations before she learns them all.

The ten retarded children in her class are good teachers. They are more tolerant of deviant behavior than normal children would be, knowing their own behavior leaves much to be desired and has not always met with acceptance. The wise and loving young woman who teaches them knows how to show them that they can help Elly and feel good about themselves at the same time. As one boy said in the first bad days, with satisfaction and surprise, "Elly can do arithmetic better than me but I *behave* better." And it is *behavior*, in its fullest sense, that Elly has now to learn. The private school, even as they excluded her, expressed dismay that she had now to be put into a class for the retarded. "She's really a bright little girl." I do not know what "really" means in this context, but I know that these retarded children, far from holding her back, are light-years ahead of her in adequacy and function. Taking my semi-weekly cafeteria duty, I listen astonished as these supposedly backward children assert their full humanity. "Hey, what're we having for lunch? You want to know what I did yesterday? What's this stuff? I hate prunes, don't you? You want mine? Will you play with me after? We need the ball, Johnny's got it. Come on, don't be mean, Johnny! He's always like that. Do you want me to pop you one?" I listen in wonder. This is retardation, these pronouns, these prepositions, these verbs with their auxiliaries and their tenses, this mastery of verbal and social idiom? Yet some of these children, at thirteen, cannot learn with constant repetition mathematical relationships that to Elly at eight are intuitively obvious. Her disabilities are no more mysterious than theirs. How can they miss these clear simplicities, when they can learn so well the infinitely more complex modes of social interaction? What have they that Elly lacks, and why do her abilities not interconnect and ramify to allow a comprehension of wider experience?

However clearly one recognizes such questioning as useless at worst, at best as premature, one is forced back on it at last. I have earned the right to my speculations and I present them here, hygienically cordoned off and plainly labeled for what they are.

It is not up to me to decide between the various labels that are offered to describe my child's condition, but there is one that I have come to think is clearly inapplicable. My child is not, I think, a "disturbed child." Now and then things happen that are too much for her capacities, and these disturb her. But the longer I watch her, the better I know her, and the more there is to know, the more I am convinced that what we are concerned with is not a disturbance but a lack. The screw is not loose, it is missing. I dredge up crude terms from the innocent past when those who took it upon themselves to describe aberrant human beings did not yet veil their uncertainties under precise terminology. These crude terms still suggest an important distinction. Elly is not crazy. She is not feeble-minded; her mind, for those aspects of the world she can make sense of, is sharp and retentive. She is *simple*-minded—and whatever the progress she has made, she is simple-hearted as well. Watching as Elly slowly refines her capacity to feel, I remember what Jacques May told me—and this doctor, whose fruitless search for help for his twin autistic sons * led him and his wife to found a school for others like them, is a sensitive and experienced guide: "Autism is only a symptom," he said. "As the child grows, if it is sympathetically handled, the autism recedes. But the child does not thereby become normal." It does not, and this leads me back to what may have seemed the least significant of the four categories under which I described the baby Elly. I now wonder if the clue to Elly's abnormality may not be found, not in her blindness and deafness, which are gone, or her isolation, which can now be breached by anyone who tries, but in the phenomena I described under the heading of "willed weakness"—in her overwhelming unwillingness to affect the environment.

Over the past five years we have watched Elly's passivity change to hyperactivity, leading us to reflect that one must be very conscious, in reading case histories, of the case *as history*, for it is not always recognized that the same child—or condition

---

* Described in *A Physician Looks at Psychiatry*, John Day, 1958.

—may present totally different aspects at different stages. Depending on Elly's state of mind, her activity may be relaxed, or tense and excited, but more likely it will be the latter, and the more she is enjoying herself the tenser it will be. Because she is so active, it takes sensitive observation to notice how rigidly circumscribed is that activity and how much energy and imagination it takes to enrich its content or extend its range—energy and imagination which normal children themselves supply but which Elly must still, for the most part, take in from outside. Spring-tight, vigorous, and wiry, Elly is in effect still weak.

Elly has learned to do most of the things she did not do when she was four. She turns knobs, she opens windows, she puts her zipper together and zips it, she unbuttons buttons if there are not too many, she will button one. She goes downstairs foot over foot as normal children do. She jumps down one step—she was seven before she became willing to do that—and recently she has jumped two. Carefully she climbs alone up snow banks and fences, if the person who is with her stays out of reach of her searching hand. She dresses herself in a finite time, if her clothes are laid out for her and she is constantly spurred on to take the next step. She toilets herself, not on impulse, but by a self-established routine night and morning. This month she took the brush and brushed her hair. Occasionally she has even come out with the proud, impatient "Elly do" so familiar to mothers of normal three-year-olds, as she mails a letter or pushes open a heavy door.

But she is eight years old. She does not ride a tricycle. Unless encouraged to do so, she does not pull a wagon, and she does not manage a sled. She will not climb a ladder or go down a slide, though she did both at three and though this summer she climbed without protest down a twenty-foot ladder into a boat in order to go sailing. She cannot snap a snap or operate a safety pin or untie a knot or tie her shoes. She still takes your hand to effect what she wants. It is no longer a denial of you as a human being;

she may be in close contact with you, talking and laughing. She may—she probably will—respond to a good-humored "You do it, Elly." But it is six and a half years now and still she tries to avoid action on her own.

Her manual dexterity, once so remarkable, appears so no longer. She has not increased it over the past four years and normal children have caught up with and surpassed her. Her letters were good at age five; they are as good today, no better. They are clearly good enough for her; she puts them down, fast and casual, and makes no further effort. At school, if her work is good, she gets a star. At first that delighted her, but now she is equally pleased with a zero or an 80. It is not that she doesn't know the difference; she does. But any notation pleases her, and the star is no longer novel enough to motivate sustained effort. In fact, Elly will sustain effort only within the framework of a stereotyped task, and even there she does so only *faute de mieux*. She herself will type out the numbers from one to fifty, but she would much rather have me do it.

Elly types easily now, but two years ago she was as weak with the typewriter as she had been at three with faucets and switches. At first she used my fingers, then I used hers. It was weeks before she would press a key hard enough to make a mark of her own. The process repeats itself with each new skill. Certainly I can teach her to tie her shoes if I try hard enough. Perhaps this year I will do it, or perhaps her teacher will, as Elly in the service of weakness mobilizes the vanished blindness and deafness, ignoring instructions, averting her eyes from the task, even closing them. We can teach her one new skill, or five, or ten; we can insist, ignore her protests; we can batter down her resistance. But there are hundreds of such skills inherent in the condition of a normal eight-year-old, and how much expense of spirit can we—or she—afford?

It is of course impossible to separate this physical inertia from the mental and emotional inertia which accompany it. Again, it is characteristic of the condition, not unique to Elly. Rosalind Oppenheim * describes her son's inability to sustain any activity— this of a child who at four endlessly rolled a ball across the floor but who at six, still speechless, could read and answer questions in writing. Unlike Elly, he read stories, if mother or teacher shepherded him through page by page, asking questions at the end of each. He enjoyed the stories too, but though the book was left temptingly available week after week he never once picked it up on his own. And so it is with Elly. Whatever she does, no matter how well it begins, peters out. There is no forward motion, no self-sustained expansion of mastery—in play, in self-help, in drawing, in reading, even in the numbers she finds so fascinating—except in completion of a routine, or sustained by someone else with a support that is in constant danger of becoming a substitute for her own activity or—if it lures her into activity that is too successful—of causing her to abandon it altogether.

Of how many remarkable feats, experienced with how much hope, have I had to record that "She did this only once," or "twice in six months," or "no longer shows interest"? Her liking for letters and her memory for their combinations is still remarkable. Another child who possessed the ability to memorize a new word overnight would have been reading within a month. Elly reads voluntarily not at all—unless we count the OFF-ON on switches or the NO PARKING signs whose nonsignificance she embraces with delight, perhaps because it does not threaten her with further progress. Elly can understand spelling too, or so I infer from the fact that for days she has been writing VAKE and GAKE and correctly pronouncing them. But when I suggested she add TAKE and LAKE she said "No?" I knew better than

* Author of "They Said Our Child Was Hopeless"; in an unpublished letter to Dr. Bernard Rimland.

to insist, but she avoids them as if I had drilled her in them daily.

Even in the area of learning where she is most at home, inertia holds her back. It would be possible, by proper selection, to make Elly appear extremely precocious mathematically. When I was still diffidently showing her that $1 + 1 = 2$, she assembled two six-inch blocks and a seven-inch one from her set and remarked, without counting them, that $6 + 6 + 7 = 19$. Yet today in school, six months later, she makes all the usual mistakes in performing far simpler three-digit sums. This summer, when someone said we needed thirty hamburgers for a picnic, Elly, who had seemingly been paying no attention, volunteered that $15 + 15 = 30$. When she was given a box of 48 crayons to add to her set of 64, she knew by some process of her own that she had 112, although she had not yet learned to perform addition that involves carrying. Watching such isolated feats, it is hard not to speculate on what she could do if she would. Yet they remain isolated, and if one tries to elaborate on them Elly resists. Inertia and passivity take new forms but they do not disappear. They ensure that Elly remains a very imperfect *idiot savant*.

To sum up: what seems impaired is not only the capacity for affect, but another capacity perhaps even more fundamental, the capacity for undertaking exploratory behavior and sustaining it. We know little about what we still call by its old-fashioned name of curiosity, still less about the qualities we describe, with more sophistication, as "motivation" or "drive." All of us know, however, that normal individuals vary enormously in the degree to which they possess these qualities. We know that curiosity, motivation, and drive are affected by the stresses of the environment, but we know also that even babies differ markedly in their desire to explore the world around them, for no apparent environmental reason. There are those from whom no medicine bottle is safe, who pull every light cord, who poke into every drawer to see if something interesting might be hiding there, and others (like my three normal children) who are much less interested in physical exploration. And there is Elly, who is not interested in exploration at all.

Families can reinforce curiosity and drive in their children, or discourage them. Societies can do the same; we all know that three thousand years of Egyptian intelligence is a very different thing from three hundred years of Greek. But however it is reinforced or discouraged, all normal human beings exhibit the drive to learn and to explore—indeed all animals do, our cousins the apes most of all. Years ago W. I. Thomas listed "a desire for new experience and stimulation as one of the instincts," * and indeed it must be so. What if it were not? If animals were born without that positive enjoyment of new experience which leads them to explore and master their environment, neither they nor their species would survive. Curiosity and drive are essential to evolutionary survival, and if we can expect any characteristics to be built into animal biology it would be these. One day we may know how such things are built in—into brain impulses, into nerve structure, into blood chemistry, into mechanisms we cannot yet suspect. Even now we—not neurophysiologists only, but all of us—know how will and motivation can be reduced, even temporarily annihilated, by physical causes such as aging, sleeplessness, or drugs. Most of us feel such a reduction as unpleasant, but it need not be. Suppose a child felt always the detachment that in certain people is produced by LSD? Such a child would not initiate action, would welcome the limits that made it unnecessary, would, as its irreversible growth engaged it inevitably with the world's complexity, seek out and enjoy the unchanging patterns that affirm stability in a world of Becoming.

The inertia of such a child might affect even cognitive func-

---

* Cited by Rimland, *Infantile Autism*, p. 209, in a discussion that readers who are interested in this possibility will find extremely rewarding.

tions, so that ideas that normal babies associate without apparent effort would be connected only with difficulty, and past experience would be only minimally available for use in new situations. All the autistic child's deficiencies could be seen as converging in this one: the deficiency which renders it unable or unwilling to put together the primary building blocks of experience. It affects the senses, it affects speech, it affects action, it affects emotion. The autistic child does not move naturally from one sound to another, from one word to another, from one idea to another, from one experience to another. Yet reality, as human beings experience it, is a web of connections to be made. The reality of persons and emotions is the most complex web of all. The baby who can make little sense of the simpler interconnections will make even less sense of these complexities; it will be "deficient in affective functions." Because this deficiency is more conspicuous than the others, it will tempt us to consider it as primary. But if over years we watch this deficiency steadily diminish, while others simply change their faces, we will begin to wonder.

Not all individuals possess all the characteristics of the species —even the essential ones. By imagining an individual born with the capacity to explore the environment, but with whatever it is that determines the drive to do so absent or grossly impaired, we can arrive at all the characteristics of the autistic child. Because of the negative survival-value of the trait, such individuals would be uncommon—as autistic children are. But such a hypothesis would explain much that other explanations leave untouched.

I have deferred discussing one last deficiency of Elly's until now, almost at the end of the story, because it is so pervasive and difficult to catch hold of that the appreciation of it has need of all that has gone before. It is directly related to the lack of exploratory drive, for it concerns Elly's signal lack of interest in future experience. My husband thought of the word for it—one day, watching as Elly moved with agonizing slowness through the hundreds of motions that were necessary before she could reach the enjoyable experience of school, he exclaimed, "It's the sense of purpose that's missing!" We began then to think about purpose and what it entails, and to relate it to a lack in Elly we had long felt without being able to give it a place in the total picture.

Purpose entails drive, and the capacity to sustain. But it entails another capacity as well, one which itself plays an obvious part in motivation—the capacity to *imagine*, to bring to mind and take seriously what is not, or not yet, present to immediate experience. The middle-class boy does not need much imagination to see himself as a stable and prosperous professional man; the boy from the ghetto, to sustain the same vision, must possess imagination to a remarkable degree. I return to Elly's simplicity of mind, the emptiness of her horizons.

She is curiously matter-of-fact. The Institute, long ago, told us she had many fears, and at the time we were quite ready to assent. Fuller experience has made us less so. Fear is not mere anxiety, such as Elly exhibits daily when some trivial thing goes wrong. Fear envisages; it imagines; it is anxiety in anticipation. It is fear, not of what is visibly present, but of what *may be going to happen*. If this distinction is granted, I cannot recall a situation in which Elly seemed to feel fear, and I can recall many in which fear seemed natural and she exhibited none. She could not, for example, be brought to fear traffic. She knows about looking both ways before crossing a street, but she never does it unasked, and if asked she looks without looking. The idea that a car might really hurt her seems to defy communication—and this though at five she was actually knocked down by a truck. I have tried to make use of a certain three-legged dog in this connection, but he conveys no realization of danger, although he provides an occasion for ritual joking. "Dog hurt! Only three legs! Go hospital!" It is not that Elly does not *know* what cars can do. It is that she cannot *imagine* it.

Her attitude toward dogs in general provides another illustration of the difference between fear, which envisages what is not present, and anxiety, which does not. Elly is anxious in the presence of rambunctious dogs, but she would never refuse to visit a house where from previous experience she might expect to meet one. Relevant here also is the absence of hallucinations that has been noted in autistic children. What is hallucination but imagination so vivid that it takes over the very mechanisms of the senses themselves? In contrast, Elly's sense of what is and is not the case is unusually sharp; it is the main source of her humor. At four, her father taught her to pretend, mimicking bedtime, laying her on the floor with a sheet of paper for a blanket, a stick for a doll, while she laughed at the ridiculousness of it all. At seven and eight she could pretend a little for herself (significantly, "real" and "pretend" were adjectives she learned very easily). Seeing her suck her thumb, I told her it was chocolate; she herself added "strawberry" and "vanilla." Recently she stroked me, giggling "Furry, furry Mama!" There could be no possible doubt that this was a joke, part of a constant and enjoyable interplay between truth and falsehood. "Is Mama downtown?" "No!" "Did Jill go downtown?" "Yes!"

No hallucinations, no fantasies. We could use some; they would make her play much richer. Nor have we ever seen any evidence of nightmares. Her focuses of severe anxiety all have the same characteristic—they are immediate and visible. I do not say that she is like the boy in the Grimms' fairy tale who could not shudder. But it is certainly true that one of the reasons it is so hard to read her the simplest children's story is that she is as yet incapable of understanding why Peter Rabbit was afraid of Mr. Mac-Gregor, because for her out of sight is out of mind.

As with fear, so with other emotions. To attain its full human complexity, emotion must include an element of imagination. Jealousy would be a minor affliction indeed if we felt it only in the actual presence of the loved one. Without the power to envisage, to interconnect, to bring to bear past and future, we should experience only a very simplified version of hatred or affection or love. And if the deficiency in imagination is relevant to deficiency of affect, its relevance to the deficiency of exploratory activity is even clearer. Recently I played hunt-the-button with Elly and discovered that she could envisage no new hiding places. Though I restricted the hiding places to my own person, Elly could find the button only if left in plain sight, or in places I had hidden it previously.

A final illustration of this matter-of-factness is her attitude toward blood. Blood can be a touchy subject for children and psychiatrists—for children, the focus of much emotion and fantasy, for psychiatrists, of much theory. Elly knows about menstrual blood. In the general lack of privacy attendant on life with Elly I made an effort to keep this inconspicuous, but over a period of years there are bound to be slip-ups. There was reason to worry about Elly's reaction to blood, especially since there were no words for explaining the phenomenon to her. I was not reassured when to "Red blood, hurt!" she added "Leave your tail alone," showing that she had made a connection between masturbation and menstruation, which I was as far from being able to discourage as I was from having suggested it. But she exhibited no anxiety, let alone fantasy or fear, and subsequent developments showed that her matter-of-factness was not a blind. There are indeed patterns to be found in reality, as plausible as those we find in psychology books, but considerably less interesting. "Brush teeth, red blood hurt," Elly remarked soon after, and it was true. Mother has only to brush her teeth to produce red blood; Elly picks a scab and red blood comes. "Don't pick-uh nose, ha' red blood!"—and Elly has in fact induced several nosebleeds in this way. It is all of a piece, and the fabric is very simple.

Where then are we now, and where are we going? The social worker at Hampstead told me we could never make up the lost years – and if there is a biological deficiency, we cannot make that up either. Yet Elly has improved and is improving. She has moved far beyond what she seemed likely to achieve in her early years, and a comparison of her case with other histories of children claimed as autistic could be used to support considerable optimism.

Elly's psychiatrist is encouraging too; a year ago he told me of a boy he knew of who seemed much like Elly and who ended up at Harvard. But then he adds that there is no point in looking even twelve months ahead. Neither he, nor we, nor anyone else knows what will become of her. The most we can say is that at one time the prognosis was nearly hopeless, and that now there is no prognosis at all.

We cannot assess the results of our work, or even understand what we have actually been doing. Were we changing Elly's assessment of the world? Were we slowly, painfully performing for the emotions what the strange new physical disciplines seem to do for damaged brains, as injured children and adults crawl themselves back to function? Were we too, by activities repeated a thousand times and more, training other brain cells and other nerves to take over missing functions? Were we indeed doing anything, or would what has happened have happened without us? There can be no controlled experiments with the same human being. We shall never know.

It is a long time since we first recognized that "something was wrong with Elly." Perhaps these common words are the best ones after all; they do not disguise under multifoliate terminology the plain fact that no one yet knows what. It has been a long siege. As a siege, it has been successful, for we have reached Elly. Whatever else she is, she is no longer walled off from affection. Yet we are not the first to discover that to reach another human being is not in itself to cure; we are not the first to learn that though the contact which seemed impossible may at length be made, it only opens the future to the work to be done. The expectation of cure is a luxury we have learned to do without. We work, and others work with us, and Elly grows and slowly she comes to do a little work herself. We work for what we can accomplish; we accomplish new things with each month that passes. We get our satisfaction from our motion forward. No more than Elly do we envisage the future.

16 ⧓ The Others

WHEN much effort is expended for a goal that remains uncertain, the detached mind is bound to wonder if it is worth it. We who are engaged in the labor learn not to ask such questions, since we can afford only such thoughts as strengthen effort and do not paralyze it, but even we cannot suppress them wholly. The child in the poem could not help asking, "And what good came of it at last?" And of course we could not go on if we had not found some answer.

If nothing more were accomplished than an expansion of the possibilities for one flawed human being, some might accept that the work was worth while. But more has come of it than that. Out of it has come, for ourselves and I hope for others, an increment of experience which is, I hope, implicit in every chapter of this book. It will not take many words to make it explicit; most readers who have penetrated this far will already have understood for themselves that what we have learned watching the slow-motion growth of one small rudimentary human being behind invisible walls has applications that go beyond this single child. We saw Elly as a citadel which it was our choice to attack, because the equilibrium she had found denied the possibility of growth. There are others, very different from Elly, who like her cannot meet the challenge of their world and who achieve an equilibrium at the expense of their potentialities. I am a teacher, and from Elly I have learned much about students—about normal students, many of high intelligence, who talk and read and understand and go about their business and yet who challenge our ideas of normal and abnormal because they are so like Elly. The severest problem of teaching—particularly in teaching those we coolly call the "culturally disadvantaged"—is in motivation, in the confrontation of the array of blocks against learning and against achievement itself. The blocks are many and their disguises are subtle—blocks against a subject, against an approach, against a necessary way of working; blocks against continuing education; blocks against seeking a job in line with ability. The personality whose major work is to deny or frustrate its own potentialities operates in ways more complex than Elly's, though hers are perhaps no less refined. I have lived with learning blocks eight years, watched their inception, seen them so potent that they can inhibit not only learning but the primary faculties of sight and hearing as well. From a child who can counterfeit deafness there is much to learn about how human beings limit or destroy themselves.

Strange Elly is so like us. In her the immobilization that afflicts us all, often or sometimes, temporarily or in full finality, before the task that seems impossible is seen magnified into full visibility. I watch her squint her eyes shut before a reality she doesn't want to look at, and recognize my students and myself.

I learn from Elly and I learn from my students; they also teach me about Elly. In the early years, I knew a student who was himself emerging from a dark citadel; he had been to the Menninger Clinic and to other places too, and he knew from inside the ways of thought I had to learn. "Things get too much for her and she just turns down the volume," he told me. I remembered that, because I have seen it so often since, in Elly and in so many others. Human beings fortify themselves in many ways. Numbness, weakness, irony, inattention, silence, suspicion are only a few of the materials out of which the personality constructs its walls. With experience gained in my siege of Elly I mount smaller sieges. Each one is undertaken with hesitation; to try to help anyone is an arrogance. But Elly is there to remind me that to fail to try is a dereliction. Not all my sieges are successful. But where I fail, I have learned that I fail because of my own clumsiness and inadequacy, not because the enterprise is impossible. However formidable the fortifications, they can be breached. I have not found one person, however remote, however hostile, who did not wish for what he seemed to fight. Of all the things that Elly has given, the most precious is this faith, a faith experience has almost transformed into certain knowledge: that inside the strongest citadel he can construct, the human being awaits his besieger.

Though I once thought of this as a long chapter, I realized in time that it could not be. I have not the right to be circumstantial here. Elly's privacy I have not respected (though I have changed her name, and the names of my other children) because I thought that the good that might come from telling her story would outweigh the hurt she might suffer if one day she should grow well enough to read it. But to tell stories about anyone else is neither right nor necessary. Other besiegers—street-workers, doctors, ministers, teachers, lovers, and friends—know what I know and will supply examples for me.

When I began this book I had an epigraph for it—the great sonnet of assault in which John Donne implored his God to batter his defenses down. I decided that I could not put it at the beginning, since it would haze over this story with an atmosphere of piety which would be totally false. Yet this book is, among other things, a personal record, and if it is to be a true one I cannot leave out these words which sustained me so many times when I had little else:

Batter my heart, three-personed God, for you
As yet but knock, breathe, shine, and seek to mend;
That I may rise and stand, o'erthrow me, and bend
Your force to break, blow, burn and make me new.
I, like an usurped town, to another due,
Labor to admit you, but oh, to no end;
Reason, your viceroy in me, me should defend,
But is captived, and proves weak or untrue.
Yet dearly I love you, and would be lovèd fain,
But am betrothed unto your enemy:
Divorce me, untie, or break that knot again,
Take me to you, imprison me, for I
Except you enthrall me, never shall be free,
Nor ever chaste, except you ravish me.

It is all in theological terms, but let them stand. They are no more false than any others. I know no better description of the terrible imperative of the assault of love, which brings us godless ones as close as we can come to the experience that others call God.

Yet it is not with myself that this book should end, but with Elly and with the others, and so I will tell one more story. I can tell it because it is not about a friend, but a stranger. One bright, warm afternoon a year ago I was working in the garden when I was accosted by a student—not a student of mine, but one of the sheltered and fortunate habitués of my husband's college. This young man, in his madras shorts, was naked to the waist and barefoot, he was leaning on a pretty girl, and he was staggering drunk. To my astonishment, he seemed to have something to say to me. All sorts of feelings rose up in me, as that college boys were losing whatever vestiges of shame they had ever had, that after all there were certain standards, that he ought to know better than to speak to a professor's wife in his condition. If Elly had not taught me to wait and listen and look beneath the surface—if I had not learned from her that dignity is the most expendable of all satisfactions—I would have told him off, or moved away. Instead I began to hear what he was saying. "You don't know me," he said, "and I wouldn't be saying this if I weren't drunk, but I think Elly's beautiful. She makes something magic out of that patch of green lawn we think is just an ordinary world."

I forgot he was drunk and disorderly. I told him she was a fairy and that's why she didn't talk, and he smiled and staggered away. The next day he wrote me a letter. I copy it here.

DEAR MRS. PARK,

I am the drunk that you were so nice to as I passed by your yard Saturday afternoon. Even though sober now, I am no more capable of explaining to you just how Elly has affected me. Elly transforms our messy back yard into a wonderland. She makes a world that you and I can only see in daydreams. Sometimes when I look out the window and see her dancing to our music I can almost see that world with her. Elly can sit and watch my friends work on their motor cycles all afternoon and never say a word. Yet she seems to be as much in tune with them as I could be with all the conversation in the world.

I know that being Elly's mother must be a very discouraging, very frustrating experience. After only a few moments of a few afternoons I have felt the need to pressure her into talking—the need to break into her world verbally. I hope that someday Elly will become well and have a happy life. I'm writing you because I'm sure that because you're Elly's mother you don't get enough chances to appreciate Elly—to only gain and not sacrifice—as I have. I thought maybe it would help to hear what I had to say. I wish I could express it better for you.

P.S. I don't usually talk like this so please don't tell on me.

It helps, of course. It helps a lot, in many ways. It helps to know that a stranger, seeing Elly, can look beyond her embarrassing defects to sense something of her strange integrity, and it helps more deeply than anything else can to know that stranger can touch stranger, in gentleness and love.

EPILOGUE, Fifteen Years After

WORDS organize experience, a book can seem to conclude it —
beginning, middle, end. A chapter, a paragraph, a sentence, a
word is presented as the last, and by the very fact, the experience
takes on shape. Elly was seven when I began this account, eight
and a half when I finished it, the last chapters opening to absorb
the very latest minute of her growing. I had not meant to write
it then, though I was so full of what was happening to us that
words poured out of me into the slightest readiness to listen,
Ancient Mariner to Wedding Guest. Someone suggested I write
a book about it — Elly was six. I remember saying I wasn't ready,
it was too soon, that we'd have to wait and see how the story
ended. Though memory tricks us often enough, that memory
must be true; I could not possibly have invented words so touch-
ingly, so piercingly naïve. I imagined, then, that the story could
have an ending. The analyst's question comes to mind: What was
I expecting?

True-life stories do not end, except with that externally imposed finality, the death of the subject — or the teller. We only
stop telling them. If we have managed to find a meaning in that
portion of the story already lived, we voice it, so the meaning
can give shape to the story, render it usable, permit it to reach a
conclusion. But the story, of course, continues.

Yet it is not easy to reopen even what was so provisionally, so fictively concluded. It would be more satisfying, more shapely, to leave Elly dancing to their music, in a vision which even today expresses its own kind of truth. Yet that would not answer the question I have been asked so often: how is Elly *now?* I have answered it before, of course — in letters to friends known and unknown, in speeches, in epilogues for foreign editions of this book. Every year the answer is fuller, richer, there is more to add. But I have never until now reread my account from first to last, re-lived the years within the words, forced myself to connect the Elly recorded here to the Elly who lives with us today, still growing, and ask if the sense I made of it all fifteen years ago makes sense still.

Yes, she still lives with us. That is usually the next question, and we are happy at the answer, and proud. She is twenty-three now, slim and shapely, but still with a child's transparency of expression. She has not had to be sent away, though once, when she was excluded from her local school,* it looked as if we might have to lose her. The climate changed, however, just in time for Elly, though too late for others. Public education for the severely handicapped was made mandatory, in our state first, then in all the country. A program was developed for her, showing that the teachers of a rural public high school, with no recondite expertise beyond the skills and goodwill they already possess, can do what still was thought impossible fifteen years ago — educate a severely autistic child in the schools of her own community. Autistic? People still said "psychotic" then, even "schizophrenic," frightening words to school administrators in those days when the kindly vocabulary of "special needs" had not yet come into being. Elly was thirteen before she was allowed to go to school

---

* The story of Elly's exclusion, and return, can be read in "Elly and the Right to Education," in R. E. Schmid, J. Moneypenny, and R. Johnston, *Contemporary Issues in Special Education*, McGraw-Hill, 1977.

for a full day — Elly, who had so much more to learn than other children.

But that is water under the bridge. Elly entered Mount Greylock Regional High School and had nine years there. School ended for her a month before her twenty-second birthday; she wore a white robe and mortarboard and sat on the stage with the rest. She had even passed the minimum competency test for our state, an astonishing tribute to the patient resourcefulness of the teachers and guidance officers who devised her individualized combination of special and regular classes, for when she entered it her speech was intelligible only to those who knew her, and she could read and write only a few words. By their help, and the hard, essential work of the staff of the CETA Job Training Program, she has passed a greater test; she has a job, part-time still, but one she enjoys and does well. Her trial period is completed and she has had two raises. She keeps her own checkbook, and her NOW account contains $2500 she has earned herself. Next year she may pay taxes. And there are other facts I could list; I will tell them later, proudly, for I suppose this is by way of being a success story. Like other true-life stories, it is not all success, though by canny suppressions I could make it sound so. The success is real, however, and it is there we should begin. But the first telling began not with facts but with a picture. Perhaps that is the way to reopen the past and connect it with the present.

Empezamos con una imagen: una pequeña niña dorada. . . . Elly sits at her desk, peering attentively at the words she is typing, slowly at first, then picking up speed. She cannot read them, for they are Spanish, but she can type them as accurately as anyone else — more accurately, perhaps, without the meanings to distract her. She types English that way, too. As she finishes a page she proofreads it, letter by letter, line by

Some sounds are "too good." At fifteen, Jessy blocks her ears as her friend sews. *Below:* Jessy tenses with delight. Psychologists would call this a "bizarre behavior," neurologists a "soft neurological sign." It has been with her since infancy.

7/26/73 Jessy
back

Above: Anna, the friend who taught Jessy to draw. Pencil sketch on computer paper. Age fifteen.

Right: The "hangman" Jessy sees in others' eyes, who hangs from trees or is pinned to clotheslines, or jumps higher or lower according to the conventional formulas of politeness Jessy finds distressing (see page 296). Age sixteen. *Opposite:* The hangman and various kinds of politeness. These childlike drawings were done a year *after* the sophisticated pencil sketch of Anna.

The hangman hangs by the clothespin because of new politeness. YOU'RE MORE THAN WELCOME
YOU'RE VERY WELCOME
YOU'RE MOST WELCOME   YOU'RE MOST CERTAINLY WELCOME
YOU'RE CERTAINLY WELCOME
YOU'RE SURELY WELCOME
YOU'RE QUITE WELCOME
YOU'RE SO WELCOME

"I'm smiling about me hanging by the clothespin."

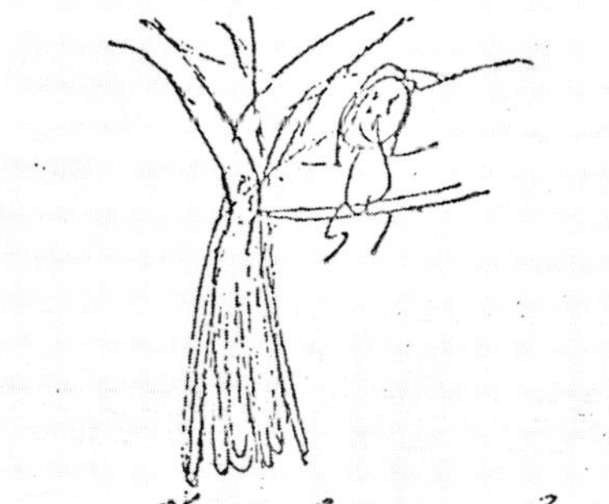

early politeness

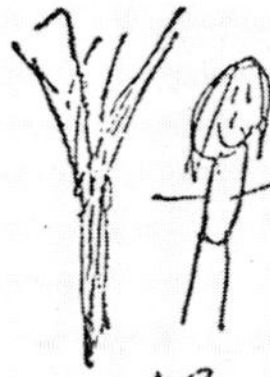

silent politeness

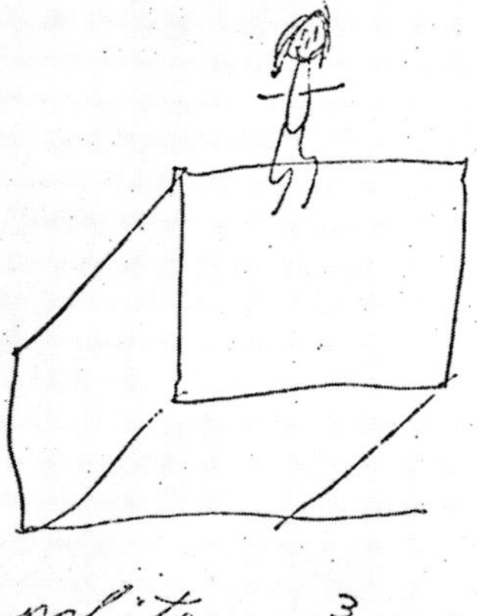

politeness^2

is smiling
and saying
"thank you"
"you're welcome".

politeness^3 smiling,
~~the~~ "thank you"
"you're welcome"

Tree in a courtyard, done for a school assignment. The students were instructed to go into the courtyard with paper and india ink only, using as drawing implements any materials — leaves, twigs — they could find there. Age sixteen.

Pencil sketch of house. Age seventeen.

Above: At seventeen, with father, mother, and brother. *Photo by Deborah Peck, one of the "Jessy-girls."*

Below: At eighteen, intent at the sewing machine.

Above and below: Jessy at twenty-three. *Photos by Mark Andres.*

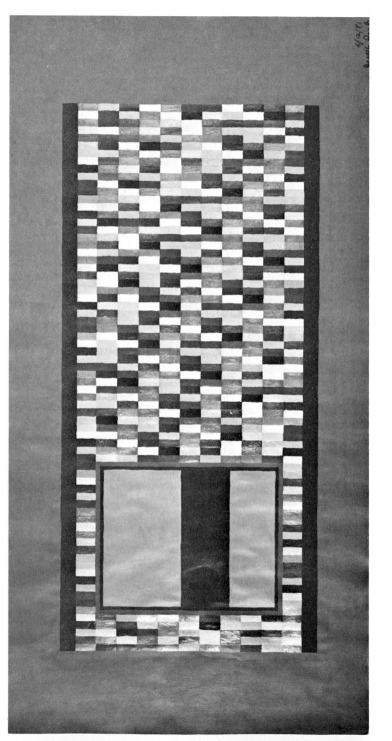

The Heater in Valerie's Bathroom, described on page 282. One of a series of acrylic paintings of the objects Jessy finds so meaningful — radio dials, railroad crossings, electric blanket controls, quartz heaters. Age twenty-three.

line. Every once in a while she finds a combination of letters she likes: E l l y. She knows that's her name in the book, and that it's different from her real name, which is Jessica, Jessy. She knows the book is about her, the way she knows that she is five foot three and weighs 113 pounds and has blonde hair and lives in a house with her mother and father and sometimes a friend — ordinary, inconsequential facts. It's nice to come across a name and know it means you. That's all it means, though. Fifteen years ago I gave her that name, in case — could I actually have thought it? — she would someday read this book and be embarrassed. I need not have worried. Jessy likes coming across her book name. She likes coming across an extra space between paragraphs, too, or unusual punctuation. She still flips through books, as that golden baby did, and smiles her secret smile, only now she is looking for spaces, or irregular quotation marks, or the longest sentence she can find. She's blasé about hyphens now, but when she was first learning to type she stopped dead at every one, shivering with delight. That made her lose points on the timed tests, and she hated that. She still doesn't *like* to type; no typing is error-free. When Jessy makes a mistake — not as often as most of us — she mumbles under her breath, and now and then her distress may intensify to weeping, unhappiness which has nothing to do with the ease or difficulty of correction. A period for a comma, correctable by a simple strikeover, may trouble her more than a whole word omitted. This is a job, however; she is being paid per page, so she masters her emotion and keeps going. She's learned to do that. Jessy typed the entire Spanish translation of *The Siege*,* from *empezamos* to *amor*, and used the money to pay for her own plane ticket to stay with friends in California.

Jessy sits at her table, bent over a sheet of drawing paper, deftly outlining a rectangle with a sable brush. At hand are some

* *Ciudadela Sitiada* (Madrid: Fondo de Cultura Economica, 1980).

thirty tubes of acrylics, but for today she has mixed only shades of green — five of them. Green is her favorite color. She is working from the pencil sketch she made at a friend's house some weeks ago, one of her quartz heater series, the successor to her series of radio dials and electric blanket controls. Her abstracting eye has reduced the heater to its essential design elements, 11 ranges of tiny rectangles, 72 to a range. For the painting she has enlarged them fourfold, but they still measure only a half-inch by a quarter. Today she will fill in only the greens, placing them unhesitatingly among the 792 rectangles according to a pattern we cannot see. But she can see it; she has already chosen the final color which will enclose the whole. Next day she will place a few dark reds near the greens, Christmas colors which look harsh against all the white space but which, joined over three weeks' work by three different oranges, three pinks, a yellow, and four shades of purple, will glow against the tan neutrality of the border with the surreal intensity of a heater in a dream.

Jessy is cooking. We all like chocolate chip cookies. They stir up easily and she makes them often, needing no recipe. But today she's pleasing herself, choosing one of the most complicated recipes in her cookbook, rolling up the plain and chocolate dough together, wrapping it in wax paper, and refrigerating it — tomorrow, when she slices and bakes it, it will come out in spirals. Or she may divide the dough five ways and color it with food coloring. We enjoy the cookies, but she enjoys the orderly complication of the process. Desserts are her recreation, but her repertoire extends far beyond. She makes our bread, she makes salads, spaghetti sauce, yogurt, omelets, applesauce, a fine fish chowder. It's been years since we've given any thought to her breakfast or lunch — she makes her own, applying the nutritional principles learned in Gourmet Cooking — like typing, a class she was able to take with normal children. If we are running out of eggs or milk, she notices, and goes downtown to buy more. She needs no help to read the recipes, with their invariant vocabulary and straightforward meanings. Cooking, like painting, is something she can do alone, in the hours when the house is empty. But it's also an activity to share with others — "auxiliary cooks," she calls them, for she has become interested in the long words she learned to spell for typing class. Then the kitchen is alive with noise and people — the extra daughters, surrogate sisters we call Jessy-girls, and Jessy simply calls her friends. They come — often they bring *their* friends — and the house hums with the activity of the years long gone, before her sisters and brother left for the larger world.

There are many pictures to choose from. Jessy is working at her job in the college mailroom, sorting letters, readdressing them for forwarding or inserting them into the two thousand numbered student mailboxes. Perhaps a postcard bears 20 cents instead of 13. That makes her happy: "Extra postage!" she chirps, all smiles. Or a student's face appears, emptying his box at the very moment Jessy is filling it. That makes her happy too. Or she sits at the calculator, figuring the long-distance charges individually billed to professors by department, fussy, exacting work she gets done, we're told, in half the time it took the previous worker. An error distresses her now and then, but she gets it under control: "I cried *silently!*" Another image: having retrieved her paycheck from the Friday mail, she is standing in line at the bank to deposit it. She is a little too close to the person in front of her, but she holds herself in check, trying not to push forward and succeeding. "Hello, Jessy." They know her at the bank; they are nice to her, with the natural niceness of women who work in offices. They do not know much about her, but they know that she is different. A person is different when it is less difficult for her to balance her checkbook than to wait patiently for her turn.

Another image — least of all to say about this one, for unless we eavesdrop on the conversation we see nothing more than an attractive young girl having a hamburger at McDonald's with a friend. And yet for anyone who knows her history, this image of success is perhaps the most important of all.

Jessy's day begins early. She rises as punctually for work as she did for school. She has laid out her clothes — colors carefully harmonized — the night before, so as to have plenty of time to shower, make her bed, and eat a leisurely breakfast, for she becomes anxious if she thinks she's going to be late. She has an alarm clock, but she doesn't need it. Her father or I may have breakfast with her, but it's for sociability, not supervision. She will leave the house on the dot, whether or not we're there. She returns from her job in midafternoon; at home she will occupy herself dusting and vacuuming, doing the laundry, ironing. She mends her clothes, on the machine or by hand. She weaves on the loom she bought with her own earnings, setting up the warp herself, not merely throwing the shuttle. She can put in a new washer when the faucet drips. At the sight of this cheerful, useful member of our household, the long, inert years might almost be forgotten.

Yet not quite. Jessy is most at ease — and appears most normal — when there is work to be done. Painting, cooking, listening to the radio (responding, however, more intensely to the station call letters than to the music), she can fill her leisure up to a point, and her repertoire of activities continues to expand. A thousand-piece puzzle can keep her occupied for an afternoon or two; a new book of mazes will last a couple of weeks. Now and then she looks at a book, even reads it a little bit. But she runs out of things to do eventually, and if no one is on hand to introduce her to a new activity and share it, we can see that the old Jessy is still there, face-down but openeyed on her bed in midafternoon, or rocking in her rocking chair, the only place where rocking is allowed — too wildly, if we don't stop her, or in the dark. Then, the vision of what she might have been, what she might still become if the world abandoned her, is made frighteningly real.

But she no longer guards that solitude. Once the hardest trial for the young people whose task was to work and play with her were the times she refused their company, to rock, or bounce a ball over and over, or sift her "silly business," home-made confetti she had cut up out of magazine pages — often, to our distress, out of pictures she had made herself. How could they not feel they had failed, when she told them to go away? It is hard, as I wrote so long ago, not to be bruised by the rejection that seems deliberate even when one knows it is not. Perhaps it is impossible. We would try to talk to Jessy about it, to help her understand that "You hurt Debbie's feelings." But though she might echo them, the words carried no meaning for her. If the road toward speech has been long and slow, the progress toward the feelings beneath speech has been slower still.

But not imperceptible. Little milestones: Jessy is fifteen. Two young women have come to see us, as interested people do come sometimes, people who have read this book. We spend a pleasant afternoon together. "Those were nice girls," I say next day. "I liked them. Did you like Jane and Kathy?" — for it is already possible to expect that Jessy may recognize even new acquaintances by name. "Yes," says Jessy, smiling and proud. "Never ever ask them to leave!"

Month by month she grows, and year by year, milestones frequent enough now so I no longer record them all. Here is another; she is eighteen. Sister Becky, long away, telephones from abroad, a great event. Summoned to the phone, Jessy, who three years before could only breathe into the mouthpiece, assembles her words: "I am missing you. I would like to see you," she says. For years, when her father was away on his sabbatical odysseys she had not seemed to notice his absence. Out of sight, out of mind. But that same year she asked for her own copy of his itinerary, "so I can keep track of my father." Last year, hearing a friend's arrival was delayed, she exclaimed, "Oh, no! When will Diana come back?" Milestones? We grow jaded; once they would have seemed miracles.

For Jessy has ceased to be autistic, if we give autism its root meaning. She is no longer immured within the self. The self — I recall some of those authoritative-sounding phrases, phrases I then did not challenge. How could anyone ever have talked of "early ego failure," of the unlikelihood of achieving "an integrated personality"? Whose ego ever had surer boundaries, whose personality was ever more perfectly integral than Jessy's? But the citadel's walls were breached long ago, and now they are down. A year ago, flying over the Sound, we looked down on a tiny island with one house on it. Speaking to Jessy's new interest in vocabulary, I remarked that the house was *isolated;* that it would be lonely living there but that it would be nice if you didn't like people. To which Jessy replied that she *did* like people.

And she does. She is all smiles and hugs when siblings return, or one of the long train of young people who have worked with her since she was four years old. Innocent and open, she would hug acquaintances too, regardless of gender, even, perhaps, strangers; she has had to be taught that she should smile and shake hands instead. Jessy lives with us now, truly with us, no longer a changeling but a human child. But she has not left the Land of Youth. For all her progress, she understands less of the subtle language of face or body than a normally perceptive seven-year-old, and far less of the manifold interchanges of the social world.

A seven-year-old knows that one does not invite unacquainted people of different sexes to sleep in the same bed. Yet that was Jessy's suggestion a few months ago when the house was full and we were discussing where to put Marilyn, up from the city. "Share the bed with Milt?" Jessy likes to talk about sharing beds. She likes to talk about sharing food, too, and for the same reason: it leads to a cheerful conversation on one of her favorite subjects, germs and the manner and likelihood of transmitting them. It is not that she is ignorant of the facts of sexual biology; she has been taught them at home and in school. She even knows enough to smile sideways and drop her voice when she says "sexual intercourse" — the same mild salaciousness with which she mentions bathroom activity, a five-year old's enjoyment of a violated social tabu. But there is none of that in the matter-of-fact good cheer with which she mentions sharing beds. How could there be? A retarded adolescent is familiar with them, but Jessy guesses nothing of the emotions that might lead to sharing beds, and though she knows something of the physical feelings, her sexual enjoyment is solitary, unconnected with the sharing of beds or anything else.

Physical feelings are easy to understand; our bodies teach them. But interior feelings are intangible, and to the unpracticed eye and ear invisible and inaudible as well. "You hurt Debbie's feelings." A seven-year-old would understand what we mean by that. But listen to Jessy as she tries to work out why it is that she should not cry on the school bus.

Already fifteen, she has been riding the bus for more than a year. There are problems, but also progress; she is beginning to try to control her distress when someone takes her preferred seat, or when she misses the special billboard she feels compelled to look at every day (or rather, the place where the billboard *was*, for it was taken down months ago). But now, as we talk, she feels no distress, relaxing into the enjoyment of things past. I remember when she could not frame the simplest question; now, laughing, and serene, she asks, "Is it hurt people's feelings when I cry on the bus?" Jessy's crying was a banshee's shrieking, a siren's wail; autistic children do not even cry like other people. In the enclosed space of the bus . . . "It hurts people's *ears*," I say. I've said that before, often; it's probably what she is thinking of. "But not their *feelings*," I add, and try to explain. Her incomprehension is plain. Ears are hurt by shrill noises; she knows that from her own experience. But people's feelings are different from ears'. I say that people's feelings get hurt when they think you don't like them; that's why you don't ask them to leave. But she has stopped listening; how can she understand that? Hers don't.

She is looking for a concrete definition, and there is none. What can I refer to? There in the Land of Youth no one is hurt, or embarrassed, or ashamed. It will be four more years before she knows what it is to be even dimly conscious of someone else's opinion.

A few months later she tries again. "Why is laugh about people crying hurt their feelings?" From three years before a memory grips me: a man in a wheelchair, skeletal, pale as death, still young, he can't be more than thirty. "Leg *broken*," said Jessy then, trying to get things clear. Distress and horror filled me, yet the educative demon in me spoke up, so automatic had it become to extract a lesson from everything that passed. "No, his leg isn't broken, he's sick — I think he's very sick." Birdlike and cheerful, mercifully out of earshot, Jessy's voice rises, in search of fuller understanding of the interesting world. "He will die soon?"

Five years later she will say to me spontaneously, "I'm sorry I pushed you yesterday." That yesterday, we had been sitting around the supper table, Jessy, her father, myself, and Lynn, the girl who lived with us the year Jessy was seventeen. Jessy had gently hit at my mouth, responding to the frustration of adult conversation that never seemed to stop and let her get a word in. Once we had waited weeks for a word, and talking was something she did only in my dreams. Now — another miracle — it seemed time to talk about interrupting, about how hard it is to wait your turn when you have something to say. Then, to turn the lesson into fun, I began to talk about when it was all right to interrupt. "Of course you can interrupt when there's a *fire*." Jessy laughs cheerily, as always when envisaging hypothetical disasters. "Then say 'Excuse me! There is a fire!'" I think of another one: water might be coming through the ceiling. Jessy is enjoying this; she comes up with her own example. "Or a flood in the cellar?" We assent with enthusiasm: "Because those things are IMPORTANT" (we're working on that word). "But," I say, "there are other things that are important." Using the comic exaggeration which Jessy understands and enjoys, her father suggests, "If Lynn got very sick and her face turned green and she fell off the chair, that would be a good reason to interrupt."

And here it comes: "*If Lynn gets sick is that important?*"

It is like living with a Martian. "She just has a distorted sense of what's important," I had told my neighbor, so long ago. My mistake was in that word "just." Jessy is our fairy child still, escaped from an alternative universe, utterly without malice or — I would once have written — without sympathy. But what we have discovered, most of all in these recent years, is that Jessy does not stop learning. We knew well enough that our normal children's learning did not stop at eighteen; why did we assume that hers would? Jessy learns more every year, and better, because she is at last learning *how* to learn — to listen, to attend, to imitate, to generalize, to pull out of the air around her a little, a very little, of what normal people are said to "pick up naturally." Jessy did not pick up speech naturally; she needed all the help we could give her. She did not pick up sympathy naturally either. In this, too, she has needed help, and it has come even more slowly. Piaget says a child is about seven when it begins to be able to put itself in another's place. As so often, it was one of the Jessy-girls who determined, the summer Jessy turned twenty-one, that she was ready to learn a new category of behavior. They wrote the words down together: THINKING OF OTHERS, and then, in colored crayons, six different ways of doing that. Jessy needs things clear and specific; we had learned already that for this child who could perceive so easily the abstractions of shape and number, even as obvious a social abstraction as "helping" was only a word, unless we aided her with the definite, concrete instances which could give it meaning. It had been four years since we had listed six kinds of helping on the behavioral chart I will describe later, in its place. "Thinking of others" would be a natural extension of the concept.

Not that six — or sixteen — instances of thinking of others could supply that missing insight into what others feel. You still have to tell Jessy when you feel sick or sad, and her ritualized "I hope you will feel better" is not really very comforting. And yet — last year she told me proudly that she was putting nutmeg instead of cinnamon in the tapioca "because you like that better." This year she plays classical records at lunchtime, "because you don't like rock music." To Joe, her friend from the special class, she exclaims, "I gave my mother and Valerie an Easter egg hunt and they both liked them!" — followed by a little sound of pleasure, a soft, indescribable squeak. *Learn to labor and to wait.* I remember the candy she fed me in the doctor's office so many years before — can it really be twenty? That gentle squeak is its true sequel, and our reward.

I've just heard from the students who are living with Jessy in our house this summer while we summer at the shore — a working girl now, she joins us only for her vacation. What they report, like everything else, tells of her progress, and its limits. She was easily upset for a day or so after I left. Whistling could cheer her up, but the new way they found was even better — "WMNB-FM," they'd say, and she'd start to smile. And then terrible news came for one of them: Tracy's father had been in a collision, was in a coma, and Tracy was crying. Jessy could see tears, she did not need to be told Tracy was sad. She put herself in Tracy's place the best way she knew. She said, not "I hope you will feel better," but "WMNB-FM."

It is like living with a Martian, or a fairy. Or better, it is like living with one of those creatures of old Russia, a Holy Fool, guileless, transparent, pure.

From what I have written, it is plain that social incomprehension is not the only mark of Jessy's condition. Autism is not one handicap but a collection, beneath them the "inability of the brain to decode its perceptions or render them usable" that I wrote of fifteen years ago, speculating then on the plight of the baby "faced with a world in which an unreadable welter of impressions obscures even the distinction between objects and human beings." At that time it seemed best to frame this explanation as a question; it was by no means generally accepted then. In fifteen years, however, much has changed. Research has not discovered the cause of autism — it seems likely, in fact, that like cancer it will turn out to have no single, simple cause — or cure. But that inability to decode, to process information, has become the strongest hypothesis, and no one in touch with the latest developments in the field any longer imagines that inside the autistic child there is a normal child waiting to get out. Though the environment surrounding the autistic person can make a difference, perhaps all the difference, it seems certain that autism is rooted in the brain. Arising from the brain's inability to decode the world, or superimposed upon it, are other impairments and peculiarities, many of them illustrated in the incidents I have described. But the most immediately obvious impairment is the one the reader will already have noted in all I have said of Jessy — the impairment in the use and comprehension of language.

Language is far more than speech. The autistic child's impairment affects not only the acquisition and understanding of speech — if that were all, the condition would not be so very different from deafness, or the kind of language disability we call aphasia. An even more primary impairment further isolates the autistic baby: it cannot use or interpret even gesture.* Gesture develops before speech. Babies wave bye-bye; they point. And the comprehension of gesture is independent of speech; animals can interpret gesture, as they can interpret facial expressions and tones of voice. But at nineteen months Jessy did not point, and though at twenty-three years she has long ago mastered such external, easily imitated gestures as pointing, I have already written how

* Lorna Wing, *Autistic Children*, Brunner/Mazel, 1972, pp. 20–21.

far she is from understanding the subtle language of our faces and our bodies. It is that pervasive handicap, directly related to the autistic lack of empathy, which more than anything else gives the autistic condition its quality of strangeness. That is why I placed it first, before commenting on her difficulties with actual speech. Beside her inability to interpret the social world her troubles with words may seem trivial. Yet her speech is still what people notice first about her, the most conspicuous mark of her condition. Her family, her teachers, her speech therapist, she herself, have all worked hard on her speech, and I must say something about it.

Anybody who hears Jessy speak more than a word or two realizes that something is wrong. She has learned English as a foreign tongue, though far more slowly, and she still speaks it as a stranger. The more excited she is about what she has to say, the more her speech deteriorates; her attention cannot stretch to cover both what she is saying and how she is saying it. Pronouns get scrambled: "you" for "I," "she" for "he," "they" for "we." Articles and tenses are confused or disappear, verbs lose their inflections or are omitted altogether.* (French autistic children, faced with the continual shifts of their highly inflected verbs, take refuge in the simple, invariant form of the infinitive — like many a tourist.) We have similar troubles with our own foreign languages when our minds are full, unless they have truly become second nature.

And we too may have difficulty picking up the intonation of a foreign language, the pronunciation of individual sounds and words, but even more, the accent, the lilt which makes the lan-

---

* Those familiar with aphasia will recognize many of its characteristics. Autistics vary widely in the extent of their speech deficit, as in other measures of retardation. Fifty percent of them do not learn to speak at all, and most autistics who function as well as Jessy speak far more fluently and idiomatically than she. Their superior speech, however, does not necessarily make them any more socially aware.

guage sound like itself and not another. So Jessy; syllables get scrambled if there are too many of them, phrases do not flow automatically into others, but are assembled slowly, with effort. But there is more to it than this. Nuances of expression escape her here too. All questions are spoken with the identical rising intonation. She has not the normal person's many ways of saying "no" or "what?", ways that can entirely change their meaning, but only two or three. Her voice takes on a special tone for each of her various emotions, for cheerfulness, for joy, for anxiety, for distress. But it sounds "different," it has some of the flatness of those born deaf. Jessy has heard our voices from birth, and every year she hears them more attentively and reproduces them better and more intelligently. But difficulty in imitation is a characteristic of autism, and she still can only approximate the shifting tones of normal human speech.

Other autistic characteristics persist. We live in the midst of that hyperreactivity to sound that so many observers have noted. Jessy has learned to control the intensity of her reactions to the clicks and buzzes and hums with which the twentieth century surrounds us. But she still notices them. "Guess what! The refrigerator turned on while the door open! A loud click!" If Jessy is tuned to a sound it pierces through to her through conversation, or distance. She hears the sound of the refrigerator — or its silence — two rooms away. Some sounds fill her with mysterious delight. Other sounds and phrases trigger an equally mysterious distress that seems, in its devastating suddenness, almost like an allergic reaction of the psyche. Stock responses like "You're welcome" or "What?", innocent words like "water" or "cricket," may set off a train of undercover mumbles, even a crisis of crying. We practice such words deliberately now, for at work, in the world, she must be able to tolerate it when somebody says "What?" or "I don't know." "I don't know" is like "partly heard song," she tells us. She hates partly heard song. Restlessly she scowls when you enter her room if certain songs are coming from the radio; your

293

presence interrupts; she is trying not to ask you to leave. "I don't know" causes the same discomfort. It's absolutely logical, if you accept the premises: the "un" of "unheard," she tells us, is like "No," and "heard" is like "Yes." So "partly heard" is to "heard" and "unheard" as "I don't know" is to "Yes" and "No"; it's in between. What could be clearer? — to a Martian.

Consider this. Jessy is fifteen. She has made herself eight pieces of bacon for breakfast. Why? "Because of good." Why good? "Because Anna cough and burp too. Sound and silence." I ask, "If Anna talked at the same time would that be sound?" "Only politeness ["excuse me," "thank you," etcetera] is sound." And ordinary talking? "That is not sound. And the bell in camp is a sound. And the boat horn. And animal noises, just like a dog." I recall the sudden bark that made us laugh so. We had noticed it long ago; it was exactly those sounds that for us carried least meaning that riveted her attention. Now Jessy herself has made the principle perfectly clear. Only nonsignificant sounds are defined as audible: burps, coughs, recurrent, automatic phrases. We catch a glimpse of what it must have been like for her in the long years when all speech was unintelligible.

Back to breakfast and bacon. Jessy still loves to categorize the world; she used to spell her name five different ways according to the kind of day. And here is another system: "Doing something fairly bad is only three and bad is two and very bad is one! Doing something bad is the most! No wonder get egg!" No wonder, to logical Jessy. A bad day means only two pieces of bacon, so naturally a supplement is needed. "If I have less than five and egg I have to cut that thin slices* of toast. If I have less than five and no egg I have to cut thick slices of toast." She has

---

* Note the key difficulty with language: the forms of words vary continually to fit their context, they are not invariant like the mathematical (and musical) notation she found easy. Why can't it be "slices of toast" in both sentences? How old is a normal child when it absorbs — "learns" is too formal a word — that "slices" in the plural must be preceded by a

thought it all out, with that brain of hers that orders as naturally as breathing.

Jessy is cheerful about the bacon. But we understand now the kind of reason that lay behind so much of her distress in the years before she had words to tell us reasons — or rather, we understand that we shall never understand. At nine, she would arrive home from school choked and exhausted with crying: "I forgot to say ha-ha to the gas pump!" To this day, she does not like to stay up till midnight, "because of the ha-ha's." Children, even normal ones, often observe compulsive rituals of their own creation. But Jessy has never been heard to say ha-ha to a gas pump, or at midnight. She answers our question: "In my *mind!*" and we get another glimpse of her inner life.

In which, be it said, distress plays only a small part. The fairies who stood over Jessy's cradle blessed her with a happy nature, and her compulsions bring her more joy than pain. She laughs and smiles more often than she cries — more often, I think, than most people her age. It is one reason people like her. ("Jokes, such as eating roads, a man has three arms, a house is upside down, and flowers are growing on a telephone, make me laugh.") She smiles socially, warmly, in normal response to pleasures and to people. But often, too, it's her smile out of fairyland, at delights we can't understand, in realms of emotion where we can't follow. As that golden baby smiled, circling her spot so long ago. That secret smile is part of her condition.

It is also part of her charm. Five years ago a psychologist gave her a complete evaluation (excerpts from it, and from earlier intelligence tests, will be found in the Appendix). In three hours with Jessy, he reported, he found "no indication of disturbed, malignant, or bizarre thinking," and indeed Jessy's thinking is not often disturbed, and never malignant. We were surprised, and

---

plural demonstrative pronoun? Of course meanings vary with context too, not to mention tone, and that is even harder.

very glad, that she could pass a whole afternoon without betraying herself; conversation and behavior which may seem charming among friends would be deeply disconcerting if encountered in a supermarket or by co-workers in a busy office. But of course Jessy's thinking is profoundly bizarre. I expect that the psychologist, as he administered his tests, didn't talk to her about bacon, and to literal Jessy, the Rorschach would scarcely have suggested crickets. He wouldn't have noticed how she avoids saying "thank you," or, pressed to say it, how she swallows the words and looks over our heads so as not to encounter the imaginary "hangman" visible in our eyes, the little fellow who hangs from trees or is pinned to clotheslines, or jumps higher or lower according to those conventional formulas of politeness which can disturb her so much more than events in the normal world. Certainly he never discovered the families of "little imitation people"* that inhabit the household appliances that buzz and hum and click around her. It is hard for Jessy to find words, though it is easier than it used to be. Concocting sentences is harder still. Except about subjects close to her heart, she has little conversation, and what there is is labored, factual, and dull. But ask her about the little imitation people and you will get an earful. "Guess what! The oven is a make-believe family also!" Jessy is firmly grounded in reality; at seven she learned the words "real" and "pretend" easily, though at that time she had few adjectives of any kind. There is nothing hallucinatory about the make-believe families. "Noise of the oven same as the buzzer of the washing machine. This part of the family has only two children and both get married and one of them has children and the other don't. And there are four parts of the family. 'Member our family has two parts. Second part are my cousins. Stove has three sets of cousins.

---

* For a glimpse of how language sounds to her, compare the word "Lilliputian." She has said — and drawn — "little imitation people" ever since we looked at the pictures in *Gulliver's Travels*, years ago.

Some of the sisters and cousins are Karens." (Karen is Jessy's favorite name.) "There are two Karens in two different sets of cousins, and both didn't get married. Too young." Later, we look at a children's book on astronomy, and the concept expands. "Every galaxy has lots of sun families. Know why I say that? Pretend the sun is the parent, and the planets are the children and the earth is *me!*" Then she senses a difficulty. "But the sun is not married."

The interest of the appliance families lies in the elaboration of their family relationships. As she describes these kinship systems, Jessy is a natural structuralist. "Third set and fourth set have Karens in it. Third set also has stepparents. Children got to be half-sisters and -brothers. The first set are the oldest, the fourth set are the youngest. Third set splits in two. Parents had three children, got divorced." (Lynn's parents did that.) "Father married another wife, three children from first wife, one from second. And there is a dishwasher family — different names. And child from third set of washing machine family is getting married to the oldest child of dishwasher family, and it will be the family-in-law." (Jessy's sister Sarah got married the year before this conversation: she met the in-laws at the reception.) "Stove, dishwasher, and washing machine. And also includes drying machine." But, I object, we don't have a drier. Jessy laughs. "Family in the *store!* And germs have family also! In the body! And insect family! Ant family!" Imaginary, I ask, or real? Jessy giggles. "Imaginary!"

First set, fourth set, third set splits in two. Eight pieces of bacon. Structures. Numbers. Ideas of order. When Jessy was nine, with blocks and rods, with groups of circles and triangles, I led her from simple counting through the basic operations of arithmetic. I doubt she needed the blocks and rods, but I wanted to make sure the concepts had meaning. We progressed through multiplication and division to fractions. Remembering my own bewilderment at Jessy's age when the teacher kept talking about pieces of pie, I drew no pie; I drew clear, abstract, intelligible circles and squares and divided them into two, three, four, five . . . twelve . . . sixteen, then translated them into the notation of halves and thirds and quarters and sixteenths and rang their changes. Was I pushing her? Now and then I still thought about that; in those days, parents were not encouraged to teach even their normal children to read. The principal who excluded her from the retarded class where she seemed to be doing so well would not even look at her sheets of addition and subtraction; they were, he told me, all done by rote. But I could see that fractions were far easier for Jessy than they had been for me. Passively, though with no particular enthusiasm, she took them in.

Two years later — she was eleven — arithmetic had become so easy that she began to play with numbers herself. Hour after hour she multiplied and divided, squaring and cubing all the numbers through 100, dividing huge numbers by 7, 11, 13, 17, 19. I have a box filled with her calculations. She worked out the fractions representing the portion of the year we had accomplished: that March 6 it was 15/73: that is, 75/365 reduced to lowest terms. Factorizations fascinated her; 60 was her favorite number, because it could be divided so many ways. In a year we discovered we could give her any odd number up to 1000, even beyond, and she could tell us at once if it was a prime; if it was not, she could supply the prime factors, so surely that she once corrected a misprint in a Bureau of Standards table. Numbers lost their neutrality; now they reached down to the mysterious sources of her emotional life. "Guess what! 70003 is a prime!" Some numbers were bad; that year 75 was one of them, which was awkward, since we were living near Paris, and 75 was the Paris license-plate number. Jessy kicked all cars that bore it. But these values were not permanent. "Guess what! 1240 change to *good!*" From the bacon conversation of three years later: "6, 4, 3, 5, 2, 1 is a magic number." Not 7? I ask. "And 7 too. And all are, up to infinity." Are some more magic than others? "1 to 8 is very magic."

Did we expect a great leap forward? A normal child with mathematical gifts welcomes new discoveries, seeks them out. Jessy's math was as autistic as the rest of her. She did not want to learn more mathematics but to do the same things over and over again, until she grew tired of them and gave them up. Even here where it was easy she did not enjoy new learning. As time went on she would tolerate only a fifteen-minute math lesson. Soon numbers became so magic that she would no longer say them. At most, with coaxing or with pressure, she would write them, or, squinting her eyes shut, speak them in a whisper. So it was with so many of the things she liked best — phrases too charged for speech, records she wouldn't play. We had long suspected what she was feeling — at twelve, she actually said the words. *"Too good."* She made a chart that year, for different kinds of records. She likes charts; they order experience. Music was classified according to the number of closed doors needed between herself and it, to protect her from her pleasure. Four doors, naturally, was the best kind — the hard rock that was too good to play. Music cooled down through two degrees of pop to classical — one door. Records of talking were no doors at all;* no difficulty in ignoring those.

She handles her hypersensitivities much better now, but they are still with us, along with the delight in system-making, the distress at order disrupted,† and the investment of emotion in exactly those areas which in the normal world least naturally

---

* Those interested in details of Jessy's elaborately correlated systems of clouds, shadows, light sources, directions, numbers, and times of day will find them described in "Light and Number: Ordering Principles in the World of an Autistic Child," David Park and Philip Youderian, *Journal of Autism and Childhood Schizophrenia,* vol. IV, no. 4 (1974), in which this chart is reproduced.

† Early morning. Jessy is eighteen. I hear crying in the kitchen. Spontaneously, she explains. The soup bowl ought to be in the top of the dishwasher, not the bottom. "Did you cry about *that?*" (Cheerfully) "Yes! Glad I didn't *break* it when I had a tantrum!"

elicit it. The normal world? I told someone once about Jessy's numbers. She was a nurse, a trained observer, and it happened that recently she had undergone several operations. Each time, she said, she had come up out of anesthesia with a number in her mind, a number she *knew* was of supreme significance. Is that the kind of thing that goes on in Jessy's brain?

Certainly she could have gone further in mathematics. In school she went through business math and accounting; like typing and art, these were classes she could take with normal children. She got an A— in accounting; although the textbook was thick with sentences she could not understand and I am sure did not read, she could perform the processes. She could have managed algebra too, possibly geometry — but few high school teachers have time to translate higher mathematics into language intelligible to a five-year-old, nor did there seem to be any practical reason to do so. Now and then, over the years, someone has been interested enough to show Jessy a new bit of math — logarithms, simple functions, the transformations of equations, Fibonacci numbers. She grasps them quickly, but she doesn't enjoy them as she did her repetitive arithmetic. She has passed beyond what I can teach her, and her father, who loves and honors mathematics, is discouraged by the contrast between what she seems able to do and the sterile iteration of what she wants to do with numbers. For the stereotyped repetition of autism still remains, though years of work, our and hers, have attenuated it. Always hot dogs in the pea soup. Always scarves on the loom. Routines unvarying, night and morning. The same conversations over and over, about station identification, road construction, germs. I recall a phrase I read once in an article about infant monkeys experimentally deprived of, I think, oxygen: "Deficiency in exploratory behavior." Jessy was nine when I was finally able to teach her to find a candy, first in my pocket, then a few inches distant, then a few feet. Then we were ready for an Easter-egg hunt; she could find the eggs in plain view, or,

"Look under the cushion, Jessy." The *next* Easter — the *memory!* — she took her basket to each of the hiding places of twelve months past, expecting to find eggs there. She looks efficiently enough now, of course, ten years later; she even finds things when we can't. "Failure to search!" she says, echoing one of our old phrases. She loves to correct us, she who has been so often corrected, and we love to hear her say the words that record and nourish the growth of that precious sense of adequacy.

I hear Jessy downstairs as I write. "Whoopsie, I missed the click of the eight-day clock." But no crisis follows. For years now we've had "flexibility practice"; the phrase itself helps her cope with the disruptions of an orderly universe. Proudly now she substitutes in recipes, varies the day she vacuums and changes her sheets. Knowing that she must replace any breakage with her own money, she restrains herself from banging the machine when she makes an error. Flexibility must be maximized and bizarre thinking minimized, since it leads all too directly to bizarre behavior.* No one at work knows, I think, about the little imitation people who undoubtedly inhabit their calculators and electric typewriters. The numbers in the departmental telephone bills must stay emotionally neutral, and I devoutly hope that in the unlikely event that her boss says "cricket" Jessy can keep her feelings under control. Yet we have not wished completely to bid farewell to these strange products of the imagination. Bizarre thinking must be discouraged, yet to suppress it entirely would be to reduce Jessy to the flatness of her ordinary conversation. and to sacrifice the individuality and charm which are among her greatest assets.

* Jessy recorded this in 1974, when she was sixteen, in one of her first sustained pieces of writing: "I went wild at the bus stop. I kicked lots of stones, leaping, rocking, jumping, running, and I tilted my head. You knew it, there are some special words. I'm afraid to have no typing class never ever again. I didn't go wild at the bus stop today."

Beyond expectation, almost beyond hope, a way seems to have opened between these hard choices. It may be that Jessy can have it both ways, that she can keep in touch with the strange springs of her emotional life, yet without threatening her adjustment to the normal world. It is time to speak of Jessy's art.*

In the long years when speech was so limited, art had been one of our chief ways of communicating.† Jessy between eight and fourteen produced literally thousands of consecutive pictures which she stapled into "books," presenting a curious, repetitive, yet attractive universe of rapid, stereotyped renditions of the adventures of herself, her family, and little imitation people among roads, dials, record players, numbers, clouds, and whatever else had mysteriously attracted to itself her emotional interest. We would spend hours together talking about them. While speech was still too much of an effort to be elicited by the commonplace events of normal life, the books could lure her to communication — but also to greater and greater elaboration of her bizarre obsessions.

At thirteen, Jessy arrived at the remarkable art department of our regional high school. For nine years, art was a continuing item in her Individualized Education Plan. It proved easy for her to learn to draw from life, and to execute assignments with increasing skill and refinement. Bizarre subject matter dropped entirely out of sight. She produced creditable still-lifes, perspective sketches of rooms and buildings, even, on assignment, Cubist compositions. But these displayed no particular individuality be-

* The following section, with some of the other material of this epilogue, was originally prepared for the chapter "Growing Out of Autism" in Eric Schopler and Gary Mesibov, eds., *The Autistic Child through Adolescence*, Plenum Press, 1982.

† Most of Jessy's art, from her first drawings through age eighteen, is in the Prospect Archive of Children's Art in North Bennington, Vermont, and may be consulted for research purposes. Her more recent paintings are in many private collections.

yond that conferred by her fine sense of line, design, and color and her tendency to render her subjects from unusual visual angles.* Nor did she produce this sophisticated art work spontaneously, as she had her "books"; it was done obediently, on demand, and in contrast to the books, she had nothing in particular to say about it. Art, apparently, was something she could do, and do extremely well. But it did not interest her, and, with regret, we assumed that the naïve spontaneity of her earlier art had been sacrificed necessarily, if indeed she had not, as normal children do, simply outgrown it.

Not so. The last two years have brought an unprecedented surge of creativity. Jessy now uses her polished technique to communicate her vision of the objects which hold for her so much obscure meaning. Radio dials, railroad crossings, electric blanket controls, quartz heaters — even crickets — transformed into nearly abstract design elements, are charged with surreal intensity through the sense of color and form she possessed before she could speak and that she can now use to render her private preoccupations public. Jessy is a natural pop artist; in the singing colors of her acrylics, common objects become both original and beautiful, and autism's stereotyped repetition is transmuted into the artist's exploration of a theme. The vision Jessy paints is not ours, but through her art we can share it, incandescent with the charged secrecy of her inner life, the hooded intensity of her smile.

So many mysteries still, so much to explain. Long ago we asked ourselves a question: was the problem cognitive or affective — rooted in Jessy's comprehension, or her emotional orientation to the world? We had decided then that for the labor of

---

* For more on her artistic development, see my review article on Lorna Selfe's *Nadia: A Case of Extraordinary Drawing Ability in an Autistic Child*, in *Journal of Autism and Childhood Schizophrenia*, vol. VIII, no. 4 (1978).

every day, it was unnecessary to decide. As time went on and Jessy grew, as we watched her slow and imperfect acquisition of speech, as the language she learned showed us more and more of the simplicity and concreteness of her perceptions, it became more and more clear that those early observers who had attributed a normal intelligence to autistic children had been wrong. The evidence of cognitive impairment could not be ignored. Jessy was as mysterious as ever, but as we learned more and more about the experience of brain-damaged persons we began to recognize characteristics of her speech, her thinking, even her behavior, which were not unique, or even unique to autism. I met a mother whose baby had lacked oxygen at birth, and was severely retarded as a consequence. But at fourteen months he had shrieked when his bottle came with a red top on it instead of a blue one; at four, speechless still, he pulled open every drawer in the house — just three inches. I remembered Jessy's playing cards, lined up so exactly along the floorboards. I read the books of other mothers of other afflicted children, among them Peggy Napear's *Brain Child*.* That child was an unquestioned case of cerebral palsy; at eight she still couldn't walk. Yet I recognized behavior after behavior I had seen in Jessy. Reading accounts of the experience of stroke victims, I learned about anomia, the difficulty they have in retrieving the noun they want, though they know it well — a difficulty we recognize in a mild version in our own aging brains. The word, the name, is there somewhere in the mind, it pops out easily enough when you aren't reaching for it, but that doesn't mean you can catch hold of it when you need it. I remembered Jessy at three, whose few words surfaced when least expected but who never used them to make something happen; Jessy at five, recognizing the word she wanted when I said it but unable even to approximate it for herself; Jessy who sang a tune, not when she'd just heard it, but six weeks after;

* Harper and Row, 1974.

Jessy who did so many things once and once only. I thought about my own semiautomatic behavior — how my typing went to pieces as soon as I became conscious of what my fingers were doing; how all I needed was for someone to enter the room where I was playing the piano and I would make a mistake. Was that why Jessy could perform only when we were not looking? Willed weakness, willed deafness, blindness, isolation. I thought I had seen these things; I had made them central to the story. Had they been merely illusions — worse yet, my own inventions? I began to question what had seemed so fundamental. Was it that she would not do what other children did, or could not?

Certainly it was plain now that Jessy *could* not learn to speak like the rest of us. If that deficit was not a matter of will, what of the others? As I reread the pages of this book, I was ready to discover that I must reconceptualize everything. *As if*, I had said — *as if* she wouldn't. I had gone further; I had written of "a tiny child's refusal of life." Had all that been wrong, a romanticization, a poeticizing of a baby's simple, sad incapacity? Had — to take an example — the refusal to drink at the table from the cup she used so elegantly in the bath been in fact no refusal, but a real inability to perform the required behavior on demand — even, perhaps, to generalize from bathroom cup to cup for drinking? Jessy generalized some things very well — her balls, her circles. But others not; she had learned, I remembered, to read so well the words on the pink cards, to refuse blankly — or was she unable? — to recognize them when she saw them in a book.

I have tried to rethink it all, instance by instance. Much of the data will support an explanation in terms of cognitive dysfunction. Some requires it. But not all. As I reread this account from the beginning, immersing myself again in so much that I had forgotten, Jessy's refusals again surrounded me. Her inertia had been real; it resisted any simple cognitive explanation in terms of incapacity. She put on her shoes and laughed. *"She won't give you the satisfaction."* She could do those things and didn't. Even with that cup, it does not seem that what we were addressing was the inability to pick up the cup in a new situation, or to recognize it was adaptable for drinking. If so, the strategy we found, the placing of the tiny cup on the chair, unaccustomed place and unaccustomed vessel, would have made it harder, not easier, for her to make the connection and act accordingly. It was rather the unwillingness to lift the cup and drink. When that was overcome — and it was not so very difficult — she could use the cup in the kitchen as she did in the bath, at will. Cognitive or emotional? We have seen both play their part. The most recent research points to what Barbara Caparulo, working at Yale in the new field of psycholinguistics, calls "a blurring of the traditional division between cognitive and affective."* It is not only unnecessary to choose between them; it is impossible.

What I have called refusal permeates Jessy's history. It was not inability that prevented her taking objects directly from our hands, or from climbing out of her crib. What of the circles she drew day after day at two-and-a-half and did not draw again — was that firm, sure grip, the pressure on the crayon, the exact closure of the figure, really something she *could* not repeat a year later? What of the faintness of her lines, the figures erased in sand, of the drawings made (at nine and ten) with yellow crayon, nearly invisible against a white ground? What of her persistent choice to use, not the blank face of the scrap paper we brought home, but the side where her little imitation people must compete with purple dittoing and mimeographed office memoranda? What of the jigsaw puzzles she abandoned at seven? Six years

---

* "Development of Communicative Competence in Autism," *Proceedings, 1981 Annual Conference of the National Society for Children and Adults with Autism*, Washington, D.C., 1982. Published yearly for more than ten years, these *Proceedings* provide an excellent record of ongoing research in autism.

later, when I coaxed her back to them, I had to repeat the same step-by-step progress against negation we had gone through when she was three — only now the puzzles had a thousand pieces and in a month she could outdo me. She had given up singing at the same time, and fussed so when I sang that I gave it up too. Years afterward, a Jessy-girl began a tune and left it incomplete; Jessy's pure, accurate tones completed it, responding to the same lure that had got her to put rings on a stick so long before. Had the music been "too good"? She did not find those words for six more years, but they tell us her refusal was neither unreal nor simple. I ask her the names of the children in the washing machine. "I know one of them," Jessy replies, "but I don't want to tell you." Of course she is smiling.

I summed it up the year she was twelve, reviewing her progress for the newsletter of that organization that had grown so important to us, NSAC, the National Society for Children and Adults with Autism.* "To paint, to play at the piano, to type, to swim, even to go for a walk — Jessy's characteristic response to any initiative is still 'No.' Yet," I wrote then, "the skilled teacher

---

* Anyone, student, parent, or professional, interested in learning more about autism should contact the society at 1234 Massachusetts Avenue, Washington, D.C. 20005, tel. (202) 783-0125. It is the parents' and teachers' best resource, and should be the professionals' first recommendation. If parents of autistic children, once excluded from their children's therapy, are now welcome partners, it is NSAC that has made the difference, with professionals like Dr. Eric Schopler, who pioneered in making parents "cotherapists." (See E. Schopler and R. Reichler, "Parents as Co-therapists, in the Treatment of Psychotic Children," *Journal of Autism and Childhood Schizophrenia*, I (1971): 87–102. If my chapters "The Professionals" and "The Amateurs" now sound out-of-date (and I hope they do), we can thank professionals like Dr. Schopler, and the dedicated parents who founded, organized, and support NSAC. The society maintains an information and referral service, and its bookstore is the best source of books on autism. Another valuable resource is the Autism Services Center directed by Ruth Christ Sullivan, whose information on autistic individuals and programs is perhaps the most exhaustive in the nation. Its address is 101 Richmond Street, Huntington, West Virginia 25702; tel. (304) 523-8269.

perseveres, in the faith that the new activity, like others before it, may at length be exercised with satisfaction." At ten she learned to tie her shoes, at eleven to make her bed. At thirteen she learned to ride a bicycle; I had thought she'd be cramped on her tricycle forever. At fifteen her friend Anna taught her to draw from life. Slowly, slowly, propelled by prodigies of patience and ingenuity (now largely other people's), Jessy added new skills, and older ones became habitual. We did not know — we could not guess — that the means for the great leap forward lay just around the corner.

I approach this section with some hesitation. Many readers will be surprised to learn those means, and some may even be shocked. For many have heard of the abuses of behavior modification, but comparatively few know its benign face. Yet it was by the methods of behavior modification — worse yet, by those that bear the ugly name of operant conditioning — that Jessy's refusal, her massive, crippling inertia, was unexpectedly overcome.

We had been aware for years of B. F. Skinner's methods — how a complex skill could be taught to those who could not previously learn it (as Skinner trained pigeons) by breaking it up into minute steps, each to be reinforced by a small reward. Similarly — and even more commonsensically — undesirable behaviors (and Jessy had so many!) could (sometimes) be extinguished by a penalty. We knew these methods were being used with autistic children, with some success — more than attended most others. At the meetings of our young society we heard yearly presentations by the pioneers in the field, Frank Hewett, Ogden Lindsley, Ivar Lovaas. I took careful notes and reported them for the newsletter. Yet years passed, and we did not use them with Jessy. Partly it was an inertia of our own; our siege had been going on a long time, and we had lost our enthusiasm for new approaches, especially if they seemed to require of us new effort and new learning. Partly it was the residual unwillingness — I have heard it from so many parents — to believe that one's own child could be trained like a rat or a pigeon. Mostly, however, it was complacency. Toilet behavior might indeed be teachable by breaking it into twenty-eight steps, but we had managed already to teach Jessy those elementary skills, and not by programmed learning, either. Now if they could program behavior for a birthday party . . . Implicit: they can't, so we don't have to think about it.

But the summer Jessy was fifteen we had a piece of luck. Another autistic child came to visit us at the shore. He was doing exceedingly well* — less impaired then Jessy from the beginning, his speech was now fluent, though (he had arrived by ferry) obsessively concerned with foghorns, the *Titanic*, and the exact temperature required to melt an iceberg in Long Island Sound. Jessy paid no attention to him, but she was transfixed by what he wore on his wrist — a golf-counter. It clicked. It added and subtracted up to 100. Golfers use them for keeping score.

This boy had passed beyond the problems we had with Jessy — the primitive speech, the shrieking, the dark mumbles, the pervasive refusal. He had progressed to ordinary small-boy negativism. The counter, recommended by a clinical psychologist, was smoothing life for the whole family; 30 points, amassed by ordinary nine-year-old good behavior, earned an evening ice cream. Jessy *wanted* that counter. We were on an island — no golf-counters there. It must be dispatched from the mainland. Days passed. "Counter?" Jessy was *waiting* for it, *asking* about it, Jessy who seemed never to anticipate, who never wanted anything but candy. So we embarked on our experiment in behavior

---

* Then, at nine, he was performing adequately in a normal fourth grade, though socially isolated; his chosen leisure activity consisted of counting to a million. Today he has completed high school, having been on the school chess team and played drums in the band; though some eccentricities remain, only those who know his history would relate them to autism. Like all medical conditions, autism can vary in severity.

modification in the most favorable circumstances possible — via a mechanism requested by Jessy herself.

Of course she wanted it. It was everything she liked: exact, numerical, easy to use. She liked, too, the clear specificity of the behavioral contracts we worked out together on Sunday mornings, behaviors plainly described and written down in words within her own vocabulary which she could watch taking shape on the paper — as she had watched my drawings take shape long before. Reading was still very hard for Jessy, and she resisted it, but she *liked* reading the lists of behaviors; they focused her attention, perhaps the very committing of them to visible phrases began the process of putting them within her control. The first brief contracts specified only five or six behaviors, with the points earned by each; I had read enough to know you were supposed to keep it simple. But the behavior therapists had reckoned without Jessy's rage for classification. The contract taught us to break "Helping" down into specific actions, but Jessy subdivided it still farther: Big job — 5 points; medium job — 3 points; little job — 1 point. Only my firm stand prevented proliferation into Very Little, Fairly Little, Medium Little, Medium, Fairly Big, and beyond. Soon we had to tape two sheets together to accommodate all the behaviors. We couldn't possibly keep track of them, but we didn't have to. Jessy could, and did, with literal accuracy. Autistic children don't know about cheating.

The children in the behavior modification literature were reinforced with tangible rewards — M & M's, potato chips, pickles. Accordingly, 100 points earned Jessy a popsicle. It was not until the day she racked up 164 points in a euphoric crescendo that we realized that the system was its own reward. She and it were made for each other; it involved everything she liked and understood best: numbers, categories, keeping track of things. We watched in amazement as Jessy, spurred on by nothing more concrete than a rising tally, acquired in weeks — sometimes days — a repertoire of new behaviors that formerly we would have been glad to see take shape over years.

At first we tried to contract for nothing that was not easily within her capacity; one of the system's advantages was that it could be adjusted to guarantee success. As Jessy became accustomed to what that felt like, we could intersperse a few hard tasks with the easy ones. Doing jobs was easy, now she had a reason to do them — it has been eight years since I have had to think about taking out the garbage. Controlling herself was very, very hard, but mumbles and shrieks, though they did not wholly disappear, were much reduced as Jessy learned for the first time to *try* to control them. She might lose 100 points for HITTING, the aggressive behavior that had never before been a problem, but which had begun to surface as life put more demands upon her and the experience of effort brought frustration as well as success. But she could redeem her points by DOING SOMETHING TO HELP, or such easily achievable feats as using the past tense or the definite article correctly. For all sorts of things found their way onto the expanding contract, as Jessy and I reviewed the week and talked about what we needed to work on next. Her repertoire of household skills began in that astonishing eighteen months, and as these were practiced and assimilated into her orderly routine, she made that most important of discoveries: that work is preferable to idleness. Task done, Jessy clicked up her points, giving herself an additional click if she had done it WITHOUT BEING TOLD. I had laughed when a particularly enthusiastic behavior therapist had told me he could program spontaneous behavior. I laughed no longer.

But the purpose of the system was not to turn Jessy into a willing household drudge, but to expand the limits of her world. TRY A NEW FOOD (3 points) and there's a good chance you'll like it. Or a new skill. For two years I had been teaching Jessy to swim, and she would still paddle only a few feet, directly into my arms and never beyond her depth. The day I promised her 1000 points to swim the length of the seventy-five-foot college pool, I thought I was setting a goal for months ahead. That same evening I heard a splash as Jessy jumped into the deep end and — with enormous inflationary consequences to the system — swam the length *eight times*.

Behavior, said Skinner, is controlled by its consequences. I recalled an example from our time in Paris, years before the counter. Jessy had refused for years to enter an elevator; living in an area where no building topped four stories, I had never made an issue of it. Appalled, I discovered our Paris apartment was on the eleventh floor. What to do? But when I offered Jessy the option of walking upstairs, she entered the elevator calm as you please. The consequence, apparently, was meaningful to her, and it was unavoidably built into the situation. Realism took over. The counter worked the same way, impersonally, automatically, through the numbers that by heaven-sent luck were meaningful consequences too.

Working through a combination of improved focus and increased motivation, the counter made it possible for Jessy to master behaviors that had never before seemed within her control. The most crippling of these was by this time so ingrained that we had resigned ourselves to living with it forever. For two years her fragmentary and labored speech had been rendered even harder to understand by a devastating verbal tic. It was allied, apparently, to her mumbles, strange collections of vocables that had once been words ("in the morning," "hang hang," "we go on," "cigar three"), now hardly recognizable even as nonsense. But this was worse. Every sentence she uttered — sometimes every phrase — was followed by an automatic "hello," more often than not trailed by a proliferation of syllables that obscured almost fatally the sound of the sentence, let alone its sense. We had, we thought, tried everything — coaxing, exhortation, the withholding of favorite foods unless properly asked for. The school speech therapist had fared no better. Now we hardly heard it anymore. People who knew Jessy picked out the sense through the nonsense; to people who didn't, it was as unintelligible as pig-Latin.

Then we went on a trip — to Japan, out of reach, three weeks, my longest absence ever. She seemed ready for that. Her brother and twin Jessy-girls stayed with her — behavior therapists with an average age of eighteen. On our return, our son asked, "Notice anything?" Then four proud young people told the story of how Jessy had been liberated from her hello's.

The young therapists had been hard taskmasters. Supporting each other, they had dared to be far tougher than we had ever been, as tough as Jessy needed them to be. They had docked her one point for each hello. Red-eyed, desolate, shaken with crying as her tally sank further and further into the red — minus 100, minus 150, minus 200* — Jessy made the effort we thought she could not make. It took, they said, not quite four hours. The hello's were gone.

The elimination of this long-standing speech pathology was the counter's most spectacular triumph. The building of constructive new speech patterns went more slowly, but we discovered that social communication, too, could be addressed by the counter. Those hello's of Jessy's had been involuntary noises, not greetings. At that time Jessy never greeted you, or looked you in the eye. So a new item was added to the contract: "Hello" earned her one point, use of proper name a second, eye-contact a third. "Hello, Mrs. Smith." (Click-click-click — plus a fourth if she had done it all "without told.") Suddenly people Jessy had ignored for years began to report their astonishment: Jessy was so much more *friendly*. And she was. Those who administer the tangible rewards of conditioning therapy take care to associate them with others less superficial; they smile, they hug, they radiate approval. And of course those Jessy greeted for the first time were all smiles and pleasure. Social reinforcement could hardly have been stronger, or more naturally delivered. With

* Jessy had never had any trouble understanding minus numbers. At eleven, seeing a friend's new baby, she had observed, "When Jessy ten, *that* minus one!"

those smiles Jessy was learning more than a new behavior, more even than manners. She was learning to enjoy social contact, effort, success. She was learning to enjoy praise — the praise that for so long had been all she needed to make her stop doing whatever it was you had noticed. If Jessy can now say, "I'm proud of myself" and mean it; if she can say, "If at first you don't succeed, try, try again" and do it, we have to thank a behavior therapist we never met, and that little counter. So, under the aegis of modern psychology, we rediscovered an ancient truth, that methods which seem external, even trivial, can reach inside to bring about lasting internal change.*

Paradoxically, it is Jessy's art, the most individual, most inward, least mechanical expression of personality, which best illustrates the operation of Skinnerian reinforcement principles. Not that she gets points for paintings — or for anything else. The counter has been shut away in a drawer for seven years. Now, at twenty-three, she gets what other artists get, when they're lucky: money. For years Jessy sketched on demand, performed her school art assignments dutifully, but without enthusiasm. What has spurred the creative efflorescence of the last two years is Jessy's discovery that paintings bring checks; she has had two shows, and banked hundreds of dollars. She no longer has to be coaxed to sketch or paint; she is now reinforced by exactly the same sort of numbers that motivate most of us.

Motivation. I come back to the old mystery of Jessy's long passivity, and the related question of the role of cognitive and emotional factors in her disabilities. Long ago we speculated about a deficiency of motivation, of drive: "It's the sense of purpose that's missing." Year after year we had watched Jessy's in-

---

* Readers who would like to pursue this idea further may be interested in the pages on behavior therapy in *You Are Not Alone*, the guide to coping with mental disorders which I wrote with Dr. Leon Shapiro (Atlantic-Little, Brown, 1976, pp. 71–88), a book whose introduction begins with Jessy, and which owes much to our experience with her.

ertia pervading her life and ours, crippling her possibilities. And then we watched the melting of that negativism we had thought so profound — which *was* so profound — for a popsicle! For a rising tally! Who could imagine that such a triviality could supply the missing drive, substitute for the sense of purpose? Yet when we thought about it we saw that Jessy had never had a reason to make an effort before.

Does a child need *reasons* to perform the myriad tasks of development, to grow? Ridiculous question. That growth is natural, automatic; the whole human race takes it for granted. But Jessy had taught us to take nothing for granted, growth least of all. Why do children grow? Of course their growth is rooted in their biology; talking, like walking, requires unimpaired muscles, nerves, brain, and I have speculated already that in drive, too, biology must play its part. But growth is social too. The baby has social reasons to pay attention to the sounds its mother makes, to make sounds in return, to notice what effects those sounds produce, to practice and refine them. It associates people with comfort and pleasure, it recognizes them, it wants to communicate with them. It imitates naturally, as Jessy did not. But it also has reasons to imitate, social reasons. It wants to do those hard things like buttoning coats and tying shoes, because that's what other people do, because it doesn't want to be a baby anymore. As it learns to do things well, it wants to do them better, whether it's mathematics or throwing a ball, enjoying the activity itself, but also enjoying the sense of progress, the recognition, the praise. Not only has it reasons to do things, it has reasons to refrain. Sooner or later, children learn not to pick their noses, not to scratch in embarrassing places. They learn to inhibit these natural activities because they have good reason to. Adults will scold; more important, their peers will think they're gross.

Cinderella, dressed in yellow,
Went downtown to meet her fellow,
On the way her britches busted,
How many people were disgusted?
One, two,
three, four. . . .

But Jessy was immune to emulation or embarrassment. Of all these natural motivations for activity and growth, not one had any meaning for her. Yet she had been faced with developmental tasks far harder than a normal child's: not only to acquire ordinary self-help skills, but to surmount a massive communications handicap, and to control her strange obsessions and the strange behavior that accompanied them. With so little comprehension of the social world, its satisfactions or its penalties, why should she labor at its difficult tasks? We saw the counter supplying her with the motivation she had so long lacked. It was not a "natural" motivation, but it was natural to her, exact, numerical, structured. It gave her the strength she needed to compensate for her genuine disabilities.

Yet though the new motivation was powerful, it would be falsely simple to ignore its limits. External reinforcers can melt inertia, supplying Jessy with reasons for doing things which she has no deep-rooted reason for not doing — and there are a great many of these. But they have less power over the world within. The delighted, shivering refusals of "too good" remain; I suspect that any success bought by external reinforcers would be temporary. Not that I have tried them. Frustrating as it still is that Jessy should buy a record and refuse to play it, that is a resistance I would rather coax than condition away. We can talk about it, laugh about it, and start the record while she's in another room; she runs out the front door, smiling. But she inches back, hands not quite over her ears, and we smile together. Jessy's inabilities, her refusals, her obsessions are a web no simple method will unravel, and no simple theory either. *Cognitive. Emotional.* The words record two ways of looking at the same experience, an experience that still resists explanation.

How much I have left out! It took nearly three hundred pages to describe Jessy's first eight years. These added pages can only sample a much more complex development. But one thing deserves far more than the small hints I have given already and I cannot leave it out. Jessy's development has for years been largely in other hands than ours — in her own hands, increasingly, in the hands of the dedicated teachers of Mount Greylock Regional High School, but most intensively and most richly in the hands of those she calls her friends.

I am not speaking of the ordinary peer-relationships that we usually mean when we speak of a child's friends. Jessy has no peers. In high school she understood little of normal adolescents' rapid talk, and none of their concerns. Her freshly acquired greeting behavior did not extend to the arts of conversation; she might ask how many sisters and brothers a new acquaintance had, but the complexities of feeling her way toward common experiences and interests was — and is — beyond her. Though some of the children were very nice to her, she made only one friend at school — or rather, Joe made friends with *her*. He comes every Sunday; they go for walks and giggle together at shared nonsense. Joe has a list of 100 girlfriends, mostly media personalities. He used to try to make Jessy jealous by telling her she was no longer Number One, but she had no idea she was supposed to feel bad and after a while he stopped. They have a good deal in common; he likes radio call-letters too. She looks forward to his visits.

But it is those other friends who have made the difference, those extra sisters and daughters — recently joined by a son or two — who over the years have supplied the stimulation and practice in social living that come so much more naturally and easily from somebody young than from increasingly middle-aged (and tired) parents. It is they who have kept our home a place of learning, even when we grew tired of teaching. More than anyone else — more, even, than the extraordinary teachers at her school — these friends have made possible her continuing progress.

I lost track of the number of Jessy-friends when the count topped twenty. For a long time one or another of them lived with us; now this is no longer necessary, though Jessy likes it better when they do. I cannot hope to list all they taught her; most of what she does today, readily and easily, she learned to do with them. They have been teachers, therapists, companions — but the best word is still friends. It is they who taught her to make her bed, to bake and wash up, to hammer in a nail, to shop for groceries, to ski, to (what a miracle!) answer the phone and write down the message. The list is endless, and built into each item has been the continuing expansion of speech and comprehension — linguistic and social — that remains her chief, her permanent task.

Most people do not hire their friends. For years that was one more of the many facts of social intercourse that Jessy did not know — as she did not know that the devotion of these friends was beyond what any money could buy. It was a measure of her progress when, two years ago, seeing the money I had left on the table for the student who was spending the afternoon with her, she asked, "Why don't I get paid for being Joe's friend?" Some friends were teachers, I told her. We talked about some of the things they'd taught her, remembered how she had screamed and mumbled and asked them to leave and sometimes even hit them when they were trying hard to help her. She and Joe had fun together, but they didn't teach each other, and so neither of them got paid. It was a simple, matter-of-fact explanation, the kind she can understand: friends who teach are paid, others not; both are precious. It satisfied her. It satisfies us all.

For all these years, it has been natural — all too natural — to be aware of how much we were giving Jessy. Far more slowly has come another awareness, of what she was giving us. They have passed through our house for nearly twenty years now, a stream of young people, sharing with us for a time their imagination and devotion, in a relation which guarantees they will be known at their most generous and most shining. Other people's children, now our own have flown, who stay for a time, leave, and — like our own — unexpectedly return. Jessy fascinates young people — her mysteries speak to them, as they spoke to that student long ago who saw her dancing in another world. I hear it from them over and over, in one version or another, as they find the words to express the discovery we all make, sooner or later:

"Mrs. Park, Jessy's given me so much more than I've ever given her." Gifts of understanding, gifts of feeling — we have long known about those, and I have tried to share them in this book. But this other gift was one we could not yet recognize, fifteen years ago — that Jessy, herself eternally young, was giving us the gift of youth, in a household rich with the young. Not that we have not sometimes received it grudgingly, like Jessy's other gifts; amid such a hum of relationships and preoccupations, of comings and goings, one might wish at times to be left alone, to grow old in ordinary privacy. But then comes a lull, the kitchen is silent, we are between friends, and Jessy, Jessy who was once called autistic, remarks that it is *boring* and *lonely*. And she is right.

Other people's children — and our own. Part of that long future which we will not share, which Jessy does not envisage but which we must. Yet we were once told to take one day at a time, and told rightly; one day at a time we have come this far. If this is a success story — and it is — it is *Jessy's* success story, the one she cannot tell, the story of her hard struggle to work and love. *Arbeiten und lieben* — to work and love — were these not Freud's measures of success? Jessy has learned to do both, and this changes the possibilities for her future. We cannot look very far ahead, even now; we can only ask questions. Should she live with us, in the home she loves, in the town she knows, a help and a sunny presence (most of the time), moving when we are gone to the sisters and brother who say, "Of course she'll always have a home with one of us"? Could that be right? Group homes exist, sheltered villages too, more all the time, and better; society, in one form or another, can take over the burden we once thought we could never pass on to children who had already borne enough. Yet Jessy is not what she was but what she is and will be. Her brother and sisters genuinely love her. So do her friends. If we live twenty more years — a reasonable projection — they will be moving into their fifties. Jessy herself will be forty-three. It must never be necessary, and it will not be, but it does not seem preposterous that among them they might want to find a place in one home or another for a busy and affectionate cook-house-keeper. For growth is endless, and our lives change and change us beyond anticipation. I do not forget the pain — it aches in a particular way when I look at Jessy's friends, some of them just her age, and allow myself for a moment to think of all she cannot be. But we cannot sift experience and take only the part that does not hurt us. Let me say simply and straight out that simple knowledge the whole world knows. I breathe like everyone else my century's thin, faithless air, and I do not want to be senti-mental. But the blackest sentimentality of all is that *trahison des clercs* which will not recognize the good it has been given to understand because it is too simple. So, then: this experience we did not choose, which we would have given anything to avoid, has made us different, has made us better. Through it we have learned the lesson that no one studies willingly, the hard, slow lesson of Sophocles and Shakespeare — that one grows by suffer-ing. And that too is Jessy's gift. I write now what fifteen years past I would still not have thought possible to write: that if today I were given the choice, to accept the experience, with every-thing that it entails, or to refuse the bitter largesse, I would have to stretch out my hands — because out of it has come, for all of us, an unimagined life. And I will not change the last word of the story. It is still love.

APPENDIX: Tests

Professional readers may be interested in Jessy's performance on standardized I.Q. tests, especially as it has changed over time. Though it illustrates vividly the impossibility of arriving at a meaningful figure, it does seem to support the frequent observation that the I.Q. in early childhood, with all its inadequacies, is the best indicator we have as yet of an autistic child's future development.

I have no reports on Jessy's intelligence tests at three, if indeed any figures were arrived at. At seven years and ten months she was given the Wechsler intelligence test. The tester's report follows.

May 10, 1966

I felt that the verbal tests of WISC [Wechsler Intelligence Scale for Children] would be hopelessly inappropriate but agreed to give Jessy the WISC performance tests. I do not regard these results as measures of Jessy's capacity in the usual sense but am sending them as an account of what the child actually did within the (for her) rather rigid framework of the scale.

Raw scores on Picture Completion, Picture Arrangement, and Coding were 6, 6, and 22, respectively. Test age equivalents for these are 5½ and 6 years. Raw Scores on Block Design and Object

Assembly were 16 and 19, respectively, with test age equivalents of 9½ and 10 years.

The half hour was apparently a pleasant one for Jessy though two or three times she appeared to be diverted from the tasks by factors of which I was not aware. Picture Completion and Picture Arrangement presented many situations wholly unfamiliar to her. On Coding, she made no errors but was slow, perhaps because of what appears to me to be some confusion of handedness.*

On Block Design, she worked rapidly, appraising and correcting her errors deftly. In Object Assembly, *Face* was disproportionately difficult for her. She placed the nose and mouth pieces correctly against the largest piece and, a few inches away, assembled a pair of the remaining parts. This required the time limit of three minutes. *Mannikin* was correctly assembled in 33" as against the time limit of 120". On *Horse,* she earned a time bonus. *Auto* was finished in 1 minute though the limit is 3 minutes. An inversion of the door piece lost a possible time bonus.

On all these tests, I adhered to the WISC directions. I felt that communication was adequate for the needs of the test situation. While I would not offer these results as a real measure of this child's ability, I find it interesting that these disparities in accomplishment add up to a Performance IQ in the lower half of the "Normal" range.

Jessy took this test in the tester's own home, where she had already visited several times. One year later Jessy was given the Stanford-Binet by her school psychologist, in the standard school testing situation. Whether because of the changed circumstances or the differences between the tests, it was not thought possible to assign her a meaningful score. The psychologist then attempted to give her the WISC of a year before, with no better success.

---

* There is no additional evidence of this. The Institute neurologist thought that, at three and a half, she was clearly right-handed.

Jessy's score on the Rimland Diagnostic Check List for Behavior-Disturbed Children (Form E-1): 43 autistic responses to 4 schizophrenic responses.

For comparison, these are her scores on the Wechsler Adult Intelligence Scale, taken at seventeen years, six months, aligned for comparison with scores on the Wechsler Intelligence Scale for Children, re-taken at ages eleven and twelve.

	October 1975	May 1970	February 1969
FULL SCALE IQ	101–106	76	87
VERBAL IQ	88–95	66	75
PERFORMANCE IQ	119	92	103
Verbal Subtests			
INFORMATION	5	5	4
COMPREHENSION	2	3	3
ARITHMETIC	13	7	8
SIMILARITIES	11	7	10
VOCABULARY	NA	5	5
DIGIT SPAN	11	10	NA
Performance Subtests			
PICTURE COMPLETION	9	7	8
PICTURE ARRANGEMENT	9	5	6
BLOCK DESIGN	17	13	17
OBJECT ASSEMBLY	18	10	12
DIGIT SYMBOL/CODING	10	11	9

NA: Not administered
Peabody Picture Vocabulary Test IQ = 77

Excerpts from the report, by Dr. David L. Singer, Director of Doctoral Training in Professional Psychology, Antioch New England Graduate School:

I gave Jessy the following tests:
Wechsler Adult Intelligence Scale (WAIS)

Peabody Picture Vocabulary Test (PPVT)

Rorschach

Tasks of Emotional Development (T.E.D.: a picture
story-telling test)

Trail Making Test (useful in assessing presence or
absence of brain injury)

Animal Projective Technique (APT)

Jessy refused to take the Vocabulary sub-test of the WAIS, and
did not complete the Rorschach. Because she was responding superficially and reluctantly to the T.E.D. after an initial refusal to tell
stories, I shortened that test for her.

Cognitive Functioning and Development:

Because Jessy's progress along differing developmental lines is so
varied, overall IQ scores mean very little in her case except as a general guideline to future expectations. Even using lowest estimates of
current functioning, Jessy's WAIS IQ scores are higher than in previous years. This strongly indicates that she is making continued
progress and that continual development is taking place. While there
is huge variation in level of ability on differing tasks, her Verbal and
Full Scale IQ are clearly within normal limits, and her Performance
IQ is in the high "bright-normal" range.

Jessy still has considerable difficulty with verbal concepts and verbal
problem solving: nonetheless, significant gains have been made in that
area. Whereas she used to have considerable difficulty transposing
verbal problems into numerical formulations, she can now do that
quite well. She is currently functioning above average on that type of
problem (Arithmetic scaled score = 13), where previously she was
well below average.

Abstract verbal problems pose the greatest difficulty for Jessy at
present. Two underlying factors appear to be involved: 1) she has
continued, but lessened difficulty encoding thought into language; and
2) she is still tied to her own perceptual experience in much the same
way as a 7 or 8 year old. Unless a problem is directly linked with an
experience she is having (or can remember) it is virtually incom-

prehensible to her. Thus, hypothetical situations or questions are usually meaningless for Jessy. This cognitive "egocentrism" or "concreteness" can often lead Jessy to say things which seem quite strange — i.e. when asked to name four presidents of the U.S. since 1900, one of her responses was "Martin Luther Kingdom." Moreover, abstract phrases (e.g. "bad company") and metaphor (e.g. "strike while the iron is hot") seem odd and confusing to her.

Interestingly though, once the basic "building blocks" of a problem are available to her — that is, if she understands the language of the problem and what is being asked of her, and if the response does not require complex verbal output — Jessy has very good capacity for verbal reasoning. This was demonstrated quite poignantly on the Similarities sub-test of the WAIS. Jessy had a difficult time at the outset in grasping the concept of "alikeness" and missed the first item. However, when given an example she went on to do quite well, giving stylistically immature, but accurate answers. (Asked how an egg and a seed were alike, she replied, "Both grow things"; a fly and a tree; "Both living.")

Jessy's functioning on non-verbal tests has also improved considerably. This is in part due to: 1) greater comprehension of the physical and social world around her; 2) an increased ability to relate picture-symbols to her own experience; and 3) excellent capacity to visually integrate and recognize the "whole" that needs to be made from the parts. In addition, she now appreciates causal and temporal sequence much better than previously.

It is also true, though, that Jessy still has considerable difficulty understanding the subtleties of social situations. On several Picture Arrangement items she arrived at technically correct solutions even though she did not understand the story or its humor. Her solution was based on sequence and time cues which she picked up quite perceptively.

As has been found before, Jessy has excellent perceptual motor coordination. She can attend to problems and tasks quite adequately when she is not anxious. On the Trail Making Test, where she was asked to connect with an unbroken line in alternate sequence 26 scattered circles containing the numerals 1-13 and the letters A-K, she performed at the 85th percentile of normals and the 99th percentile of brain damaged adults.

Jessy was reluctant to take any of the projective tests, and when she did cooperate her responses were guarded.* There was no indication of disturbed, malignant or bizarre thinking. Jessy's responses were quite conventional, though in form and content developmentally quite immature. Her own self image is also that of a child, not a young woman.

Jessy is a remarkable 18-year-old who may have been an autistic child, whose development has certainly been atypical, and whose current functioning is marked by tremendous unevenness in cognitive and emotional development. Her overall IQ is well within normal limits and her potential – once the long process of development and compensation is completed – may be considerably higher.

* Author's note: Knowing Jessy, I would say rather that she was nonplussed. Open-ended responses of this kind are still extremely difficult for her.

A Short Bibliography

Since 1967, when *The Siege* was first published, ideas of infantile autism have changed so profoundly that many of the references in the footnotes are now only of historical interest. The books and articles below provide a reliable introduction to current thinking on autism's nature, causes, and treatment. Most of them are available from the bookstore of the National Society for Children and Adults with Autism, 1234 Massachusetts Ave., N.W., Washington DC 20005. Telephone: (202) 783-0125.

DeMyer, Marian K. *Parents and Children in Autism.* New York: John Wiley & Sons, 1979. A small encyclopedia of information on children, parents, and families.

Greenfeld, Josh. *A Child Called Noah.* New York: Holt, Rinehart, & Winston, 1972.

———. *A Place for Noah.* New York: Holt, Rinehart, & Winston, 1978. A father's absorbing narrative of life with a very severely impaired autistic child.

How They Grow: A Handbook for Parents of Young Children with Autism. Washington, D.C.: National Society for Autistic Children, 1981. Practical guidance, and a larger bibliography than this one.

Kosloff, Martin. *Reaching the Autistic Child: A Parent Training Program.* Champaign, Ill.: Research Press, 1973. An introduction to behavioral methods.

Morgan, Sam B. *The Unreachable Child: An Introduction to Early Childhood Autism.* Memphis, Tenn.: Memphis State University Press, 1981. A comprehensive, fair, and readable survey of what is known of autism today.

Rutter, Michael, and Eric Schopler, eds. *Autism: A Reappraisal of Concepts and Treatment*. New York: Plenum Press, 1978. Authoritative articles by the foremost specialists in the field.

Schopler, Eric, and Gary Mesibov, eds. *The Autistic Child through Adolescence*. New York: Plenum Press, 1982. Surveys what is known about the later development of autistic children.

Schopler, Eric, and R. J. Reichler. "Developmental Therapy by Parents with their Own Autistic Child." In *Infantile Autism: Concepts, Characteristics, and Treatment* (ed. M. Rutter). London: Churchill Livingston, 1971. Parents as co-therapists.

Wing, Lorna. *Autistic Children: A Guide for Parents and Professionals*. New York: Brunner-Mazel, 1972. A clear and practical introduction.

The complete file of the *Journal of Autism and Developmental Disorders* (formerly the *Journal of Autism and Childhood Schizophrenia*) is the best source of more specialized articles on autism published since 1971, when the *Journal* was founded.

25-5